COMMISSION OF THE EUROPEAN COMMUNITIES

D1798123

Audiovisual production in the single market

by Matteo Maggiore

DOCUMENT

This publication is also available in the following languages:

ES   ISBN 92-826-0264-8
DA   ISBN 92-826-0265-6
DE   ISBN 92-826-0266-4
GR   ISBN 92-826-0267-2
FR   ISBN 92-826-0269-9
IT   ISBN 92-826-0270-2
NL   ISBN 92-826-0271-0
PT   ISBN 92-826-0272-9

Cataloguing data appear at the end of this publication

Luxembourg: Office for Official Publications of the European Communities, 1990

ISBN 92-826-0268-0

Catalogue number: CB-58-90-481-EN-C

Acknowledgements

Very special thanks go to Mary Rose Byrne, responsible, among other things, for all the logistics related to the writing of this book.

Nicola Bellieni and Johanna Maas, of the Commission of the European Communities, must be thanked for their patience and assistance.

I also thank Carlo Ripa di Meana, Member of the Commission of the European Communities, for his support. I am especially grateful to the whole of the audiovisual production and policy division, without exceptions, in the Directorate-General for Information, Communication and Culture of the Commission of the European Communities.

Of all the persons toward whom I feel a debt of gratitude I must recall Roberto Barzanti, MEP; Mariella Braccialini, Sintesi; Antonino Cascino, RAI; Jacopo Giola, Fininvest; Renee Goddard, European Script Fund; Ekkehard von Koch, Deutsche Condor Film; Dieter Kosslick, EFDO; Carlos Alberto Martins, former consultant at the CEC; Frank Naef, EBU; Alberto Pasquale, Anica; Raymond Ravar, EAVE; Alessandro Silj, CISS; Gaetano Stucchi, RAI; Alastair Tempest and Joan Vandersande, EAT; and Frederic Young.

I owe many thanks to Frederic Cobau of Edimedia, Antonio D'Angelo, formerly responsible for documentation with the Media programme, and Sergio Diana of Cesemaan, for the documentation they kindly put at my disposal.

Last, but certainly not least, I thank Diederik Bangert for his friendly support.

Brussels, 15 October 1989

Contents

List of tables

Chapter III: The protagonists

Chapter IV: The technological challenge

Introduction

The audiovisual sector is the new-born child of traditional activities such as film production, broadcasting and the electronics industry. These sectors are both public and private and fall under the categories of both industry and culture.

Culture, economics and industrial production all represent aspects fundamental to audiovisual production. They cannot be separated and none of them may be forgotten or left behind. No cultural activity was ever in the past as conditioned by industrial and economic factors, and no industrial activity has ever depended so much upon its cultural content and mission. As a single sector, audiovisual production is new in the sense that the activities involved in it are undergoing such changes as to alter their nature and mould them into something new.

The dimensions of the sector are not impressive as yet. In 1985, its turnover was estimated at ECU 15 400 million in Europe, representing 0.4% of the GNP of the European Community. Television accounts for 58% of this total, and 120 000 people are employed in the whole of the industry.

Apart from the fact that this figure is rapidly growing (it could attain ECU 27 000 million by 1990), audiovisual production is closely connected to other economic and industrial sectors (electronics, and information industry, advertising, etc.) and is, therefore, more economically relevant than figures can tell. The audiovisual revolution to which reference will be made in this book was brought about by technological innovation.

Satellites and cables turned the broadcasting landscape from a small and crowded one into a vast expanse of air-time. This space is still virtually uninhabited, and many wonder whether the resources needed to fill it exist and even if there is any demand for it in the first place.

It is the writer's opinion that such demand and resources do exist, but that audiovisual production and the services offered will be radically different a short time from now from what they have been in the past.

Film and television images are incomparably more effective than any other means of expression. As soon as it becomes practical to use them for all purposes, private or public, they will relentlessly take over where sound or writing have operated until today.

This does not necessarily imply that these other techniques will die. For practical use, however, audiovisual means are likely to become the paper and ink of centuries to come.

The European audiovisual industry sees the light in a highly unfavourable position. The main drawback is fragmentation.

The first effect of the audiovisual revolution is the transborder circulation of programmes and films through broadcasting via cable and satellite. The unification of Europe is an accomplished feat as far as air-time and broadcasting areas are concerned.

This circulation has just seen the first attempt at regulation on a transborder and continental scale. Before, regulation only existed at the level of national States; it was not consistent and did not apply to products originating in other States.

Europe's production and investment potential is also lost because of scattering and division. The primary actor on the audiovisual scene developing a single strategy for the European market, and operating simultaneously in all European countries, is the USA; Japan follows.

While European television's main problem lies with programme production, the cinema should solve primarily the question of distribution and financing. A distinction should

Table 0.1
Household penetration of basic amenities

Country	Number of H/hs (1986) (1 000)	Year	Own toilet (%)	Bath or shower (%)	Central heating (%)	TV set (1987) (%)
Austria	2 863	1987	92.3	87.7	55.2	97.1
Belgium	3 620	1985	90.5	99.3	92.8	89.1
Denmark	2 260	1985	95.7	86.1	88.1	97.3
Finland	2 052	1980	92.3	81.1	80.2	87.7
France	20 976	1984	97.2	84.7	69.7	95.3
FR of Germany	26 850	1981	87.0	84.0	51.0	87.6
Greece	3 444	1981	78.0	69.0	30.0	87.1
Ireland	1 004	1981	89.8	82.0	39.0	93.8
Italy	19 947	1984	96.0	87.6	39.7	98.6
Luxembourg	130	1981	97.2	86.1	73.9	99.0
Netherlands	5 643	1985	100.0	96.0	72.3	98.3
Norway	1 620	1980	78.5	82.2	91.0	95.7
Portugal	3 300	1983	63.4	46.8	10.0	73.5
Spain	14 329	1981	91.0	70.0	21.0	74.6
Sweden	3 680	1980	96.0	93.0	93.0	90.6
Switzerland	2 701	1986	100.0	97.0	78.0	85.5
UK	21 005	1984	97.0	97.0	66.0	98.0
Turkey	9 090	1975	67.2	45.1	40.0	66.0

Source: European Advertising Tripartite (EAT).

Note: H/hs = Homes/households.

be made, however, exclusively between software (programme and film) and hardware (equipment) production, as all the others, including that between cinema and television, are bound to disappear.

Any national policy in the field of audiovisual production is insufficient. The main effort should be displayed on a continental scale, within European Community institutions and the Council of Europe.

In the last few years, the European Community has committed itself greatly to the development of a successful audiovisual policy. Its action follows three main directions:

(i)   regulation, with the drafting of minimum rules, in the form of a directive, on transborder broadcasting;

(ii) support to European hardware production, consisting in the setting of common standards within Europe as well as coordinating diplomatic and promotion action throughout the world; and

(iii) support to European software production, notably through the European Commission's Media 92 programme.

Table 0.2

Basic European television statistics (1986)

Country	Population (million)	Total homes (million)	TV homes (million)	Colour sets (% homes)	VCR (% homes)	Teletext (% homes)
Austria	7.55	2.77	2.61	81	9	2
Belgium	9.86	3.61	3.50	77	11	6
Denmark	5.12	2.27	2.18	79	16	5
Finland	4.88	1.80	1.79	80	17	7
France	54.72	19.56	19.48	73	13	4
FR of Germany	61.30	25.70	23.12	80	29	5
Greece	9.87	3.05	2.87	41	13	0
Ireland	3.59	0.99	0.93	80	24	1
Italy	56.98	18.54	17.50	65	4	1
Luxembourg	0.36	0.14	0.13	na	na	na
Netherlands	14.39	5.49	5.30	90	25	14
Norway	4.14	1.50	1.32	94	23	11
Portugal	10.13	3.15	2.35	32	4	0
Spain	38.40	10.65	9.48	62	15	0
Sweden	8.34	3.61	3.09	92	24	10
Switzerland	6.48	2.67	2.16	89	18	14
UK	56.60	21.25	20.61	84	38	16
Total	352.71	126.75	118.92			

Source: Logica.

Notes: [1] Insignificant.
na = not available.

The idea of an audiovisual Eureka, formulated by the French President François Mitterrand in December 1987, is the occasion to draw a balance of the developments that have taken place to date and for the sketching of a global policy. A series of proposals and guidelines for this programme were issued at the 'Assises de l'audiovisuel', a meeting involving over 800 experts of the sector from all over Europe and observers from overseas. The conference was held in Paris between 30 September and 2 October 1989; as yet, it is too early to assess its outcome. Nevertheless, the audiovisual Eureka has acquired by now certain definite traits that will be summarized in the last part of this publication.

Table 0.3

TV population in Europe

Country	Population (million)	TV homes (million)	TV homes (%)
Austria	7.6	2.9	94
Belgium	9.9	3.5	98
Denmark	5.1	2.2	94
Finland	4.9	1.7	95
France	55.2	19.5	95
FR of Germany	61.0	23.1	97
Greece	9.9	2.9	81
Ireland	3.6	0.9	95
Italy	57.2	19.8	96
Luxembourg	0.4	0.1	98
Norway	4.1	1.5	96
Netherlands	14.4	5.3	98
Portugal	10.0	2.8	80
Spain	38.4	9.5	96
Sweden	8.3	3.3	96
Switzerland	6.5	2.1	89
UK	56.6	20.6	97

Source: Antennes – June 1989.

Chapter I

Carriers

The audiovisual landscape has been dramatically modified by technological change in the first place. This affects primarily the carriers, the vehicles for image and sound. Evolution in viewers' attitudes and responses depend on the nature and volume of space, or air-time, available for activity.

Satellites, cables and terrestrial frequencies, although none of them represents a new factor, have developed in such a way as to call for a substantial reconsideration of the audiovisual environment.

1. Satellites

The European scene

The role of satellites in future developments of the European audiovisual landscape, one way or another, will definitely be a major one.

The original role of satellites was that of improving telecommunications, and to this day the majority of existing satellites are for telecommunications, used primarily for telephony and other types of data exchange.

Since the early 1980s, however, the majority of geo-stationary telecommunications satellite transponders are allocated to television broadcasters and a kind of satellite-rush has gripped the European broadcasting landscape. Table I.1.1. provides a list of television programmes distributed by telecommunications satellites in Europe.

Telecommunications satellites can normally reflect a signal originated from the ground to various receiving points on the ground on different channels. Signal power at reception is between 15 and 20 watts. It is a fairly weak signal which needs to be amplified in order to be functional for service at ground level. This was never thought of as a handicap as long as users were powerful public structures such as the national PTTs and the signals carried bundles of single-voice conversations. Even in the early stages of the use of satellite transponders for television signals, public-service broadcasters had no trouble in providing the voluminous and costly equipment needed to receive weak signals, amplifying them and redistributing them through cable networks.

Table I.1.1

Television programmes distributed by telecommunication satellites in Europe

Service	Hours per day	Language	Homes	Finance source	Ownership
3-Sat	8	German	3 432 280	public	ZDF/ORF/SRG
AFRTS	24	English	na	US govt.	US govt.
Arts Channel	3	English	3 000	public	W.H. Smith, TVS, Commercial Union, Equity & Law
BBC 1/2 mix	8	English	na	note	BBC
BR3	10	German	1 900 000	licence fee	Bayerischer Rundfunk
Canal 10	24	Spanish	na	public	Fininvest, Thorn EMI
Childrens' Channel	10	English	887 000	public	British Telecom, DC Thomson, Thames TV, Central TV, Thorn EMI
CNN	24	English	233 209	public	Turner Broadcasting
Eins Plus	4-5	German	2 860 000	licence fee	ARD
Eureka	12-18	German	2 520 000	public	Medi-Media GmbH
FilmNet	24	Dutch	65 000	subscription	Esselte, UIP, VNU
Info Film	varied	Norwegian	na	licence fee on receipt	na
Kindernet	3	Dutch	60 000	na	Telecable, Benelux WH
La Cinq	17	French	92 150	public	Fininvest, Hersant
Lifestyle	6	English	203 300	public	W.H. Smith, TVS, Yorkshire TV, DC Thomson
M6	16	French	20 780	public	CLT, Compagnie Lyonnaise des Eaux
MTV Europe	24	English	2 212 425	public	Maxwell Communications
NRK	9	Norwegian	10 000	NRK	NRK
Première	12	English	40 000	subscription	Maxwell, Columbia, 20 Fox, HBO, Showtime/The Movie Channel
RAI Uno	18	Italian	1 500 000	RAI	RAI
RTL Plus	7	German	2 868 280	public	CLT, Bertelsmann
SAT-1	12	German	2 873 280	public	PKS (Kirch 51%, DG Bank 49%) APF, Springer, von Holtzbrink
Screensport	9	English	241 000	public and licence fee	W.H. Smith, ESPN, ABC, RCA 3i's
Sky Channel	19	English	10 869 773	public	News international, Ferranti, Ladbroke, DC Thomson, Equity & Law
Super Channel	20	English	9 660 000	public	ITV (RU) exc. Thames & TVam, Virgin

Table I.1.1 *(continued)*
Television programmes distributed by telecommunication satellites in Europe

Service	Hours per day	Language	Homes	Finance source	Ownership
SVT1 & 2	14	Swedish	na	na	SVT
Teleclub	6	German	30 000	licence fee	Beta Taurus
Tele-fünf	24	German	2 860 000	public	KMP/Fininvest
TV3 (Scansat)	6	Swedish/ Norwegian	850 (1987)	public	Kinnivik (96 %) & Nora (4 %)
TV5	7	French	7 029 685	na	TF1, A2, FR3, RTBF, SSR, Radio Canada
TVE1 (Spain)	18	Spanish	na	TVE	RTVE
WDR3	10	German	1 900 000	WDR	Westdeutscher Rundfunk
Worldnet	5	English	3 542 212	USIA	USIA

Source: Europe 2000: *Quelle télévision?*

Note: na = not available.

In fact, for any satellite system, investment in ground segment equipment (i.e. signal receivers and/or redistribution infrastructure) is substantially more important than investment in the satellites themselves.

Control and coordination of satellite programmes and frequency allocation still lies with international organizations gathering representatives of the national PTTs. These organizations are essentially Intelsat and its regional equivalents, the European one being Eutelsat. All domestic satellite systems have to coordinate technically with the international systems, so as to ensure that there is no interference in transmissions.

Both the regional and the global international satellite systems are, in fact, strictly 'international': frequencies are assigned to PTTs which, in turn, can sublease them to broadcasters. Thus, to the basic leasing cost are added PTT charges for link-up and administration.

However, even on the first Eutelsat satellite, ECS-1, launched in June 1983, all nine active transponders were allocated for television broadcasting, and in 1987 over 70 % of the organization's revenue came from its TV leases. Details of Eutelsat satellite transponder use can be found in Table I.1.2. The main use for satellite links in television has not, until recently, been actual broadcasting, or what is technically defined as point-to-multipoint broadcasting. In spite of the unique advantages of satellites for sending TV signals to large geographical areas, their immediate relevance to broadcasters was point-to-point exchange of news material. Since the first satellite TV relay effected on Telstar in July 1962, the main video application of satellites, until quite recently, has been the relay of TV news and event material.

Table I.1.2

Eutelsat satellite system details

	ECS-1	ECS-2 (Primary)	ECS-4
Launch date	June 1983	July 1984	To be launched
Transmission date	February 1984	November 1984	
Life span	7 years	7 years	7 years
Orbital slot	13°E	7°E	16°E
Uplink frequency	14.0-14.5 GHz	14.0-14.5 GHz	14.0-14.5 GHz
Downlink frequency	10.95-11.2 GHz 11.45-11.7 GHz	10.95-11.2 GHz 11.45-11.7 GHz 12.50-12.75 GHz	10.95-11.2 GHz 11.45-11.7 GHz 12.50-12.59 GHz
Transponders	12 (9 in sunlight)	14 (all operable in sunlight and eclipse)	14 (all operable in sunlight and eclipse)
Status	Pre-emptible	Pre-emptible	Pre-emptible/Non-pre-emptible
Transmission power	20 watts/channel	20 watts/channel	20 watts/channel
Transmission standard	PAL	PAL	PAL
Users	FR of Germany (1 transp.) UK (2 transp.) Belgium (1 transp.) France (1 transp.) Italy (1 transp.) Luxembourg (1 transp.) Netherlands (1 transp.) Norway (1 transp.) Switzerland (1 transp.)	EBU (2 transp.) Telephony (3 transp.) SMS/Business (2 transp.) NW/NRK (1 transp.) Occasional video (1 transp.)	UK (2 transp.) Italy (2 transp.) Denmark (1 transp.) Norway (1 transp.) Spain (1 transp.) Sweden (1 transp.)
Beam allocation	*Spot West* RAI Worldnet TV5 Sky Channel Teleclub Filmnet SAT1 Super Channel 3 SAT *Spot East* RTL Plus *Spot Atlantic* Spare Spare	*Spot West* NRK TV Occasional video Telephony *Spot East* Telephony/business Spare *Eurobeam* EBU EBU *Spot Atlantic* Telephony/business	

Source: Logica.

Note: GHz = gigahertz.

In 1982-83, however, the Luxembourg Government raised the by then inevitable question of satellites specifically designated for television transmission.

Telecommunications satellites, as previously mentioned, retransmit weak signals to the ground. The size (and the cost) of the aerials needed to receive satellite signals depend on the signal power. Low-power signals such as the ones transmitted by telecommunications satellites (20 watts) need huge aerials in order to be received. TV broadcasting via telecommunications satellites implied a centralized powerful receiving and distributing structure, such as only public-service television stations were traditionally capable of providing.

The use of satellites for broadcasting is in fact conditioned by the expansion of cable networks and by the regulatory environment.

The large-scale use of low-power telecommunications satellites for television broadcasting raised the question of satellites conceived specifically for television. It was the Luxembourg Government that opened the debate in 1982-83 by introducing the idea of a medium-power satellite for European TV distribution. In 1985, while the SLS (Société luxembourgeoise des satellites) became the Société européenne des satellites (SES) and signed a contract with RCA Astro Electronics for a satellite with 16 operational 50-watt transponders and six spares, Eutelsat announced new specifications that would bring the power of its satellite transponders up to 50 watts. Throughout the following year a debate took place between SES and Eutelsat, which considered at first that the company had 'submitted insufficient information for a debate on "significant economic harm" to Eutelsat', and eventually ended up by rejecting all SES proposals as 'completely unacceptable'.

This was the origin of the two European medium-power television satellites, Astra and Eutelsat II. Table I.1.3 contains details on the various types of satellite.

Table I.1.3

Comparison of low-, medium- and high-power satellites

Satellite	Low-power	Medium-power	High-power
Transponders	9-10	16	4
Output power	20	45-50	120-230
Downlink frequency (TV) – GHz	10.95-11.2 11.45-11.7	11.2-11.45	11.7-12.2
Design life	7 years	10 years	7 years
Median transponder cost (TV)	USD 3 million	USD 5 million	USD 15 million
Potentially accessible homes	< 20 million	80 million	> 100 million

Source: Logica.

Astra was launched in December 1988. Both satellites will carry 16 24-hour television channels receivable by 60 to 90 cm dish aerials. They will therefore introduce relatively cost-effective satellite broadcasting for individual reception.

Six of the Astra transponders are taken by Rupert Murdoch's Sky Television, two have been leased to W.H. Smith (Lifestyle and Screen Sport), two to Scansat (including the Scandinavian TV3 commercial station) and MTV. Three transponders still have to be allocated, and are being promoted especially with German broadcasters, in an effort to 'Europeanize' the satellite.

As far as the commercial success of Astra is concerned, a crucial role is likely to be played by British Telecom (BT), which has agreed with SES to market 11 of the 16 transponders and to help develop the ground equipment market (it is remarkable, in this respect, that BT is one of the three main signatories of Eutelsat).

Table I.1.4

European DBS satellites

Satellite	Country of origin	Launch date	Launcher	Potential number of TV channels
TDF 1	France	launched October 1988	Ariane	4
TDF 2	France	December 1989	Ariane	5
TV-SAT 2	Germany	June 1989	Ariane	4
TELE-X	Scandinavia	February 1989	Ariane	2
Olympus 1	ESA	July 1989	Ariane	2
BSB 1	UK (private funding)	nominal August 1989 expected spring 1990	Delta-2	3
BSB 2	?	spring 1991	?	
Astra 1	Luxembourg (private funding)	8 December 1988	Ariane	16
Astra 2	?	not known – satellite for 1991 delivery	?	16
DFS-Kopernicus	Germany	May 1989	Ariane	8
Eutelsat II A	Pan-European	January 1990	Ariane	16
Eutelsat II B	?	March 1990	Ariane	16
Eutelsat II C	?	September 1990	Atlas	16
Spanish satellite	Spain	October 1991	not known	6
Sarit 1	Italy	1991	?	
Sarit 2	?	1992	?	?
European satellite	Pan-European	mid-1994	?	20-28

Source: European Commission.

Note: ? = not yet decided.

Since the late 1970s, however, the idea has emerged of very high-power satellites (200 to 250 watts per channel) capable of direct-to-the-home TV broadcasting thanks to the comparatively small dish aerial needed to receive signals 10 times as strong as those coming from telecommunications satellites. This philosophy was called direct broadcasting by satellite (DBS).

DBS satellites have only four transponders and fall under the scope of the 1977 World Administrative Radio Conference (WARC) allocation of frequencies on a country-by-country basis. Such regulations, designed to prevent as much transborder 'spill-over' as possible, are evidently redundant in the face of satellites conceived with a view to reaching larger, international audiences. In fact, broadcasting by satellite within the borders of a single State makes one think of something like shooting a fly with a cannon.

The first European DBS satellite, the French TDF1, was launched in October 1988. Apart from the government-owned cultural channel La Sept, Canal Plus will be using this satellite for both a French- and a German-language channel. Launch dates for European DBS satellites, as well as characteristics of some of them, are given in Tables I.1.4 and I.1.5.

The Italian-British Olympus followed in July 1989, after the German TV-SAT1, launched in 1987, failed to open in orbit and was lost. Olympus will certainly carry one channel of Italian television (RAI). For the second transponder, originally assigned to the now ceased Europe TV channel, there are talks of allocation to the British BBC for

Table I.1.5

Main features of some European DBS satellites

	TDF-1	Olympus	TELE-X	Atlanticsat	BSB
Life span	9 years	5 years	5-7 years	—	10 years
TV transponders	4	2	2	5	3
Transmitting power	230 watts+	230 watts	230 watts	100 watts	230 watts
Transmission standard	D2-MAC	C-MAC	C-MAC	—	D-MAC
Construction costs (two satellites)	UKL 350 million	UKL 135 million (one sat.)	UKL 120 million (one sat.)	UKL 300 million	UKL 150 million
Manufacturer	Eurosatellite	British Aerospace/ Selenia Space	Aerospatiale	Hughes	Hughes

Source: Logica.

Note: — = not operational.

a 'Best of BBC' channel. TV-SAT2, the successor of TV-SAT1, is likely to carry the same channels that should have been on the first German DBS satellite: SAT1, RTL-Plus, and the public service Drei Sat and Eins Plus.

Economics

Apart from regulatory considerations, however, the economics of DBS programmes should not be taken for granted. All of them except for the British BSB are heavily State-funded as significant 'technology demonstrators'. The case of BSB is in itself impressive: 100% privately financed, the company will, according to most estimates, have to invest some ECU 700 million over the 10 years' lifetime of its satellite. With five channels, this stands for ECU 14 million a year per channel!

Even State-backed programmes face perplexity where, as in France, private industry showed extreme caution in joining ambitious government programmes for the launch of DSB and the marketing of the necessary home-receiving equipment, not to mention technical setbacks such as the mishap which occurred with the German TV-SAT1, and the delays in the launch of Olympus. High-definition television, however, could represent a factor in favour of DBS in the future. (The link between the two will be treated in a later section.)

In the future, technology and, especially, competitivity and the decreasing rate in consumer prices for receiving equipment, will be crucial to success in the various television satellite programmes. Much will depend on the timing and degree of industry commitment to the production and marketing of the necessary hardware.

Some forecasts on TVRO (television receive-only equipment) penetration are shown in Tables I.1.6 and I.1.7. Such forecasts are evidently vital to all commercial DBS ventures.

Table I.1.6
Satellite reception to end-1994: Installed TVROs

(1 000)

Year end	SES and Eutelsat I and II	TDF-1	BSB	TELE-X
1988	25	7.5	—	—
1989	120	20	—	6.0
1990	220	50	35	12
1991	300	100	120	25
1992	700	180	220	50
1993	950	280	350	100
1994	1 075	400	600	175

Source: Logica.

Table I.1.7

Satellite dish penetration estimates

Country	1990 (1 000)	(%)[1]	1995 (1 000)	(%)[1]	2000 (1 000)	(%)[1]
Austria	30	1.1	325	11.7	675	24.3
Belgium/Luxembourg	5	0.1	10	0.1	20	0.2
Denmark	60	2.7	250	11.4	300	13.6
Finland	50	2.8	175	9.7	200	11.1
France	308	1.5	1 888	9.4	2 250	11.3
FR of Germany	53	0.2	1 095	4.7	2 772	11.8
Greece	10	0.3	20	0.7	40	1.4
Ireland	11	1.2	140	14.9	200	21.2
Italy	5	0.0	10	0.1	20	0.1
Netherlands	100	1.8	250	4.5	400	7.2
Norway	100	6.5	325	21.0	450	29.0
Portugal	10	0.3	20	0.7	40	1.4
Spain	25	0.2	50	0.5	100	0.9
Sweden	100	3.2	525	17.0	825	26.7
Switzerland	30	1.3	140	6.1	250	10.8
UK	1 500	7.2	7 000	33.5	9 000	43.1
Turkey	1	na	5	na	10	na
Europe[2]	2 398	1.9	12 228	11.2	17 552	17.6

Notes: Estimates for southern European markets are extremely tentative.
[1] % of all TV homes in 1987.
[2] % figures excluding Greece, Italy, Portugal, Spain and Turkey.
na = not available.
Source: EAT.

A case in financing: the British arena and the Japanese example

(a) *United Kingdom*

The United Kingdom, the first full-scale DBS-user country in Europe, is to this day the battlefield for Rupert Murdoch's Astra-based television channels and the British Satellite Broadcasting (BSB) DBS programme.

It is also going to become the testing ground for the European success of DBS.

The battle brought to the fore a major consequence: the adoption, for the UK alone, of two different transmission and encryption standards; in the whole of Europe there will probably be three.

The standards for transmission will be PAL, D-MAC and D2-MAC, the standards for encryption (needed in order to exclude non-subscribers from signal reception) are called Palcrypt, Eurocypher and Eurocrypt. Astra transmits Murdoch's four channels in PAL, while BSB will use D-MAC.

The economic success of direct-to-the-home satellite broadcasting is closely related to advertising investment in television. This is dependent on the audience which, in turn, is only likely to grow if:

(i) equipment costs are low,

(ii) programming is sufficiently attractive.

The existence of two different standards for satellite broadcasting reception makes it necessary to buy two different kinds of reception equipment or else to choose between two sets of programmes. This reduces the decrease in costs.

The incentive for individual receiving equipment manufacturers is not very high at the moment. Forecasts talk of 1.6 to 2.2 million homes in the UK receiving satellite broadcasts by the end of 1991. Of these, only 45% will actually own DBS receiving equipment, as most will be connected to cable networks or communal reception systems.

Further damage will be caused by the lack of a unified subscription management system.

In the United Kingdom as elsewhere the final battle will be fought therefore, on programme quality. (This is an issue which we will address in later sections.)

Consideration of the British situation suggests that the winner of the Murdoch-BSB war could be, to a certain extent, the cable industry. If two different aerials are needed to receive the full DBS service, more people are likely to choose cable connection for the two of them.

In fact, 20 new franchises were advertised for cabling by the British Cable Authority last year.

At the moment, however, satellite television does not play an important role in British advertiser strategies.

Less than 25% of them will buy satellite airtime. On average they allocate at present about 2% of their budget to satellite television space.

In fact, according to a February 1989 survey, only 3% of British viewers declared that they were definitely going to buy DBS receiving equipment, with an additional 12% of probable buyers; 78% said they were definitely not going to spend their money on it.

These figures might change, but for the time being advertisers seem to rely on them.

Their interests seem to lie with single-theme channels, which would allow for more reliable targeting.

(b) *Japan*

Direct broadcasting by satellite was born in Japan on Christmas Day 1986. Nine months later, in September 1987, the audience for the two additional channels (one educational) totalled only 8 000 viewers. By June 1988 the figure had grown to 750 000.

The dramatic decrease in equipment costs seems to have been decisive for DBS success. The price of the 70 cm-diameter aerial and converter needed for signal reception shrank to a quarter of its original value (YEN 70 000 instead of the initial 300 000).

NHK, the Japanese public-service broadcaster, is planning to introduce a special licence fee for the reception of satellite broadcasts. The Japanese DBS programme remains, however, heavily State-funded and will, according to Japanese sources, keep losing money at least for the next five years. The relevance of DBS to high-definition television makes the effort worthwhile in the view of the government.

Perspectives

Satellite broadcasting is undoubtedly bound to expand.

The first generation of high-power satellites was born with Astra and the French TDF1 and the British-Italian Olympus. The German TV-SAT2 and the British BSB will follow during the summer.

All are part of national satellite programmes. Every country will have its own DBS satellite, or satellites; every country seems ready to pay incredible prices for the independence of its DBS programme.

The advantages of satellites in broadcasting are obvious: distance-independent cost, immediate service over the whole coverage area from the start of operation, no additional cost for coverage of areas of difficult geographical access, etc.

Satellite signals can carry various independent soundtracks for each video message, making multilingual broadcasting possible and easy. Every programme can be received in different languages just by turning a switch.

All these characteristics point to the quality of satellites as international cross-border signal distributors. Along with other technological, economic and cultural changes, they provide a powerful impulse for an overall continental philosophy of communications which is fundamental to the present evolution in the audiovisual industry. National satellite programmes seem in fact a contradiction in terms: the value of satellites lies with their scope of coverage. The point was not missed by private investors, such as the large European as well as non-European media groups that launched ambitious programmes for transnational broadcasting.

A revision of the WARC 1977 agreement seems indispensable, as it is only reasonable to think in terms of common continental satellite programmes rather than of single national ones. The merging of resources would rationalize expenditure on these systems, which show a clear transnational vocation. National DBS programmes, we could say, are definitely pointless. The only reasonable perspective would seem to be that of a pan-European second generation of direct broadcasting satellites. In the light of the present experience, a viable option would seem to be a compromise between the medium-power, multichannel, Astra-like satellites and the first generation DBS satellites with improved signal power and easier ground receivability.

We are sketching a satellite carrying 10 to 14 channels of 100 to 125 watt power each that would provide good quality television to 60 to 90 cm dishes, at the same time improving cost-effectiveness. Such plans come under the label of Europesat-type proposals. The actual Europesat plan was developed within Eutelsat from 1985, then put aside due to concern over Eutelsat 2. The Europesat plan was proposed again by Eutelsat in a recent study contemplating the launch of two or three satellites of this kind. The proposal is being actively discussed in various European countries, notably in Germany and the UK.

All this requires a high degree of coordination between the States and organizations involved in the planning and regulating phases of future programmes. The chosen arena of Eutelsat definitely needs some adjusting for this new continental kind of discussion.

Independent action on the part of Eutelsat signatories depends on demonstrating that it will cause no economic harm to the organization. The notion of economic harm remains quite vague, as became clear during the debate between SES and Eutelsat on Astra.

Eutelsat has, moreover, no capacity to deal directly with satellite-user parties. The signatories insist on being the sole national points of contact. Thus, channels are allocated 'blindly' to PTTs, sometimes without even knowing whether or not they will be used. This makes rational planning objectively very difficult and causes paradoxical distortions such as occur, for example, in Britain, where companies owning licences for point-to-multipoint data and video distribution, and thus potentially in competition with British Telecom, have to apply to BT for satellite capacity.

The European institution is still embryonic in character, and that should be taken into account when devising measures to improve its efficacy and mechanisms for continental satellite planning. It must be remembered that Intelsat, the international global agency that provided the model for regional groupings such as Eutelsat, first had to cope with the appearance of competing systems while it was implementing and planning its sixth and seventh generations of satellites and boasted a long record of profitability.

Eutelsat will probably retain a monopoly in the province of its original mission, i.e. the provision of satellite capacity for telephony and telecommunications, whereas competition should be foreseen in the field of satellite television broadcasting.

What is more important still, national borders should be dismantled within Eutelsat, so as to allow channel users to deal directly with the organization's executive as far as broadcasting is concerned. Reality, as will be discussed in the following chapters, tends toward deregulation and the loss of monopoly in television broadcasting on the part of public institutions. Organizations responsible for the coordination of activities that are transborder in nature cannot but adjust to this reality if they are not to be bypassed in unorthodox or paradoxical ways. The success of satellite programmes ultimately depends, however, on the attractiveness of the services they carry and, in the case of traditional broadcasting, on the quality of productions.

The very low degree of penetration for innovative reception techniques like cable in Italy, for instance, certainly depends on the vast offer of programmes broadcast terrestrially. It is questionable, however, whether Italian or Spanish viewers will be interested in satellite channels broadcasting exclusively in English, German or French.

DBS penetration is also more likely to take place in countries with low cable diffusion. Considering the lack of attraction of the foreseen satellite channels for non-English, non-German and non-French-speaking countries, this leaves the United Kingdom and France as the development arenas for DBS-receiving equipment. Until quite recently, the demand for satellite relays on the part of broadcasters concerned the punctual and occasional exchange of video news feedback and even material. As of today, not all satellite channels available in the foreseeable future have found users, and this in spite of the hectic activity of media investment groups. Europe certainly does not have the software production capacity to fill in a portion of the available broadcasting 'room' that can be considered acceptable from the cultural point of view. This will be the subject of the next chapter.

2. Cable

TV distribution through cable networks developed at first as a remedy to difficult broadcasting. In the 1940s, broadcasters in the United States started distributing their programmes via cable in small rural areas where the terrain interfered with their signals. Cable TV retained its rural and restricted nature until 1976, when a pay-TV channel, Home Box Channel (HBC), started using a transponder on the Satcom 1 satellite to connect to various cable networks. HBC met with instant success and started something

Table I.2.1
Growth of cable television in the USA, 1975-85

	1975	1980	1985
Number of cable television systems	3 681	4 225	6 400
Cable subscribers *(millions)*	9	16	39
(% US households)	13	24	46
Pay cable subscribers *(millions)*	na	9	23
(% US households)	na	12	na
Primetime audience share of cable-originated programmes services	na	3	12
Subscribers receiving 30+ channels (%)	na	15	na

Source: TV broadcasting in Europe and the new technologies.

Note: na = not available.

very close to a revolution: 10 years later about half of all US homes were linked by cable. A summary of cabling evolution in the USA is given in Table I.2.1.

In Europe, cabling developed especially in connection with the same geographical preoccupation as well as in countries with populations of different languages and cultures. Most cabling took place in Belgium, Switzerland, the Netherlands and, to a lesser extent, in Denmark and Ireland. In these countries the interest in broadcasts coming from neighbouring countries put an end *de facto* to State monopoly in television services.

The relevance of cable lies primarily with the redistribution of satellite signals. It is foreseeable that the success of commercial satellite programmes will depend heavily on the expansion of cable networks.

Forecasts of this expansion are an important factor in commercial enterprises such as Astra and BSB. These tend, however, to be cautious: Astra owner SES (Société européenne des satellites) gives an estimate of 17.3 million cable links for 1990 and of 21.8 million for 1995 (about 17.6% of TV owners).

Advertisers' forecasts tend to be even more optimistic: their figure for 1995 shows 31.6 million connections, or 25.5% (see Tables I.2.2 and I.2.3).

Table I.2.2
Forecast of European cable homes

(1 000)

Country	1987	1988	1990	1995
Austria	350	423	500	625
Belgium/Luxembourg	3 100	3 150	3 200	3 290
Denmark	600	650	850	1 200
Finland	420	450	650	1 300
France	100	140	350	1 900
FR of Germany	3 200	4 600	6 500	13 200
Greece	na	11 [1]	na	na
Ireland	300	320	400	520
Italy	0	0	na	na
Netherlands	3 350	3 850	4 100	4 600
Norway	370	420	475	625
Portugal	na	49 [1]	na	na
Spain	na	293 [1]	600	1 500
Sweden	360	500	625	1 150
Switzerland	1 270	1 426	1 570	1 731
UK	41	63	530	1 486
Europe [2]	13 461	15 992	19 750	31 627

Source: EAT.

[1] Sky television homes (i.e. not necessarily only cable).
[2] Excluding Greece, Portugal and Spain.
na = not available.

Table I.2.3

Forecast of European cable homes

(% of all TV homes)

Country	TV homes (1987) *(1 000)*	1987 *(%)*	1988 *(%)*	1990 *(%)*	1995 *(%)*
Austria	2 780	12.6	15.2	18.0	22.5
Belgium	3 354 [1]	92.4	93.9	95.4	98.1
Denmark	2 200	27.3	29.5	38.6	54.5
Finland	1 800	23.3	25.0	36.1	72.2
France	20 000	0.5	0.7	1.8	9.5
FR of Germany	23 510	13.6	19.6	27.6	56.1
Greece	2 900	na	0.4	na	na
Ireland	942	31.8	34.0	42.5	55.2
Italy	19 667	0.0	0.0	na	na
Netherlands	5 547	60.4	69.4	73.9	82.9
Norway	1 550	23.9	27.1	30.6	40.3
Portugal	2 900	na	1.7	na	na
Spain	10 693	na	2.7	5.6	14.0
Sweden	3 090	11.7	16.2	20.2	37.2
Switzerland	2 308	55.0	61.8	68.0	75.0
UK	20 886	0.2	0.3	2.5	7.1
Europe [2]	124 127	10.8	12.9	15.9	25.5

Source: EAT.

[1] Including 129 000 TV homes in Luxembourg.
[2] Excluding Greece, Italy, Portugal and Spain.
na = not available.

By the end of 1988 around 16 million European households were linked to cable networks. That amounts to about 18% of the total 130.1 million TV households. Developments differed greatly in the various countries.

In Italy, Greece, Spain and Portugal, for instance, cable penetration was minimal. In Spain, where a significant number of commercial television channels will be launched in the near future, cabling in connection with the Barcelona Olympic Games in 1992 could be the springboard for further development. The Spanish Government plans to cable 1.2 million homes in the Barcelona area for that occasion.

Italy and Portugal give as yet no sign of cable development. On the other hand, the Benelux countries are likely to reach saturation in cable expansion by the mid-1990s.

The German Government plans to have 80% of households in that country cabled by the year 2000. The attraction of additional programming on the part of the three German-language cable TV stations (SAT1, RTL Plus and Tele 5) seems to be providing a certain impulse in cabling. Most of it relies, however, on the Bundespost's plans to offer interactive service.

In France, cable development has not fulfilled the hopes expressed by the Government in the 1982 'Plan Cable'. The privatization of TF1 and the initial success of Canal Plus increased the percentage of entertainment programming receivable traditionally, while attractive programmes to be received by cable are still few.

In the UK, Astra and BSB programming are likely to give a boost to cabling, which has been stagnating until recently. The adoption of different transmission standards for the two satellites is also likely to induce the public to connect their receivers to cable networks rather than buy two different kinds of aerials.

In most European countries, however, what cable expansion there was took place principally in connection with information technology and telecommunications. The goal of European PTTs is ultimately ISDN (Integrated Services Digital Network), that would combine telephony and a series of interactive data and information exchange services on a national, and later European, scale.

While television broadcasts per satellite are by nature transborder and continental, cabling remains a PTT affair: strictly national. Regulation on licensing for cable distribution of satellite programmes is therefore largely inconsistent within the European Community.

Another feature of cable is the slowness, complexity and costs of network construction, maintenance and upgrading or expansion. The recent development of optical fibres should, however, bring about conditions that may prove decisive for cable expansion. Two hair-thin strands of exceptionally clear glass (optical fibre) can carry 1 920 simultaneous telephone conversations or one colour television broadcast in the form of light pulses that translate the message in binary form.

With such an improved capacity, cable retains a great competitivity. Given an attractive offer of broadcasts and services, cable allows for flexible charging, easily controllable and tailored to the service supplied.

Cable removes the problem of spectrum scarcity (i.e. the availability of frequencies). On the other hand, its versatility raises the question of competition in services which are to this day the monopoly of PTTs.

A major role could be played by outcomes similar to the double transmission standard adopted in the UK by Astra and BSB, resulting in the choice for the consumer between buying two or more aerials and connecting with a cable network.

The upgrading of cable networks, however, is a costly and lengthy affair, liable to take place under substantial demand pressure. Ultimately, in satellite as in cable broadcasting, success depends on the attractiveness of programmes.

3. Terrestrial broadcasting

This most traditional means of broadcasting was itself the carrier of some major changes in the European audiovisual landscape.

Hertzian distribution generates inevitably some 'natural' border-crossing on the part of national broadcasts. In some cases, however, commercial TV channels have based their strategy on deliberate distribution across the border of their State of origin through terrestrial distribution and cable, the most famous being, of course, that of RTL. The Luxembourg channel aimed at the Belgian market, diverting important investments on the part of Belgian advertising companies and generating a protectionist attitude in Belgian institutions and broadcasters. On the other hand, hertzian distribution was the base for Italy's extraordinary development in commercial television. In the absence of consistent regulation on the exploitation of frequencies, the multiplication of local TV stations peaked in 1982 at the figure of 1 200 before the concentration of stations in the hands of large groups (mainly Silvio Berlusconi's Fininvest) brought about a reduction in the number of single stations.

Factors in the future development of hertzian TV distribution are primarily of a regulatory nature. The success of many 'young' commercial stations depends heavily on the possibility of being allocated hertzian frequencies while waiting for a substantial expansion of cable networks and of VSATs and individual TVROs for DBS.

At the same time, the strategy of large groups such as Fininvest and Hachette keeps relying on the development of terrestrial distribution on a national scale in various countries. Their success depends on the developments in national legislation.

4. Internationalization and deregulation

Technological progress resulted in borders being rendered ineffective. National regulation of broadcasting gradually lost effectiveness as international investment made State monopoly in television a thing of the past.

State monopoly in broadcasting was justified by the scarcity of frequencies. Satellites and cables simply removed the issue. Satellites, as noted before, are a transnational and regional (in the broader sense of world regions) means of broadcasting.

Terrestrial frequencies were also exploited so as to make them a vehicle for broadcasting to large areas, and obstacles posed by legislation could not prevent a free economic activity like investment in television from establishing itself in most States of the European Community.

Finally, cables brought national television services from one country to another (normally, to neighbouring countries), besides providing yet another channel for the diffusion of commercial television.

Investment is the activity linked to broadcasting best provided for in EC and international law, being of an economic nature. It was also the aspect of broadcasting that developed more rapidly on an international scale. Investment in commercial television came in many EC States, such as Italy, France, the United Kingdom and Germany, even before commercial television was authorized and regulated by law.

The case of Italy, where broadcasting remained non-regulated for over 13 years, provides a unique experience of uncontrolled development in television, and is a reminder that deregulation is not, and should not be, identical with the absence of regulation.

Deregulation is, in fact, the process under way in many European countries and originating from the consideration of the inadequacy of rules drawn up under a *de facto* monopoly in broadcasting services. It consists mainly in the modification of law with a view to opening an often very strictly regulated space in the business to the private sector. Radical as it may be in certain countries, deregulating always boils down to dismantling the monopoly of public television.

The national logic was still dominant in 1977, when the World Administrative Radio Conference allocated satellite channels, orbital positions and frequencies for direct broadcasting by satellite essentially country by country. Twelve years later the inanity of such a regulatory framework should be perfectly clear. A healthy legal environment for the production and the circulation of TV programmes must be developed on a continental scale.

In its absence, the perspective is that of the reproduction of the Italian case in European television, i.e. the law of the jungle followed by belated regulatory efforts succeeding only in endorsing the existing situation.

EC priority: A legal framework

In the audiovisual field, where economic and cultural factors are so closely interwoven as to be in fact inseparable, regulation is the least questionable among the competences of European institutions. This is the principal framework in which a suitable legal environment has to be worked out for the new aspects of broadcasting and AV software circulation on the old continent.

Unifying the market and providing for the free circulation of goods are the very reason for its existence. Among all the actions undertaken by the European Community, the effort to establish a legal framework for transborder broadcasting must be seen as the starting point for a European audiovisual policy.

EC Directive on broadcasting

(a) *Historical background*

The Commission of the European Communities report to the Council, 'Trends in broadcasting in Europe: Perspectives and options' (COM(83) 229) in 1983 marked the starting point for involvement on the part of European institutions in audiovisual policy. The document called attention to two main points:

(i) the enormous increase in the demand for audiovisual programmes in the very near future; and

(ii) the need for consistent action in support of European programme production.

The first priority consisted in the creation of a common legal framework that allows programmes to circulate freely within the Community. As the Adonnino report on a people's Europe put it, every European must be granted 'access to the largest possible number of programmes' broadcast in Europe.

The European Commission's Green Paper on 'Television without frontiers' (COM(84) 300 of 1984) was followed, in March 1986, by a draft Directive on broadcasting. It became known as the 'Television without frontiers' Directive.

Its aim is that of providing for sufficient coordination and harmonization in Member States' legislation for the free circulation of broadcasts within the Community.

Following a troubled itinerary across the various Council Committees (notably, the Cultural Affairs and Internal Market and Industrial Affairs Committee), the Internal Market Council reached a common position on the draft on 14 April 1989. The draft was approved with a qualified majority and was submitted to the European Parliament for a second reading and further amendment.

Then, on the eve of the June elections, internal political factors and external pressure on certain delegations destroyed the majority within the Council for the adoption of the amended draft. In June the European Council charged the Council to approve the amended Directive proposal within three months.

On 3 October, in the aftermath of the Paris 'Assises de l'audiovisuel' and following some bilateral compositions on the part of the French Presidency of the Council, the Directive was finally approved by the General Affairs Council in Luxembourg by a majority vote: even then, Belgium and Denmark opposed it.

(b) *Principles of the Directive*

The 'Television without frontiers' Directive is based on two fundamental principles that represent two separate spheres of legislation in broadcasting:

The first sphere is that of a measure providing regulation in transborder broadcasting. Its aim is to allow programmes to circulate throughout the Community.

The second sphere is dominated by concern for the state of programme production in Europe and the intent to support domestic production in a competition which it is not at present able to sustain. It is guided by the so-called 'cultural objectives'.

(i) Free circulation

Article 2 imposes on all EC States the acceptance of broadcasts originating from another Member State. This is consistent with the principle of applicable law: if a programme complies with regulations in one State of the Community, it must be considered acceptable, and must therefore be accepted, in all the others.

Most of the text is devoted to providing a minimum harmonization between national legislations in order to render Article 2 applicable in practice. It lays down parameters for the percentage of advertising tolerated in programming as well as for the protection of young persons.

In fact, only the repeated violation of the article forbidding the transmission of programmes 'bringing serious harm to the physical, mental or moral development of minors' (Article 22) is considered legitimate grounds for the interruption of broadcast reception from abroad on the part of a receiving State.

Advertising was a controversial point up to early 1989. A maximum percentage of advertising in programming had to be set as well as a tolerable frequency for the interruption of programmes with advertising.

An agreement was finally reached between countries with a fully developed private sector depending heavily on advertising (Italy first of all) and countries where public television retains a near-monopoly. Draft Article 11 allows for the interruption of feature films and television films (excluding series, serials and documentaries) once every 45 minutes. Otherwise advertising must in general be inserted between programmes, except in those longer than 30 minutes and provided it does not bring harm to the programme's integrity and value, and that it does not go against the right-holders.

A compromise is expressed in Article 20, allowing each State to set independent rules for programmes broadcast uniquely for national and internal reception, and that cannot be received in any other Member State. The article was introduced following an initiative of the Italian delegation to the Council.

The maximum volume of advertising was set at 15% of daily broadcasting; 20% of a single hour was also given as a maximum for advertising spots.

In this way, minimum harmonization had been reached in regulation and the free circulation of broadcasts was possible in an orderly legal environment.

(ii) Cultural objectives

The cultural objectives of the Directive are expressed in the articles and paragraphs concerning the quotas of broadcasts that should be reserved for European productions.

Chapter III of the original draft invited Member States, 'whenever possible and by appropriate means', to make television stations reserve most of their transmission time to European productions, excluding news, sport, games, advertising and teletext (Article 4).

The European Parliament, in its second reading, removed the words 'whenever possible'.

On the eve of the French elections in June, the French delegation to the Council opposed the Directive on the ground that it considered the quota provisions too feeble and vague even after the Parliament's amendments.

Agreement on the draft Directive text had been possible in April after a rather precarious compromise had been reached at a meeting for the drafting of a European Convention on transborder broadcasting within the framework of the Council of Europe. The phrase 'whenever possible' had provided for a temporary consensus between those States that wished for a more definite promotional function for European agreements on broadcasting (notably France and Italy) and those that abhorred the quota principle and remained faithful to market laws for the solution of any problem.

Among these, Germany, Denmark and Belgium maintained their opposition to the draft text, which was approved in April by the Council by majority vote.

The turning point was represented by the shift in the French attitude at the Council. Following pressures on the part of the French producers and authors, on the eve of the European elections the French delegation received instructions to withdraw their support for the draft text at the internal market Council in June on the ground that the provisions concerning quotas were not sufficient to promote effectively the European production.

Another factor was the pressure which the United States applied on some States, and which induced notably the Dutch authorities to express doubts about the compatibility of certain Directive provisions and the GATT.

At this point, the approval of the Directive by the Council for the term set by the European Council (at the latest, within October) became a challenge for the French, who were at the origin of the delay in its approval and held, at the same time, the chairmanship of the Council until the end of 1989.

The shift in the French attitude caused irritation in the delegations who were opposed even to the original formulation on which a common position had been reached in April.

However, not only does the final text read, as the original draft did, 'whenever possible', but the German delegation insisted on obtaining a written statement on the part of the Council and the Commission qualifying the provision on quotas as 'politically binding'. The statement, included in the Council minutes, is interpreted by the Germans as 'not juridically binding'. This was made clear by Commission Vice-President Bangemann in the speech he delivered in the European Parliament in Strasbourg on 11 October 1989: the Commission, he said would not proceed against Member States unless 'very extreme cases' of non-compliance with Article 4 of the Directive occurred.

This odd consideration for the adjective 'politically', read as, in fact, 'not to be taken too seriously', is bound to create confusion in the interpretation of the Directive.

Other provisions concerned the percentage of broadcasting time (10%) to be reserved for productions realized by European independent producers (Article 5).

Apart from quotas, the problem of the chronology of the media is also included among the cultural objectives.

In order to guarantee a balance between the various forms of release for feature films and fiction production, the Directive provides for films to be shown in theatres for a certain time before they can be broadcast on television. The time was set at two years, or one year when a television station is a co-producer of the film.

The French delegation was once again the main promoter of this measure, stemming from the preoccupation with the extinction of movie theatres.

(iii) Copyright

The 'Television without frontiers' Directive does not mention copyright. It did originally, but a long battle between authors' associations in the various Member States and the European institutions brought the issue to a standstill.

The EC began from the principle that copyright should not restrict the free circulation of goods in the Community. A too-complicated licence system is resented also by third countries, and notably by the USA, as an impediment to extra-European companies (i.e. broadcasters) freely retransmitting programmes by cable.

The Commission proposed, in its first draft Directive, to adopt the system of non-voluntary licences for the EC.

This system, in use in various European countries, implies the licensee's right to reproduce and broadcast a programme or film with proper remuneration to the right-holder, who renounces the possibility to forbid the diffusion of his work.

Following dire opposition to this on the part of authors and right-holders throughout Europe, provisions on copyright passed various stages.

A system based on licences conceded 'automatically' to associations of authors for them to deal collectively with distributors and broadcasters was opposed on the ground that it would have forced authors and right-holders that were not members of those associations either to join them or to be represented by an organization of which they were not part.

The final rejection of the principle of individual dealing on the part of authors brought the matter to a dead end.

The copyright issue was simply put aside, and it is likely to be the object of a separate Directive in the future.

The stakes of effective and consistent European legislation on copyright are very high. New technologies have quite abruptly brought about a *de facto* abolition of national borders and thus rendered the territorial application of national copyright law obsolete.

The possibility of diffusing intellectual works much more rapidly and effectively than ever before brings both opportunities and risks. If the protection of intellectual production must not obstruct its free circulation, it must remain effective enough to guarantee authors and creators the full return of resources invested in it. The problem is particularly relevant in connection with the pirate copying of videograms (i.e. video cassettes), and this will be the object of further consideration in Chapter II.

Convention of the Council of Europe

A draft Convention on transborder broadcasting was developed by the Member States of the Council of Europe parallel to the EC draft Directive. European Cultural Convention (ECC) States (the Vatican and Yugoslavia) and the European Community are also involved in its elaboration. Work takes place within the 'Comité Directeur sur les moyens de communication de masse' (CDMM) of the Council of Europe.

The European Council at Rhodes (2 and 3 December 1988) invited the Commission and the Council to conform the Directive to dispositions contained in the draft Convention. The two texts have since been made consistent with each other on all major points (free circulation of broadcasts, quotas, advertising).

Compared to the Directive, the Convention would:

(i) have the advantage of extending the Directive provisions to the geographical area of the Council of Europe; but

(ii) represent a multilateral agreement rather than a definite regulatory means and be, therefore, potentially less effective.

The draft Convention was signed by Austria, Liechtenstein, Luxembourg, the Netherlands, Norway, San Marino, Spain, Sweden, Switzerland and the United Kingdom on 5 May 1989. It will only become effective, however, when the Parliaments of seven signatory States have ratified it. Its entry into force is, therefore, rather distant.

Conclusion: Regulation and the identity of Europe

'Culture is not a set of goods like any other. We cannot deal with it as we do with refrigerators or cars'. These words were spoken by the President of the European Commission, Mr Jacques Delors, at the Paris 'Assises de l'audiovisuel' on 2 October 1989. They touch the substance of the problem: can a cultural policy exist on a continent where the only institutions are those of an economic community?

Technology destroyed national frontiers. This happened so rapidly that the traditional regulatory institutions have to cope with an absolutely extraordinary urgency and pressure to prevent the situation from slipping out of control and developing outside any given set of rules.

At the same time, there is no institution that can explicitly deal with the cultural aspect of this development. The European Community is still dominated by an economistic approach: the only European institutions have, on the basis of the Rome Treaties, purely economic competences. The Community is still under the spell of major setbacks in its attempts, in the 1950s, to become a real community, i.e. political. Its profile is kept meticulously low. Its partial (economic) nature is emphasized in an effort on the part of the national ruling classes to retain their authority and their control of a sovereignty that, being national, borders on insignificance.

The accelerated unification of the European market will bring along evident political responsibilities in the world arena, no matter how hard the Europeans try to avoid them. Responsibilities call for competent and effective institutions, none of which are at hand in Europe.

The market approach to European film and programme production is a result of this absence.

Quotas are definitely not an adequate and proper method for the support of an industry. When adopted, they are evidence of an extreme weakness in the sector involved. As a remedy they are, in fact, extreme.

Increasing quotas, such as those provided for in the 'Television without frontiers' Directive, seems particularly clumsy. In fact, if the Directive contained provisions for a progressive decrease in the percentage of European programmes to be shown by European television stations, it would have shown much better its intention to support European production only initially and given a very special situation in production.

The USA put impressive pressure on Community institutions and on Member State authorities on this issue. US officials stated repeatedly that the EC Directive on broadcasting represents the present administration's main worry in relation to 1992.

Special consideration, however, must be given to the status of audiovisual production. Quite suddenly, technological progress in broadcasting and telecommunications turned television into a media that is not only dominant, but will also represent in the very near future the alpha and omega of social communication. Interactive audiovisual services and thematic TV stations will replace sheets of paper with screens as broad-band telecommunications via cable and/or satellite will make even private audiovisual transmissions possible. The audiovisual technique and industry will be the medium through which ideas are circulated, in mass communication as in the creation and the rendering of services.

This revolution is taking place at an impressive speed. Some areas of the world, notably the USA, will be less affected by it than others. Because of their dimension and linguistic as well as legal uniformity, the USA developed a large-scale production for a large market right from the beginning of activity in the field.

Europe is fragmented: linguistically, politically and economically. A European policy in any field must take this fragmentation as its starting point.

The European countries see their culture, their history and their identity threatened by the sudden opening of the frontiers. Dealing with audiovisual production, it is not merely a matter of market competition. Broadcasting will soon be the principal instrument for expression. No one can be expected to deliver exclusive control of such an instrument to someone abroad.

Free competition on the unified market four years from now will mean competition between the United States and the individual European countries. This is something the Americans do not fail to grasp when they point out that a European culture as such does not exist and that the cultures in Europe are the French, the Italian, the Spanish, etc., coming to the conclusion that the motive for any quota is the protection of an industry and not the defence of culture.

Some European countries, however, will introduce quotas for broadcast fiction nationally (as France and Italy plan to do) regardless of what the Community does or does not do. Others already do so. Even in the United Kingdom, where no statutory quotas exist, the BBC and ITV voluntarily limit the percentage of non-EC material broadcasts to 14%!

Quotas seem, in fact, an asset to guarantee real freedom of choice on the part of the 'consumer'. Considering the sudden changes occurring in the structure of production and the urgent need for finished products on the part of new enterprises — commercial television stations, public broadcasters in a new state of competition in order to guarantee their survival — a free market would result in the immediate and absolute supremacy of that national industry which happens, thanks only to the country's dimensions, to be better prepared for the new situation.

This supremacy could divert investment from a crisis sector in Europe: programme production. Developments would in the near future kill European fiction production. In an environment in which audiovisual fiction will be substitutive of all other principle forms of creative expression, this will not simply mean the end of any industrial sector, it will amount to the death of an independent cultural production in Europe.

National film and television industries in Europe must change: they will have to adopt transnational forms of production, financing and distribution which will necessarily alter their present nature. They will have to become competitive economically in order to survive and retain their role as a means of cultural impression. But they must be given a fair chance. Free competition will imply that in a very near future European users will not be free to choose European products; even before, that is, they have had a chance to express a judgement or a choice.

A German, Gutenberg, invented printing. In the course of the sixteenth century the technique spread, and in every European country books could be printed and diffused.

The new techniques in broadcasting have brought about a revolution in communication and cultural production comparable to the introduction of printing. The environment is substantially different, however, and it is important that in the near future not all the 'books' have to be written in the language of the person who invented the technique.

Chapter II

Programmes

Change in technology rapidly brings about diversification in resources and distribution methods for audiovisual products. It is a painstaking adjustment resulting in some traumas and in enormous opportunities for programme production (the so-called 'software') and for artistic creation specifically.

Theatre attendances fall dramatically; in the meantime, since 1976, the whole of the world's feature film production, from the Lumière brothers to the present day (with the possible exception of Indian films), was screened three times on Italian television!

Video and broadcasting increase their share in financing for feature films. Video itself and advertising radically modify viewers' habits. To American distributors, Europe already is a single market for products whose costs are wholly recouped on the world and domestic market before they arrive on the old continent. The European programme production could virtually disappear and leave the continent with no ink with which to write.

A — The problems of fiction

The unification of the European audiovisual industry began with a consumer approach. Quite suddenly, the public's demand for entertainment and the profits available in advertising encouraged investors to put their resources into the audiovisual entertainment and service market. Technology is ready, the demand has been increasing constantly, and law has not represented, in most cases, an insuperable barrier to expansion and the breaking of State monopoly in access to distribution infrastructures.

Entertainment primarily means fiction. By fiction we understand programmes which are different from event portrayal, news or sports. The category includes, therefore, documentaries, series and serials, and, above all, short and feature films.

Supposing that in the very near future each European country will receive on average 30 cable channels, three DBS channels and three traditional channels. This is a conservative estimate, and does not take local stations into consideration.

In this situation, a base of 10 broadcast hours per day would amount to 1.5 million hours of broadcast per year.

On the basis of the present percentages, the proportion of fiction can be estimated at a third to half of the total programming. Keeping figures low, we can assess the number of fiction hours at 500 000 yearly.

Half of this production can, and indeed should, come from extra-European countries. Of the remaining 250 000 hours, a good half will probably be employed for the re-transmission of films shown previously.

This leaves us with over 100 000 (if not the exact total of 125 000) hours per year of fiction programming that ought not to be filled in by productions which, if they were to come from extra-European countries, would reshape substantially the present relation

Table II.A.1

Production of feature films, 1970-87

Country	1970	1975	1980	1981	1982	1983	1984	1985	1986	1987
Austria	7	6	7	na	13	11	17	11	3	na
Belgium	4	9	6	7	6	12	8	7	5	12
Cyprus	0	0	0	0	0	0	1	1	3	na
Denmark	20	19	13	11	13	10	11	12	10	na
Spain	105	98	114	137	118	99	102	75	77	70
Finland	na	na	na	na	16	13	20	15	28	na
France	110	138	189	231	164	131	101	151	134	133
Greece	88	38	25	46	37	47	40	38	20	18
Ireland	5	2	0	1	1	3	2	2	1	na
Iceland	na	na	na	na	na	na	4	na	2	na
Italy	235	198	163	103	114	110	103	89	114	116
Luxembourg	0	0	0	0	0	0	2	0	1	0
Norway	11	12	10	10	na	6	5	10	9	na
Netherlands	4	16	7	11	13	15	12	16	11	na
Portugal	8	16	11	9	8	4	8	9	6	na
FR of Germany	113	73	49	76	70	75	80	65	64	70
UK	86	69	29	14	45	44	53	58	46	51
Sweden	22	23	22	25	23	23	17	12	20	24
Switzerland	5	30	na	11	na	na	20	15	22	na
Turkey	na	na	na	na	na	na	na	80	na	na
Yugoslavia	na	na	na	na	na	na	na	na	26	na
EEC	778	676	606	646	589	550	522	522	489	500
USA	443	425	321	338	307	342	313	330	515	578
Japan	423	335	320	332	322	317	310	300	319	311

Source: 'L'avenir de l'industrie audiovisuelle européenne'.

Note: na = not available.

between domestic and foreign cultural productions on television. As television is bound to become an almost exclusive means for social communication, this would amount to a major cultural revolution.

The production of feature films in the four largest EC countries — France, Germany, Italy and the United Kingdom — amounts to roughly 1 000 hours per year (see Table II.A.1). Even including fiction production for television, an optimistic assessment would be that, in less than five years, nine-tenths of the films broadcast in the old continent could be non-European. This does not take into account the inevitable decrease in investment in European productions as they become less economically competitive.

Of all kinds of programmes, fiction is by far the most expensive. It is, at the same time, the most attractive for audiences and the one for which the demand is highest (Tables II.A.1 to II.A.4). It is the sector in which European production is in dire crisis.

Table II.A.2
Television fiction as a proportion of total broadcast hours (1987)

(1 000 hours)

Country	Fiction	Total hours
Belgium	2.5	8
Denmark	1.5	2.5
France	10	16.5
FR of Germany	4	13.5
Greece	2	7.5
Ireland	2	4
Italy	17	36
Luxembourg	3	3.5
Netherlands	2	4
Portugal	3	8
Spain	2.5	8.5
UK	7.5	25

Source: IIC; 'Stories come first'.

Table II.A.3
Programme structure: A comparison of public and private channels

	Public channels	Private channels
Information	17.5	16.0
Films/series	21.0	44.0
Culture/education	29.0	17.5
Entertainment	13.0	16.0
Sport	9.0	8.0
Others	5.0	9.0

Source: Commission of the European Communities.

Table II.A.4

Hours of fiction by channel (1987)

Country	Channel	Total output (hours)	Total fiction (hours)	Total fiction (%)
Belgium	BRT	3 848	1 404	36.4
	RTBF	4 836	968	20.0
Denmark	DR	2 600	962	37.0
France	TF1	5 668	1 758	31.0
	A2	6 032	1 509	25.0
	FR3	4 472	994	22.2
	La Cinq	7 280	6 770	92.9
	M6	6 136	2 516	41.0
FR of Germany	ARD	5 252	1 627	30.9
	ZDF	5 200	3 328	34.0
	WDR3	2 964	532	17.9
Greece	ERT1	4 680	889	18.9
	ERT2	2 756	964	34.9
Ireland	RTE1	3 774	1 648	43.6
Italy	RAI1	5 928	1 660	28.0
	RAI2	5 200	1 820	35.0
	RAI3	4 524	1 221	25.0
	Rete 4	6 448	5 159	80.0
	Canale 5	7 072	3 465	48.9
	Italia 1	6 552	3 932	60.0
Luxembourg	RTL-TVI	3 744	2 246	59.9
Netherlands	NOS1	3 538	919	25.9
	NOS2	3 068	674	21.9
Portugal	RTP1	5 304	1 856	34.9
	RTP2	3 120	na	na
Spain	TVE1	6 188	1 733	28.0
	TVE2	2 444	708	28.9
UK	BBC1	6 656	1 730	26.0
	BBC2	4 888	1 076	22.0
	ITV	9 516	3 425	36.0
	Channel 4	4 056	1 461	36.0

Source: IIC, 'Stories come first'.

Note: All annual figures are extrapolations based on a sample week. Figures include repeats.
na = not available.

The sudden expansion of demand for programmes on the part of broadcasters in the first place concerns fiction production. The new media groups have an interest in occupying as quickly as possible as large an audience as possible. At the same time, the only definite regulatory obstacles to private broadcasting activity concerned news and services, while entertainment remained a relatively free-action area.

It is only natural that private broadcasters should turn towards the source of cheap and plentiful productions, ready for the taking and with a healthy record of audience attraction: the United States. Tables II.A.5 to II.A.8 show the imbalance in the export/import relations between Europe and the USA. As an IIC report reads: 'Fiction makes up approximately 37% of all programmes transmitted in Europe ... On average, only about 27% are home-produced. Only Germany and the UK produce more fiction than they buy. In all cases, the prime source of imported material is the USA' (*Stories come first*) (see Tables II.A.9 to II.A.11).

Only 8% of the transactions for programme acquisition on the part of European broadcasters concern internal European exchanges. Half of the world's programme exchange transactions, accounting for a volume of business of USD 3 100 million are concluded with European partners: four-fifths of them consisted in the acquisition of US programmes. To conclude this rather impressive set of data, we will recall that in 1985 exports were 3.25% of the European audiovisual turnover. Between 1985 and 1986, the audiovisual trade balance for Western Europe fell from USD −911 million to USD −1 260 million. As a comparison, the figure for the USA rose from USD +1 546 million to USD +1 961 million. On average, American programmes represented 44% of the imports in Europe in 1986. They also gathered, on average, 40% of the audience!

Table II.A.5
Amount of audiovisual exports of EC countries in 1985

(million ECU)

Belgium	1
Denmark	12
Spain	1
France	50
FR of Germany	10
Ireland	10
Italy	60
Luxembourg	0
Netherlands	0
Portugal	10
United Kingdom	335

Source: Commission of the European Communities.

Table II.A.6

Origin of fiction programmes broadcast by European channels in 1985

(%)

Radio broadcaster	National production	EC production	National production + % EC	American production	Other production
RTB	na	na	51	49	0
BRT	21	46	67	33	0
DR	7	43	50	46	4
RTVE	23	30	53	35	12
TF1	22	34	56	37	9
Antenne 2	34	26	60	35	5
FR3	37	22	59	28	13
RAI	11	28	39	57	2
NOS	7	30	37	56	7
RTP	7	34	42	38	20
ZDF	17	33	50	36	13
SAT-1	20	31	51	48	0
RTL Plus	0	86	86	9	4
BBC	38	7	45	55	0
ITV	57	5	62	38	0
Sky Channel	na	na	12	72	16

Source: 'L'avenir de l'industrie audiovisuelle européenne'.

na = not available.

As the price for their acquisition rose according to the increase in demand, coming near to production costs, their success record explains why broadcasters still prefer to acquire them rather than produce programmes themselves.

In fact, the multiplication of channels has led to an actual explosion in the diffusion and distribution segment of the audiovisual industry. New technologies brought about the internationalization of investment in an effort to maximize profits. Broadcasters need to reach vast audiences rapidly so as to attract the advertising revenue necessary for them to survive. The demand they generate can only be satisfied by production structures apt to survive in a large market. The new broadcasting space could only be filled by productions that guaranteed success and were available at low prices.

Nothing like that exists in Europe. The initial booming phase of the audiovisual industry did not bring any substantial impulse to the fiction production structures in the Community. Quite the opposite: as television becomes the main distribution outlet for fiction, the invasion of American television productions (serials, films, sitcoms, etc.) threatens the very survival of European fiction production.

While investment in broadcasting enjoys a more mobile and transborder status because of its economic quality, fiction production is rooted in national cultures. From this point of view, not only does a European single market not yet exist, but the very idea

Table II.A.7

Origin of films broadcast by the European channels in 1985

Radio broadcaster	Number broadcast	Domestic	Other European	Total European	USA
ORF	33	15	na	na	na
RTBF	na	na	na	52	na
CyDC	128	na	na	16	na
DR	122	na	na	41	na
TVE	443	21	24	42	na
YLE	300	20	38	48	na
France (4 channels)	922				
TF1		55	5	60	na
A2		75	11	86	na
FR3		60	6	66	na
RAI	1 100	25	24	49	50
Italy (private channels)	5 000	na	na	35	65
RTL	na	na	na	61	na
NOS	262	3	32	35	na
NRK	78	12	41	53	na
RTP	210	6	30	36	na
ARD + ZDF	1 324	25	20	45	50
BBC	810	19	na	na	na
ITV	360	na	na	na	na
Channel 4	380	na	na	na	na
STV	231	21	35	56	na
SSR/SRG	853	12	43	55	na

Source: 'L'avenir de l'industrie audiovisuelle européenne'.

Note: na = not available.

faces opposition in most EC countries. Therefore, in the European Community there exists a nearly unified television channel market and 12 single, separate and relatively small production-offering markets.

Revenue for private television comes principally from advertising, and the stake of programming is a large audience. This turned the traditional vertical link between production and distribution into a horizontal programme-acquisition/diffusion/attraction-for-advertising chain, with a strong emphasis on the acquisition of fiction and entertainment productions. A large demand for fiction in a non-regulated and divisive environment is leading to a dominant position for producers better equipped to supply more quality material at lower costs. Those producers are not in Europe, and this dominance might easily become a near-monopoly.

Table II.A.8
Origin area by type of programme

(%)

Programmes	France	Italy	Germany	UK	Sweden	USA
Information			10	38	23	12
Documentary	6		13			19
Education			10	30	18	23
Cultural	29		26	17		
Religious	16	60				25
Childrens'			5	8		46
Films	8		7	7		62
Films for television			8	19		51
Musical			20	22	11	21
Entertainment			7	15		46

Source: Commission of the European Communities.

Table II.A.9
Imports of fiction by country in hours (1987)

Country	Total fiction	Domestic	Foreign
Belgium	2 372	328	1 089
Denmark	962	78	442
France	10 125	733	7 712
FR of Germany	3 927	1 460	1 260
Greece	1 853	380	741
Ireland	1 648	25	1 208
Italy	17 257	1 023	11 357
Luxembourg	2 246	0	1 610
Netherlands	1 593	188	1 019
Portugal	2 792	412	2 115
Spain	2 441	295	1 482
UK	7 692	2 640	2 387
Total	54 908	7 562	32 422

Sources: IIC, 'Stories come first'.

Notes: All annual figures are extrapolations based on a sample week. Figures include repeats.
Domestic and foreign hours exclude feature films.

Table II.A.10

Imports of fiction by channel (1987)

Country	Broadcaster	Total fiction	Domestic (hours)	Foreign (hours)
Belgium	BRT	1 404	231	750
	RTBF	968	97	339
Denmark	DR	962	78	442
France	TF1	1 758	227	1 304
	A2	1 509	362	845
	FR3	994	144	358
	La Cinq	6 770	0	6 479
	M6	2 516	0	2 148
FR of Germany	ARD	1 627	577	525
	ZDF	1 768	676	676
	WDR3	532	207	59
Greece	ERT1	889	187	328
	ERT2	964	193	413
Ireland	RTE1	1 648	25	1 208
Italy	RAI1	1 660	711	534
	RAI2	1 820	312	676
	RAI3	1 221	0	588
	Rete 4	5 159	0	3 611
	Canale 5	3 465	0	2 475
	Italia 1	3 932	0	3 473
Luxembourg	RTL-TVI	2 246	0	1 610
Netherlands	NOS1	919	35	743
	NOS2	674	153	276
Portugal	RTP1	1 856	318	1 273
	RTP2	na	94	842
Spain	TVE1	1 733	124	1 238
	TVE2	708	171	244
UK	BBC1	1 730	799	399
	BBC2	1 076	293	196
	ITV	3 425	1 142	1 427
	Channel 4	1 461	406	365

Sources: IIC, 'Stories come first'.

Note: All annual figures are extrapolations based on a sample week. Figures include repeats.
Domestic and foreign hours exclude feature films.
na = not available.

Table II.A.11

Imports of fiction by source (1987)

Country/Channel	EC imports *(%)*	US imports *(%)*
Belgium		
RTBF	51.3	48.7
Denmark		
DR	35.5	58.6
France		
TF1	1.7	44.1[1]
A2	4.0	29.3[1]
FR3	6.8	30.9[1]
FR of Germany		
ARD[2]	14.3	37.1
ZDF	33.2	36.1[1]
SAT-1[2]	31.5	48.1
Italy		
RAI	27.6	57.4
Luxembourg		
RTL-TVI[3]	45.0	55.0
RTL-Plus[2]	86.0	9.3
Netherlands		
NOS	30.0	56.0
Spain		
RTVE	27.2	48.0
TV 3 Catalan	11.7	20.1
United Kingdom		
BBC1[4]	4.0	24.0
BBC2[4]	5.0	9.0
ITV	5.8	13.8
Channel 4	5.0	12.0
Sky Channel	5.8	35.6

Sources: IIC, 'Stories come first'.

[1] 1988 figures.
[2] Films only.
[3] Includes domestic Belgo-Luxembourg production.
[4] Films and series only.

1. Cinema and television

From the point of view of production, there is no competition between cinema and television. Quite the opposite: all that happened was that people loved cinema so much that they decided to take it home.

Theatrical attendance in Europe decreased constantly since the appearance of television. In the last 10 years there were 25% fewer cinema-goers in Germany, 70% in the United Kingdom and 75% in Italy. Since 1958 cinema admissions fell by 85% (Tables II.1.1 and II.1.2). One of the long-term reasons for this dramatic decrease is the fall in the number of young people that provide the bulk of cinema audiences (Tables II.1.3 and II.1.4).

However, in the United States the trend swings back towards increase: in spite of the higher degree of penetration of VCRs and the early development of television with a much wider offer in channels than Europe, the number of sold box-office tickets went

Table II.1.1

Trend in cinema admissions: 1987 v 1980

Country	1980 (million)	1987 (million)	± %
Austria [1]	22.3	15.5	− 30.5
Belgium	21.6	16.9	− 21.8
Denmark	15.9	11.4	− 28.3
Finland	9.9	6.5	− 34.3
France	175.0	133.0	− 24.0
FR of Germany	143.8	108.0	− 24.9
Greece [1]	77.6	54.0	− 30.4
Ireland	na	na	na
Italy	241.0	109.0	− 54.8
Netherlands	27.9	15.5	− 44.4
Norway	17.5	12.4	− 29.1
Portugal [1]	40.8	28.4	− 30.4
Spain	176.0	148.7	− 15.5
Sweden	22.1	15.5 [1]	− 29.9
Switzerland	19.1	23.5	23.0
UK	102.0	75.0	− 26.5
Turkey	49.6 [1]	34.5	− 30.4
Europe [2]	1 162.1	807.8	− 28.8

Source: EAT.

[1] AIT estimates: official figures not available.
[2] Excluding Ireland.
na = not available.

from 720 million in 1970 back to 1 100 million in 1986. (For a comparative view of the share of box-office revenue in global income for feature film distribution, see Tables II.1.5 to II.1.7.)

In fact, the 'consumption' of fiction has increased. People have a choice of literally thousands of films on television every year (Tables II.1.5 and II.1.9).

Table II.1.2
Evolution in box-office attendance in the principal world markets

(million spectators)

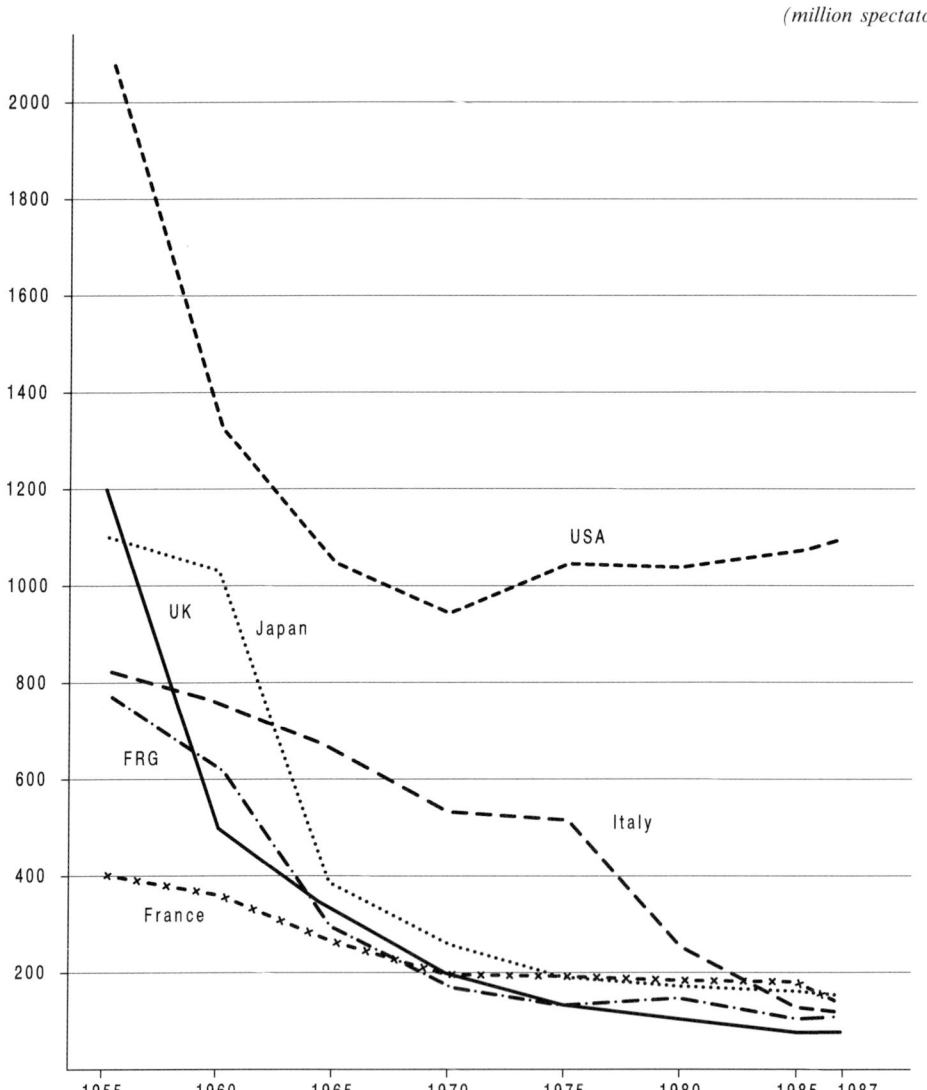

Source: 'L'avenir de l'industrie audiovisuelle européenne'.

52

Table II.1.3

Trends in the age distribution of European populations

Country	Age range	1985 (1 000)	1990 (1 000)	1995 (1 000)	2000 (1 000)	2025 (1 000)	Index (2025 v 1985)
Austria	15-24	1 259	1 100	926	891	807	64
	60 +	1 496	1 501	1 490	1 540	2 005	134
Belgium	15-24	1 520	1 391	1 274	1 235	1 177	77
	60 +	1 892	1 982	2 053	2 095	2 704	143
Denmark	15-24	788	762	690	604	480	61
	60 +	1 030	1 035	1 029	1 043	1 395	135
Finland	15-24	751	668	635	656	564	75
	60 +	843	895	924	962	1 397	166
France	15-24	8 524	8 251	7 758	7 518	6 833	80
	60 +	9 749	10 150	10 733	11 111	15 131	155
FR of Germany	15-24	10 081	8 214	6 282	5 948	5 284	52
	60 +	12 217	12 509	12 887	14 258	16 645	136
Greece	15-24	1 507	1 474	1 411	1 417	1 350	90
	60 +	1 771	1 948	2 132	2 269	2 570	145
Ireland	15-24	647	692	698	712	761	118
	60 +	510	522	525	533	904	177
Italy	15-24	9 100	8 859	7 944	6 774	6 587	72
	60 +	10 654	11 427	12 069	12 855	15 348	144
Luxembourg	15-24	55	49	43	42	36	65
	60 +	65	68	72	75	97	149
Netherlands	15-24	2 494	2 297	1 966	1 810	1 467	59
	60 +	2 391	2 534	2 666	2 810	4 422	185
Norway	15-24	651	649	581	530	466	72
	60 +	875	876	851	829	1 153	132
Portugal	15-24	1 766	1 688	1 657	1 650	1 599	91
	60 +	1 548	1 677	1 790	1 863	2 730	176
Spain	15-24	6 442	6 571	6 621	6 042	6 012	93
	60 +	6 049	6 678	7 355	7 814	10 072	167
Sweden	15-24	1 192	1 184	1 077	992	830	70
	60 +	1 900	1 894	1 849	1 833	2 241	118
Switzerland	15-24	1 011	887	759	713	565	56
	60 +	1 254	1 285	1 354	1 426	1 832	146
UK	15-24	9 036	8 263	7 163	6 984	6 566	73
	60 +	11 737	11 622	11 475	11 461	14 386	123
Turkey	15-24	10 208	11 151	11 419	11 828	14 465	142
	60 +	3 154	3 849	4 655	5 391	11 810	374
Europe (Total)	15-24	67 032	64 150	58 904	56 346	55 849	83
	60 +	69 135	72 452	75 909	80 168	106 842	155

Source: EAT.

Table II.1.4
Trends in the age distribution of European populations

(% of total population)

Country	Age range	1985	1990	1995	2000	2025
Austria	15-24	16.7	14.7	12.3	11.9	11.1
	60+	19.8	20.0	19.8	20.5	27.5
Belgium	15-24	15.4	14.0	12.8	12.3	11.7
	60+	19.2	19.9	20.6	20.9	26.9
Denmark	15-24	15.4	14.9	13.5	11.9	10.2
	60+	20.1	20.2	20.1	20.5	29.8
Finland	15-24	15.3	13.5	12.7	13.0	11.3
	60+	17.2	18.0	18.4	19.0	28.0
France	15-24	15.5	14.9	13.8	13.2	11.7
	60+	17.7	18.3	19.1	19.4	25.9
FR of Germany	15-24	16.5	13.6	10.5	10.0	9.9
	60+	20.0	20.7	21.5	24.0	31.1
Greece	15-24	15.2	14.6	13.7	13.6	12.5
	60+	17.8	19.3	20.8	21.7	23.8
Ireland	15-24	18.3	18.0	17.1	16.5	14.3
	60+	14.4	13.6	12.9	12.3	17.0
Italy	15-24	15.9	15.4	13.7	11.6	11.5
	60+	18.6	19.9	20.8	21.9	26.8
Luxembourg	15-24	15.0	13.6	11.9	11.7	10.6
	60+	17.7	18.8	20.0	20.9	28.6
Netherlands	15-24	17.2	15.6	13.1	12.0	10.0
	60+	16.5	17.2	17.8	18.6	30.1
Norway	15-24	15.7	15.5	13.8	12.6	10.9
	60+	21.1	21.0	20.3	19.7	27.1
Portugal	15-24	17.3	16.0	15.2	14.7	13.0
	60+	15.2	15.9	16.4	16.6	22.1
Spain	15-24	16.7	16.5	16.1	14.3	13.1
	60+	15.7	16.8	17.9	18.5	21.9
Sweden	15-24	14.3	14.3	13.1	12.1	10.8
	60+	22.8	22.8	22.4	22.4	29.1
Switzerland	15-24	15.5	13.9	11.9	11.2	9.8
	60+	19.2	20.1	21.2	22.5	31.7
UK	15-24	16.0	14.7	12.7	12.4	11.7
	60+	20.7	20.7	20.4	20.3	25.7
Turkey	15-24	20.5	20.4	19.0	18.1	15.7
	60+	6.3	7.0	7.8	8.2	12.8
Europe	15-24	16.6	15.6	14.1	13.2	12.4
(Total)	60+	17.1	17.7	18.1	18.8	23.7

Source: EAT.

In spite of the crisis in the traditional film industry, fiction production should, if it develops the necessary large-market philosophy, ultimately benefit enormously from the expansion in broadcasting.

Television stations began as early as the 1970s to give a substantial support to the production of feature films. Just to quote a few cases, both ARD and ZDF joined the German State film-funding institution, the *Filmförderungsanstalt*, in 1974 and have since contributed to the production of over 400 films; in Italy, RAI invested LIT 120 to 140 thousand million in the production of feature films, while Silvio Berlusconi's

Table II.1.5

Market shares of theatrical release according to country of origin in the EC Member States

(%)

		D/F/UK/I	Rest of EC	Rest of Europe	USA
Belgium A 1985; (Brussels only)	0.8	F :23.1	—	11.7	61
Denmark B 1985	5	21	—	—	62
Germany AA 1986	22.1	F/UK/I: 12.1	—	—	62.5
France B 1986	32	D/UK/I: 11	DK/E: 4	—	32
Greece A 1985, estimated	—	—	—	—	40
United Kingdom B 1986	15	D/F/I: 15	2	2	58
Ireland C 1985	2	UK: 20 F/I: 5	—	—	63
Italy A B 1985	31.8 22.5	— D/F/UK: 22.9	— 2.5	— —	48.6 44.1
Netherlands A B 1986	14.2 4	5.6 16	— —	— —	78.8 71
Portugal B 1985	1	—	—	—	80
Spain A 1986	13	12	—	—	66

Source: Distribution and export.

Note: A = box-office takings; AA = distributor's turnover; B = film premières; C = all screened films; — = no figures available; D = Federal Republic of Germany; DK = Denmark; F = France; UK = United Kingdom; I = Italy; E = Spain.

Fininvest brings in 30 to 40 % of the global investment in the Italian film industry. In a less traditional way, the British Independent Broadcasting Authority (IBA) and Channel 4 are a strong support for film producers in the UK, while in France all television stations are contributors to a central film-industry support fund.

Cinema-television relations are changing even in another respect. In March 1987 the Committee of Ministers of the Council of Europe deemed it necessary to express its wish for good relationships between the box office and the small screen in a detailed and passionate recommendation. Now the fear that theatres will soon disappear because of television seems unjustified. A film's successful theatrical release is the precondition for its attractiveness on television. A production shown in 'première' on television will hardly attract any large audience, and theatres retain, even in the face of impending qualitative equality with television, their event-generating value. Broadcaster investment in cinema production and distribution also stems from this preoccupation.

Table II.1.6

Financing of feature films in the USA

(%)

	1980	1990
US box office	45.8	23.0
Foreign box office	32.7	15.0
Pay-TV	5.0	19.0
Pay per view	5.0	4.0
Network	6.3	3.0
Syndication	9.0	5.0
Video	1.2	31.0

Source: Commission of the European Communities.

Table II.1.7

Chronology of revenues of US films

(%)

Sources of revenue \ Years	1st	2nd	3rd	4th	5th
Total box-office receipts	90	10			
Total foreign box-office receipts	40	50	10		
Video	90	10			
Pay TV			100		
Network			65	25	10
Syndication					100
Pay per view	90	10			

Source: Commission of the European Communities.

Competitiveness between television stations is, therefore, a guarantee for the survival of movie theatres. While in a situation of monopoly or near-monopoly a broadcaster is safe in its production and programme-acquisition investments, in competition even broadcasters need at least minimal guarantees of success for the programmes they are

Table II.1.8

Number of films broadcast by European television channels in 1985

Austria	ORF	769
Belgium	RTBF	235
	BRT	143
Cyprus	CyBC	120
Denmark	DR	971
	The voice (Pay-TV)	50
Spain	RTVE/TV3	396
Finland	YLE	180
	MTV	120
	HTV (Pay-TV)	570
France	TF1	130
	Antenne 2	158
	FR3	212
	Canal Plus	2 300
	TV5	52
Greece	ERT 1/2	500
Ireland	RTE	395
Iceland	RS	146
Italy	RAI	830
	Reteitalia	2 500
	Other commercial channels	3 000
Luxembourg	RTL	250
	RTL Plus	470
Norway	NRK	75
Netherlands	NOS	200
	ATN-FilmNet	1 480
Portugal	RTP	210
FR of Germany	ZDF	345
	ARD	379
	3rd channel	992
	SAT-1	570
UK	BBC	810
	ITV	360
	Channel 4	380
	Sky Channel	500
	Première	1 560
Sweden	STV	224
Switzerland	SSR/SRG/TSI	845
	TeleClub	720
	Téléciné Romandie	105
Turkey	TRT	312

Source: 'L'avenir de l'industrie audiovisuelle européenne'.

going to buy. The theatrical performance of a film will determine its value as a catalyst of audience and, consequently, its attractiveness to advertisers and broadcasters.

The problems for fiction production do not lie with the competition between cinema and television. Although in many countries cinema professionals resent financing on the part of broadcasters as a sort of intrusion and limitation to their creative freedom by

Table II.1.9
Hours of feature films by channel (1987)

Country	Broadcaster	Total fiction	Feature films
Belgium	BRT	1 404	423
	RTBF	968	532
Denmark	DR	962	442
France	TF1	1 758	227
	A2	1 509	302
	FR3	994	492
	La Cinq	6 770	291
	M6	2 516	368
FR of Germany	ARD	1 627	525
	ZDF	1 768	416
	WDR1	532	266
Greece	ERT1	889	374
	ERT2	964	358
Ireland	RTE1	1 648	415
Italy	RAI1	1 660	415
	RAI2	1 820	832
	RAI3	1 221	633
	Rete 4	5 159	1 548
	Canale 5	3 465	990
	Italia 1	3 932	459
Luxembourg	RTL	2 246	636
Netherlands	NOS1	919	141
	NOS2	674	245
Portugal	RTP1	1 856	265
Spain	TVE1	1 733	371
	TVE2	708	293
UK	BBC1	1 730	532
	BBC2	1 076	587
	ITV	3 425	856
	Channel 4	1 461	690

Sources: IIC, 'Stories come first'.
Note: All annual figures and extrapolations are based on a sample week. Figures include repeats.

the principle of audience attraction, the expansion of television represents in general a great opportunity for fiction production. The adoption of similar technical means for both cinematographic and television productions will bring the two areas even closer; from the production point of view, it will lead to virtual identity.

Problems for fiction production start with the so-called 'fragmentation of the market'.

Discussion here borders dangerously on a philosophical debate between economic liberals and interventionists. Policy models for support to national audiovisual production come in all varieties and in all degrees of efficacy. From the British deregulation and blind faith in market forces to the French hyper-regulation, *cahiers de charges*, Soficas and centralization of financing, all the Member States of the Community are enacting support or impulsion policies according to the political colour of their governments. When the discussion turns to a European audiovisual policy, everyone simply tries to transfer their internal solutions to the general arena of the continent, and this is a major difficulty in devising a genuine large-market attitude. In the next section, these philosophical factors will be discussed. The fragmentation of European fiction production structures is evident in all sectors. Major problems arise from the absence of a healthy EC-wide distribution and financing system.

Table II.1.10

Origin of films distributed in various European countries in 1985

	USA	F	UK	I	D	USSR	Other European countries	Co-pro-ductions[1]	ROW[2]	Total
Austria	192	57	18	16	48	na	na	na	14	384
Belgium	81	33	na	na	na	na	17	na	5	136
Cyprus	40	4	3	10	6	0	21	0	0	87
Denmark	129	8	15	11	8	2	16	0	9	198
Spain	204	52	19	44	14	6	17	na	25	484
Finland	125	7	17	5	2	na	19	20	11	206
France	121	124	25	20	7	24	na	34	45	456
Greece	342	30	10	15	14	0	0	0	16	427
Italy	117	26	24	81	8	0	0	0	24	280
Norway	150	21	22	4	5	0	37	0	25	266
Netherlands	192	25	19	10	28	0	20	0	6	301
FR of Germany	146	30	26	16	46	0	6	18	18	308
United Kingdom	123	12	51	3	0	0	11	19	37	256
Sweden	138	26	18	4	7	1	16	3	11	228
Switzerland	171	81	15	21	42	0	0	0	16	346
Yugoslavia	102	20	6	15	8	na	na	na	74	235

Source: 'L'avenir de l'industrie audiovisuelle européenne'.

[1] National statistics are not measured in the same way for co-productions.
[2] Rest of world.
na = not available.

The figures for film distribution in Europe have become by now sadly infamous. 80% of the over 500 feature films produced in the 12 EC countries every year are not distributed beyond the borders of their country of production. European products do not circulate. Theatres in almost all EC countries show a majority of US productions with national feature films following; productions from other EC countries never account for more than 25% of any country's theatrical releases of films (Table II.1.10).

Language barriers obviously play an important role (see Table II.1.11). Apart from that, however, American movies are safer: the most different audiences seem to like them. They are normally perfect present-time cinema products, rich in effects and famous names, with a big emphasis on all the aspects of fiction with which television cannot as yet compete. They are costly productions.

Again, (possibly the same) 80% of European films are what has become known as 'low-budget' productions: most European films, that is, do not cost more than ECU 2 250 000. A film with such a modest production budget can certainly not afford a launch comparable to that of American films, some of which devote up to half of their fabulous production prices on the launch (Table II.1.12).

Table II.1.11

Languages spoken in European countries

(%)

Country	English	French	German	Italian	Spanish	Flemish, Dutch
Austria	na	na	na	na	na	na
Belgium	26	71	22	4	3	68
Denmark	51	5	48	1	1	1
Finland	na	na	na	na	na	na
France	26	100	11	8	13	1
FR of Germany	43	18	100	3	1	3
Greece	na	na	na	na	na	na
Ireland	99	12	2	1	1	0
Italy	13	27	6	100	5	0
Luxembourg	na	na	na	na	na	na
Netherlands	68	31	67	2	4	100
Norway	80	10	20	4	2	0
Portugal	na	na	na	na	na	na
Spain	13	15	3	4	100	0
Sweden	68	13	35	1	6	0
Switzerland	26	55	81	17	3	0
UK	100	15	6	1	2	1
Turkey	na	na	na	na	na	na

Source: EAT.

Note: na = not available.

Table II.1.12

Relation of low-budget films to the total production in the EC Member States

	Total production	Films of Cat. I (up to ECU 0.75 m)		Films of Cat. II (up to ECU 2.25 m)	
		Total	% of total production	Total	% of total production
Belgium	10	6	55	4	45
FR of Germany [1]	126	93	74	26	21
Denmark	11	2	14	8	77
France	142	31	22	62	44
Greece	14	13	93	1	7
United Kingdom	46	5	11	14	30
Italy [2]	100	31	31	58	58
Netherlands	15	9	63	5	30
Portugal [3]	7	7	100		
Spain [4]	73	49	67	12	16
Total	544	246	45	190	35

Source: Distribution and export.

[1] On the basis of a special survey undertaken for this study; the data collected by the SPIO records the premières of 70 films. It is generally accepted that in all countries there are more films produced than is statistically recorded, by whatever criteria. Thus, this finding seems more applicable if one wants the absolute number of films produced in the EC to be as near to reality as possible.

[2] Including 10 co-productions with estimated budgets of over ECU 2.25 million.

[3] Not including co-productions, of which there were five between 1984 and 1987.

[4] Including 12 co-productions with estimated budgets of over ECU 2.25 million.

The American 'majors', controlling all the links in the audiovisual chain from production to distribution, are the only actors equipped to distribute a film in all the European countries simultaneously. European distributors are only active on a national scale. Thus, the American cinematographic industry export revenue (around USD 1 600 million) is three times higher than the film export revenues of all the EC States together.

Any effective support for European film production must set out from the necessity for a European global distribution system. The problem of financing is just as crucial. No State aid to national film industries will make up for the absence of a Europe-wide circulation and potential accumulation of investments in production. With few exceptions, as stated in a recent report, 'the banking sector still hesitates in getting involved with production, while it is active in the new commercial television enterprises'. Production in itself qualifies as the province of culture.

The development of a European audiovisual industry depends, however, almost entirely on competitiveness in software production. Fiction should be seen, in this respect, as a segment of an industrial sector in need of support.

Thinking of a remedy to insufficient financing on a continental scale led, first of all, to improving the opportunities for co-production. In the last few years there has been a plethora of projects in this field. Among the most concrete we may recall Eurimages, a fund for co-productions set up within the Council of Europe and operational since the beginning of 1989; the European Production Group, resulting from an agreement between six broadcasters (ZDF, ORF, RAI, SRG/SSR, Antenne 2, Channel 4) for the production of fiction series; SEPT, which undertook a policy of European co-productions; and, in the private sector, the consortium formed in 1985 by Silvio Berlusconi, Jerome Seydoux and Leo Kirch in Luxembourg.

Although regulated by bi- and multilateral international co-production agreements, co-production cannot be substitutive of financing with global continental resources for any European production.

As stated in various European Commission documents, the lack of coordination between measures of support for national film industries and in regulation on financing in the different Member States is a source of further complication in co-production and the establishment of a common financing system. Again we face the problem of a change in basic philosophy.

The financing of European productions must go beyond the occasional cumulation of resources that remain separate and national in nature. It has to be continental in scale. It must have constant, unchanging European dimensions and a European working range. It must also become substantial: fiction production needs as much resource investment as the broadcasting and electronic component segments of the audiovisual industry.

Talking of fiction production in such terms often brings confusion. It is not, however, in any way equivalent to saying that fiction and cultural production in general must be reduced to a factory-like environment where creative freedom is abolished in favour of an assembly-line logic. The expansion of diffusion and distribution means represents an immense opportunity for creativity. An American director was once reported as saying to Jean-Luc Godard: 'European directors have something we don't have in America: freedom', to which Godard allegedly replied: 'American directors have something we don't have in Europe: money'.

The money is there, now. It must not be poured only into the distribution pot, regardless of what is distributed. Money, investment money, must go to software production as it goes to satellite launching, the electronic component industry and to the acquisition of rights for programmes and films. This must happen if Europe does not want to see its main social communication media devoid of European products.

The basic problem is to create conditions throughout Europe for investors to put money into fiction production as they would into an industrial sector.

Single aspects of production need special attention. The whole phase of pre-production, for example is widely neglected in Europe because of lack of, or poor, funding. Thus, the development of scripts from original ideas is the poorest moment in the genesis of a film: a paradox, if one considers the importance of a good script for film quality.

In all sectors, continental-scale thinking is a condition for any affective action in support of fiction production.

2. The Media 92 philosophy

As noted above, most misunderstandings and opposition in the discussion on the best policy for the audiovisual sector are, at present, generated by differences in philosophical approach. The debate is too young, and the data and the methods for its evaluation are still too ambiguous to allow for a discussion on solid results. Media 92, however, is an exception.

Started at the end of 1986, Media 92 is a programme of the Commission of the European Communities included among the so-called 'punctual actions' of the Commission: a project with a relatively restricted aim, a year-by-year budget and a relatively short life.

The Media 92 approach to the question of providing an effective support to the European audiovisual industry consists of two basic assumptions: first, that the professionals themselves must determine the form that aid to production must assume; and second, that the support has to result in the establishment of independent agencies and/or structures. Having set certain sectoral priorities, the programme limits itself to organizing consultations among the professionals on the problems of each sector and making elaborate proposals. The proposals assume the form of pilot projects financed up to 50%, in a proportion that must decrease in time, by Media 92. The rest has to be provided by others: institutions, professionals, private sponsors, etc.

The Commission's 50% works as seed-money. The structures set up within the programme have to prove efficient and start functioning by their own means as quickly as possible.

In the initial phases of the programme four sectors were easily identified in the fiction production chain as the ones in direct need of support. They are distribution, financing, production and training.

Pilot projects

Consultations have led to the establishment of seven pilot-project structures. Each of them is autonomous and they all seem to be doing relatively well; all are the issue of preoccupations expressed by pools of members of the European film and television professions.

The number of pilot projects will probably grow. The present list is therefore provisional:

1. European Film Distribution Office (EFDO). The first of the pilot structures, it is based in Hamburg. Its basic principle is to give loans up to 50% of distribution costs for low-cost European feature films getting a commitment to distribute them in at least three EC countries.

2. Broadcasting across the barrier of European languages (Babel). Based in Geneva, Babel provides financial support for dubbing and subtitling.

3. Euro-AIM. This Brussels-based structure offers various services to independent producers, including assistance in marketing and production promotion as well as 'umbrellas' (joint European independent producer stands) at the main world markets.

4. Media investment club for advanced technologies. The Media club brings together industrialists, broadcasters and financial institutions. Its aim is to promote the use of advanced technology in audiovisual production. It is based in Paris.

5. European Script Fund. Script supports the pre-production phase of select ideas for feature films and television fiction productions. Its headquarters are in London.

6. Cartoon. This structure gives financial and structural support to European cartoon production. It is based in Brussels.

7. European audiovisual entrepreneurs (EAVE). EAVE organizes training seminars for young producers with an emphasis on the acquisition of management skills and entrepreneurial conception.

Three more projects should become operational this year: Media Venture, including a guarantee and a financing fund for production, and EVE, concerned with the circulation of video cassettes.

Balance

The future of the Media programme is uncertain. In 1990 its pilot phase will be concluded, and no budget for it is foreseen for 1991. Early in 1990 a document assessing the programme's results will be issued by the Commission of the European Communities, which has also committed itself to propose to the Council that the Media programme be included, under one form or other, among the long-term actions of the Community.

The final outcome of this will certainly depend, among other things, on developments in the audiovisual Eureka initiative, as will be noted in the concluding part of this book. Alleged inequalities in the distribution of the programme's initiatives between the Community member countries generated political problems that added to the spice of Media's life, as the programme's staff often put it, and threatened at some stages its very survival.

Media 92 was born as a small action plan. Its budget for 1987 amounted to ECU 1 million. In 1988, the figure was already 5 million, and in 1989 the Media 92 staff administer ECU 7.5 million. It is likely to touch the 10 million ceiling in 1990. Media 92 works, and the political problems it met with are a symptom of the interest it arises.

The programme's dimensions are such that, no matter how successful, it cannot in itself represent an adequate solution to the problem of supporting European fiction production.

Media 92 has, however, set a precious example for a new model in institutional behaviour. In an environment as hostile to public and institutional intrusion as the film industry, the Media attitude has won trust, commitment and even friends.

The Media consultations have also served to create an informal kind of club of personalities in the film and television industry that, albeit restricted and somewhat partial, is already an almost autonomous agent in the European audiovisual landscape.

Media 92 acts from a global European point of view, and this is its principal virtue. It is the living proof that the European institutions are the only convenient seat for the development of a genuine and effective European audiovisual policy.

Nobody's perfect. Media 92 is far from perfect. It was until now too small to be anything but an example, or a laboratory. It is, however, for the time being, the most successful model for a European audiovisual policy as far as the support to software (i.e. fiction) production is concerned. The studies produced for the preparation of its pilot projects are among the most accurate and complete pieces of literature on audiovisual topics produced in Europe.

Its philosophy is wholly new, and it can be adapted for use on an adequate scale.

Media 92 was acclaimed as the most concrete contribution any European or national institution could produce at the 'Assises de l'audiovisuel' in Paris at the end of September 1989. No one has as yet come up with anything better. It is not by pure chance that the Eureka priorities are the same as Media's: the distribution and financing of productions.

Whatever form the programme may take beyond 1990, everyone in the audiovisual sector wishes for it to become, in the words of the Chairman of the Committee of the European Parliament on Culture and the Media, Mr Roberto Barzanti, 'what Erasmus became for the EC education policy'.

3. Other initiatives

In the course of the European Film and Television Year, an initiative developed by the Commission of the European Communities in 1988, the need emerged for the establishment of points of reference for professionals in Europe. Databank was the key-word, an expression that occurred at least as often as a gut-cry as in the form of rational projects.

During the year professionals repeated endlessly to themselves, to the representatives of institutions and to the world that it is unthinkable to have European directors or movies or distribution networks if information on different legislation in European countries is not centralized, but must be collected 'manually' in each capital before any action is planned, let alone undertaken.

From the point of view of the situation overview, the proliferation of partial studies on audiovisual topics, often redundant, never coordinated, has led to repetitiveness of information on certain topics and its absence for others. This generated the notion of a permanent structure for the analysis of the audiovisual market. Such a structure is badly needed, especially because of the incredible rate at which information on audiovisual issues ages: data become obsolete, so to speak, in the time taken to note them down.

Proposals for a European film foundation, on the model of the American Academy, generated reactions ranging from enthusiasm to worry and disgust. It was, however, itself the product of a general need for points of reference in continental-scale activity.

At the 'Assises de l'audiovisuel' in Paris the Committee of Coordinators of the audiovisual Eureka was charged with the creation of a European audiovisual 'observatory' capable of providing up-to-date, in-depth information to professionals and decision-makers.

4. Home video

Home-video cassette recorders (VCRs) will play an increasingly important role in fiction distribution. For its potential as a source of revenue to the film industry and the problems it generates in connection with copyright, home-recording equipment must be treated separately.

In the evolution of sources of revenue for audiovisual production, home video is currently estimated to play the most dramatically increasing role in the near future (Table II.4.1).

Table II.4.1

Different sources of revenue of the audiovisual industry: Evolution 1985-90

(%)

	1985	1990
Box office	13	8
Cable	2	2
Export	2	2
Video	10	17
Subscriptions	1	4
Licence fee	36	25
Cable advertising	1	1
Advertising	35	41
Subventions	1	1

Source: Commission of the European Communities.

[1] Less than 1%.

Since the mid-1970s the diffusion of video recorders has developed steadily at impressive rates in Europe, Japan and the United States. Around 40% of television owners in Europe also own a video recorder (see Table II.4.2 to II.4.4).

Uneven growth in the diffusion of videos in the different EC countries is probably due to various factors. Certainly the wide offer of TV channels accounts, for example, for the very low penetration of video equipment in Italy (only 800 000 machines); in general, northern European countries are in the lead for video diffusion on the continent, the UK rating first with 9 800 000 machines or 46% of households.

Confronted with dramatically decreasing numbers for theatrical attendance, the film industry turns with growing interest to this new and flourishing means of distribution for feature films.

Table II.4.2
Penetration of VCRs in homes (at year end)

Country	1985		1986	
	Households (%)	Number (1 000)	Households (%)	Number (1 000)
Belgium	14.9	471	18.7	595
Denmark	23.0	430	28.5	545
FR of Germany	22.0	5 250	26.0	6 250
Greece	6.9	200	8.3	250
Spain	13.8	1 500	18.4	2 000
France	14.0	2 800	17.0	3 500
Ireland	22.0	220	27.0	250
Italy	3.0	500	5.0	800
Luxembourg	26.4	24	34.0	31
Netherlands	29.0	1 500	35.0	1 850
Portugal	10.0	200	15.0	300
UK	40.0	8 500	46.0	9 800

Source: Commission of the European Communities.

Table II.4.3
Consumption of feature films on video and at cinemas, 1980-84

(million UKL)

	1980	1984
Sale and rental of video tapes	8	350
Cinema admissions	165	95
Total	173	445

Source: 'TV broadcasting in Europe and the new technology'.

The private character of video-cassette fruition is, however, the origin of new preoccupations.

Video cassettes are, of course, in competition with theatre attendance. Film consumers have now an easy opportunity to screen films at home at a relatively low price, and enjoy all the advantages of choice, free interruption and feet on the table!

As with television, however, video products are best advertised through public theatrical release. From the point of view of production, cassettes provide a new enormous outlet for distribution, thus encouraging investment.

Table II.4.4

Development of VCRs in the EC, USA and Japan

(millions of units)

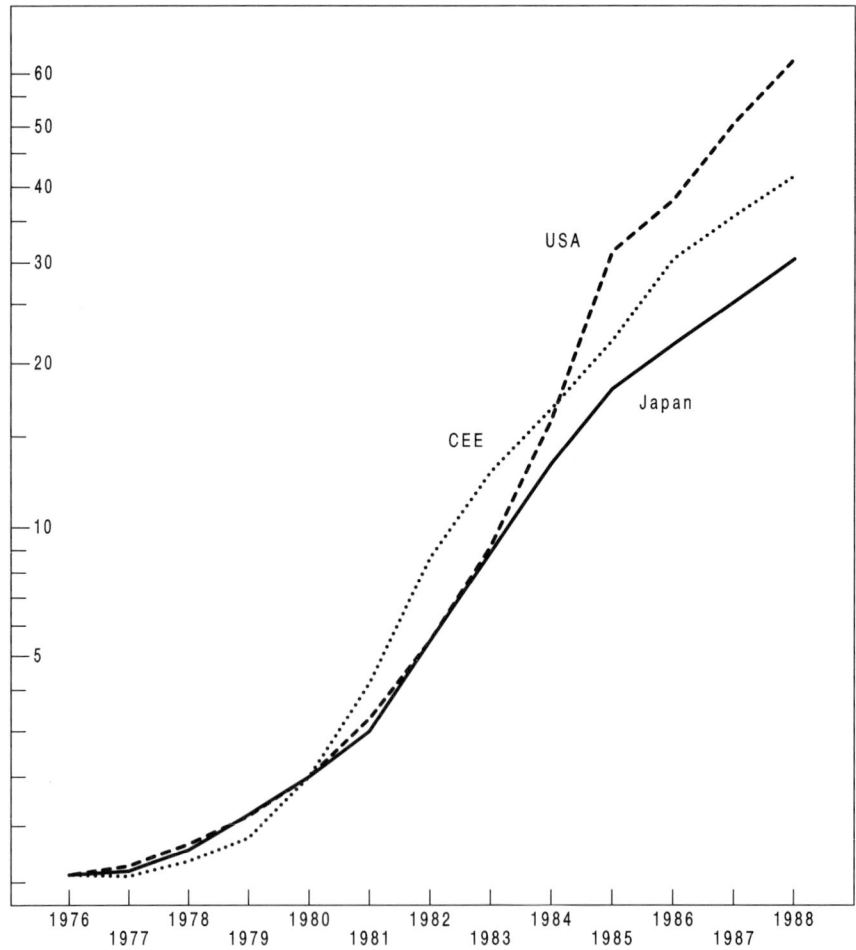

Source: 'L'avenir de l'industrie audiovisuelle européenne'.

VCRs seem to compete also with television. The audience-hunting broadcasters have to cope with the substraction of audience to broadcast programmes during video-screening time. Even worse, they have to repair the possible repercussions on advertising. The practice of recording programmes and viewing them in recorded versions at later moments ('time-shifting') allows the viewers to skip all the advertising contained in the original broadcast, jeopardizing the advertisers' confidence and, therefore, the broadcasters' revenues.

This preoccupation has been the impulse for broadcasters to put an emphasis on live broadcast, which is in many countries still the monopoly of public television stations.

The phenomenon of illegitimate copying of audiovisual products protected by copyright evidently spread with the diffusion of home-recording equipment. It earned the label of 'piracy' and attained, at some stages, awesome dimensions: in 1983 60 to 70% of all video recordings in the United Kingdom were pirate products! In 1986 unauthorized copies of video cassettes caused economic damage of USD 200 million a year in EC countries (see Table II.4.5).

While forbidding recording for private use (the so-called 'home-taping) is the object of articulate debate, there can be no doubt that the reproduction of films for commercial use, be it sale or rental, is subject to consent on the part of the copyright-holder.

Video recordings circulate mainly through the rental of cassettes. The sale of pre-recorded films still has a relatively limited relevance, both because of what has been defined as the 'saturation effect of repeated playing' and of their still relatively high price.

Table II.4.5

Extent of video piracy in the EC

(%)

	Market share of video pirate products in the Community			
	1983	1984	1985	1986
Belgium and Luxembourg	30-40	30-40	25	25
Denmark	5-10	5-10	5-10	5-10
FR of Germany	40-50	40-50	65	45
Greece	60-70	60-70	50	50
Spain	60-70	40	35	30
France	30-40	20-25	30	25
Ireland	80	60	40	30
Italy	50	50	50	40
Netherlands	50-65	50-60	45	40-45
Portugal	90-95	90-95	75-85	70-75
UK	60-70	35-40	under 20	—

Source: Commission of the European Communities.

The Commission of the European Communities' Green Paper on copyright called for the introduction of 'a rental right for ... video recordings in all Member States of the Community' as the best way to remunerate copyright holders.

The phenomenon of piracy, however, is more the concern of professional and industrial representatives in the software producing sector of the audiovisual industry. The dangers are those of a missed chance for a much-needed expansion in distribution. As the European Commission's Paper puts it:

'... if in a number of Member States, effective action is not taken to eliminate audiovisual piracy, the benefits of a Community-wide internal market will be denied to the European production industry since it will not be able to operate successfully in those parts of the market where it will be undercut by unfair competition from pirate products'.

Piracy jeopardizes revenues from the distribution of feature films in the form of video cassettes, leaving the film industry without an alternative to the decreasing flow of cash coming from box offices or television distribution.

Impending progress in VCR technology will make the situation worse. Digital recording techniques, although still some years away from commercialization, will allow for the 'cloning' of original products. The loss of quality from the master to the new copy, inevitable with the present means of analog recording, will disappear completely. It will be possible to produce a whole generation of new perfect copies from every copy of an audiovisual product. Control will be impossible other than by technical means. These include disabling commercial digital equipment from copying from another digital 'reader', so as to avoid perfection in private recording.

B — Information

Television is certainly the most effective vehicle of information. Information portrayal on television represents, in turn, the mirror of political and cultural choices. In Europe such choices were, until a few years ago, the monopoly of public, State-owned television stations. Commercial television caused public television to lose its monopoly. Information, however, at least on a national scale, remained a State television service.

At the same time, the first Europe-wide news service was started by an American commercial broadcaster, Ted Turner's Cable News Network (CNN). As was noted at the Paris 'Assises de l'audiovisuel' the fragmentation of Europe goes to the sole benefit of those willing and equipped to consider it a single space: anyone but the Europeans themselves!

The Japanese NHK started recently a news-only satellite channel, and the Canadian Broadcasting Corporation has a similar project, both in English and French. Televisa, the powerful Mexican commercial broadcaster, also started a current affairs satellite programme receivable in the whole of the United States and in Europe.

In short, there will soon be various information programmes broadcast in Europe, none of which will be European. Most of them will be run as businesses and sources of revenue; none of them will be conceived as a public service.

In the past, attempts to coordinate efforts for the organization of a European television information service were unsuccessful. The most important was developed within the Europa TV experience between 1986 and 1987.

1. Europa TV

In 1986 a consortium of European public television stations launched a European channel produced in common and broadcast via satellite. 'Europa TV', as the channel was called, stopped transmissions in November 1987.

The Pan-European Satellite Broadcasting Consortium was formed by ARD (Germany), RTE (Ireland), RAI (Italy), NOS (Netherlands) and RTP (Portugal).

Thirteen people, based at Hilversum in the Netherlands, were responsible for the production of six hours and 44 minutes of original programming per week.

The failure of Europa TV was brought about by financial complications. However, the lack of commitment on the part of many important public television stations, such as the British BBC or France's Antenne 2, represented the project's structural weakness.

The development of an editorial news policy meets even at national level with political problems related to power control. At the European level, these problems are, if anything, magnified and complicated by international relations.

The basic lines of a news strategy were, however, sketched within Europa TV.

The news-team was carefully structured to avoid the dominance of any single national group. It involved four Dutch, four English, three Portuguese, two German, two Irish, one Anglo-Dutch and one Dutch-Italian journalist.

A comparative approach became the essential feature of Europa news portrayal. A non-national perspective was encouraged by all available means. Events were covered by journalists purposely chosen among non-nationals of the country in which they occurred.

The results were, according to persons involved, less than satisfactory. Journalists tended to retain their national point of view and technique, and the news style was not homogeneous.

The Europa experience showed the need for initiative at the root, i.e. in relation to the training of journalists.

2. Eureka and the training of European journalists

In the past few years the Commission of the European Communities has begun approaching the problem of training journalists in delivering a genuinely continental, European news service.

The need for a European perspective in information is expressed in all countries. However, the logistic and technical complications still hamper progress in this field.

The Europeanization of courses in schools of journalism throughout the Continent are only a first step. The teaching of subjects such as European integration and European law is evidently no substitute for a radical innovation in teaching methods and training perspectives.

A project involving seminars for senior reporters and for heads of news-teams, as well as exchanges of junior reporters between TV news departments in different countries, was organized by the European Commission in collaboration with the French INA in 1987. It gave poor results, in particular due to the reluctance on the part of young journalists to leave their first assignments.

A proposal including exchanges of reporters between news-teams in television stations in different countries was recently formulated by the European Commission. Journalists would acquire knowledge of working methods in different EC countries and establish useful contacts for the eventual development of regular channels for work exchanges.

The proposal was born of consultations started by the European Commission among the professionals. Obstacles appear to include the need of junior reporters for constant and substantial involvement in the work of the team they are going to be ultimately assigned to, and that deters them from foreseeing periods of work abroad in the early stages of their career. Senior journalists, on the other hand, are likely to be hindered by full agendas, and are in general less inclined to be trained.

Another major impediment, however, is certainly the lack of knowledge of foreign languages and, on the other hand, the high degree of language proficiency needed in journalism. Training in journalism can only take place effectively when the working language is mastered at a degree of proficiency.

At the Paris 'Assises de l'audiovisuel' conference of September 1989, the 'Information' subgroup proposed the yearly attribution of 18 one-year scholarships to as many talented European journalists between 25 and 40 years of age. They would study a subject of their choice related to Europe in one of possibly three European universities and be committed to returning to the job they leave, their employers being committed to taking them back.

This scheme is based on the highly successful Neiman Foundation, John S. Knight and Reuter grant systems.

At present, however, European initiative in common information programmes is limited to the exchange of video news material through the EBU, the only exception being the Euronews project.

3. Euronews

Euronews is the project for a satellite broadcast TV news-only channel. It is a project initiated by the European Broadcasting Union (EBU) and closely followed by the Commission of the European Communities.

Early in 1988 a working group was established within the EBU to study the possibility of creating a wholly European news station. The group used the results obtained by the EBU in 1984 in assessing the possibility of introducing a current affairs section in programming a general European satellite station.

The EBU group's final report was presented at a meeting at the end of July 1989. Euronews should initially broadcast eight hours per day of news in five languages (English, French, Italian, German and Spanish), which could be increased to eight in the not too distant future if suitable financing is available.

The filmed material should be provided by all the European public television stations and by agencies. News flashes would be inserted every half hour. However, programming should be flexible enough to allow for the live transmission of any important events.

Euronews should be broadcast via one of the 16 Eutelsat 2 transponders starting in 1991. Eutelsat 2 will retransmit signals of 40 to 50 watts, receivable at present by 70 to 140 cm-diameter aerials. The size of aerials could be reduced to 50 to 120 cm by the time Eutelsat 2 is operational. Euronews would thus be broadcast potentially directly-to-the-home.

The cost for operating Euronews was estimated at around FF 100 million (about USD 18 million) per year. A strong emphasis was put by the EBU on the need for Euronews to be a public service, financed principally by public resources. Different sources are not excluded, and the EBU proposes to find advertising revenue for up to a third of the operational costs. It is indispensable, however, to guarantee the channel's independence from commercial and/or political pressures.

A task force was created in July for the development of the project. Eight public broadcasters are represented in it (ARD, ZDF, Antenne 2, France 3, RAI, TVE, RTB and Swedish television).

The intention on the part of the British news agency Reuters of transforming the television news agency Visnews, the largest in the world, into an autonomous, 24-hours news television channel on the model of CNN, must also be mentioned.

Visnews provides abut 75% of all transatlantic video news feeds. Reuters control 55% of it.

World News Network, as the new channel should be called, would provide Europe with a native news channel, but not with a public information service. Its cost would be in the order of at least UKL 10 million per year.

The need for such a service is strongly felt on the old continent, where long years of public monopoly on broadcasting have induced a perception of television as a public service which is hard to kill in spite of the sudden and massive progress of commercial television.

C — Other contents of European television

1. Eurosport

In May 1988 14 members of the EBU formed a consortium to broadcast a 100% sports channel. Its Chairman is Cas Goossens, of BRT. The channel became known as Eurosport.

A company — Satellite Sports Services — was created to manage production for the channel. 50% of Satellite Sports Services is in the hands of News International, in turn practically owed by Rupert Murdoch's Sky Channel.

Eurosport is broadcast via one of the four Astra transponders acquired by Murdoch, as well as by Sky Channel's Eutelsat transponder.

Although representatives of the EBU consortium deny it, Eurosport represents a major score for the commercial media group involved in it.

In fact, exclusive rights on sports broadcasts is one of the EBU's most noticeable features. For all non-EBU member broadcasters, the retransmission of sports events depends on authorization of the competent EBU Committee, and such an authorization is not easy to obtain.

The participation of Rupert Murdoch's group in Eurosport was at the base of contestation on the part of other commercial broadcasters, who claimed that the creation of a channel programming 100% sports and managed by the EBU and one commercial broadcaster would make access to sports material practically impossible for other broadcasters and would create a *de facto* monopoly.

Notably Screen Sport, a TV station in the W.H. Smith group, registered a complaint with the EC Commission because they could not obtain filmed sports material any more.

The opinion prevailing within the EC Commission is that Eurosport represents, in fact, a sort of monopoly and is therefore contrary to the rules of free competition. The case is an example of a controversial issue between the Commission and the EBU.

2. Education

The problems posed by the expansion of the audiovisual media can be turned into as many opportunities.

While the linguistic fragmentation becomes evident with the diffusion of broadcasting, the possibilities for unifying Europe culturally are multiplied precisely by the new means of communication.

Apart from the technical possibility of transmitting simultaneously in a number of languages on different sound channels, satellites bring about new openings in the field of education, especially for the teaching of languages.

Present plans include notably the use of some DBS satellite channels, for example on Olympus, for educational programmes based on the BBC Open University model.

The main problems in educational broadcasting remain financing, access to broadcasting facilities and continuity. Financing for educational TV is scarce, and the principle of a minimum contribution on the part of public and regional broadcasters seems widely accepted.

The means for diffusion of these programmes were, and will be, multiplied by the growth of cable and satellite broadcasting. Education is specifically and beneficially affected by the progressive integration of informatic and audiovisual technology. The importance of programming slots in the conventional sense decreases as the emphasis shifts from receiving to storing programmes, and production consequently concentrates on programme packages rather than on single broadcasts.

At the Paris 'Assises de l'audiovisuel' the importance of television for education was stressed, and the working group on television and education proposed a number of initiatives. The starting point was set by a distinction between a direct and an indirect educational function for television. The former is evidently represented by educational programmes (for schools, university and professional training), while the latter consists of the educational role of the audiovisual environment created by the general programming on television.

Specific proposals concerned:

(i)   the creation of a joint production centre gathering representatives of educational institutions and broadcasters to allow for the realistic conception and effective coordination of productions;

(ii) charging a European Foundation for Educational Broadcasting with the conception of television programmes;

(iii) creating a European study and observation centre on the relations between television and education, with the task of gathering information;

(iv) forming a commission counting at least one representative for each of its member countries with a supervisory task on the Foundation's activity and the role of proposing regulatory measures to the European institutions.

As far as the general programming environment is concerned (indirect approach), it was proposed to form a European education broadcasting support service providing a general infrastructure at European level.

Chapter III

The protagonists

This section describes the actors involved in developments taking place in the arena described in the preceding chapters: the personae.

The European starting point, as we have seen, includes:

(i) a rapidly expanding availability of air-time on satellites and cable networks as well as on deregulated (or re-regulated) terrestrial frequencies;

(ii) a production sector that does not immediately benefit from this expansion and could even receive a fatal stroke as a result of it;

(iii) a growing volume of investment going into television and media as well as in the closely related sector of advertising; and

(iv) a deeply rooted mental habit to consider television a public service, a habit which makes deregulation and re-regulation a lengthy process.

The monopoly of public television on broadcasting is over, as a result of the internationalization in broadcast reception. A number of commercial television channels either exist or are being discussed in every European country.

New agents either have long experience in the media business or have made their fortunes elsewhere and enter the media market by the sole weight of their financial input. Their strategies vary accordingly: they go from concentration to specialization, and shift from competing to merging with impressive speed.

From being a principally money-seeking profession, fiction production suddenly turns into a large money-making investment. National institutions cannot be considered the sole source of regulation any more, and this implies new competence and responsibility for international bodies that are not equipped or prepared to face them.

Roles have to be reassigned in a situation of primordial fluidity.

1. General features

The crisis in cinema attendance paradoxically corresponds to a dramatic increase in the 'consumption' of films and fiction. Major changes occurred quite suddenly in viewers' habits, in the structure of revenue for films and fiction in general and in legislation and aid systems for production.

Revolution in the audiovisual field started with television. New media groups and international investors appeared in connection with improved opportunities for broadcasting and they concentrated, at first, only on the diffusion of programmes they acquired at the cheapest possible price. The stake is a large audience capable of attracting advertising investment.

No commercial television station had either the means to produce 'in house' the necessary software, or the time to acquire them before they could show a substantial profit record or disappear. At first, therefore, there was a horizontal kind of concentration and connection between capital accumulation from sectors not necessarily related to the media and acquisition of broadcasting space.

A few multi-media groups appeared, like Bertelsmann or Hachette, which entered the audiovisual business coming from the printed media along with others that had made their fortunes in sectors like building (Berlusconi).

In an increasingly competitive environment, public television stations also have to turn to advertising to improve their income and provide more attractive programming. Their share of the audience shrank noticeably wherever commercial television developed.

The very concept of attractiveness in programming had to mould itself anew on the present and immediate taste of the public. This implies a revisitation of the concept of public-service broadcasting, and public stations face the problem of keeping their viewers, retaining at the same time the role of informers, means for collective social communication and, to a certain extent, educators.

Eventually, as the initial dust seems to be settling on the battlefield, a certain degree of vertical integration seems to be developing. Television stations have become the main producers of fiction. They also became directly involved in the theatrical distribution of feature films, which proved to be the only effective show-window for productions to be shown effectively on television.

The absence of consistent regulation for transnational broadcasting in Europe, in the field of the acquisition and management of diffusion structures as well as in that of copyright, where individual dealings remain the only means of agreement, represents a direct benefit for organizations capable of dealing packages of rights. The American 'majors' are the only ones on the European market entitled to simultaneously treat rights for the theatrical, public and commercial television release of productions.

The actors on the European audiovisual scene can be classified as follows:

(a) public and commercial television stations and media groups, qualifying also as cinema producers and distributors;

(b) international institutions; and, last but not least,

(c) advertisers.

Institutions responsible for the measuring of audiences will assume an increasingly important role in relation to advertising. Considering the different origins of media groups and their numerous connections with various markets not necessarily related to the media, the complexity of the general picture becomes evident.

2. Media groups

European actors

The emergence of new commercial forces was the immediate result of technological developments and deregulation in broadcasting: it was the first effect of the audiovisual revolution.

As far as large private groups are concerned, however, this seems to be one of those moments when 'disorder can be a great historic event', as the French historian Marc Bloch said of the Middle Ages. In the dust of battle, we squint and try to identify a pattern of change.

Strategies seem to divide into three actual or possible moments:

(1) conquering a portion of the market and qualifying as an operator;

(2) adjusting programme supply to the demand; and,

(3) getting involved in programme production.

(1) and (2) are part of that horizontalization of connections which substituted the traditional vertical relationship production/distribution (or transmission).

The involvement of commercial broadcasters in production, already developing notice-ably in several cases, serves among other things the aim of legitimizing their image as proper parts of the audiovisual environment. The involvement in theatrical distribution of feature films, on the other hand, is inspired by the consideration of the efficacy of movie theatres as show-windows; finally, in-house production (or steady and lasting alliances with producers) are ever more necessary as programme acquisition and production costs become similar and regulatory provisions about compulsory quotas of in-house or domestic production in programming seem probable.

In fact, the first strategic step is determinant to attain a 'critical size' capable of guaranteeing a station's survival in differentiation. Technical choices on means for diffusion (e.g. Murdoch's option for satellite TV v Berlusconi's choice of traditional hertzian distribution and simultaneous involvement in a number of countries) assume strategic relevance.

Concentration is still random and fragile. However, it seems inevitable that the European audiovisual scene will be dominated in the not too distant future by a few giants controlling the whole spectrum of the sector segments, from production to distribution. Vertical concentration will represent the actual formation of an audiovisual sector in the first place. Companies will have programme production and diffusion as their main object. Television and programme production will thus become autonomous and not simply the diversified or specialized aspect in the activity of groups originally active in other fields.

Table III.2.1 gives a list of groups involved in the European audiovisual field. Appendix I provides brief information on some of them.

It is hard to point to any qualities which the new investors in the audiovisual field might have in common. Some of them accumulated capital doing business in building and real estate (Berlusconi, Bouygues, Lyonnaise des Eaux, Compagnie Générale des Eaux),

Table III.2.1

Media groups involved or potentially involved in European commercial TV in 1987

Australia	— Bell Group		UK	— Carlton Communications
	Bond			Central TV
	Holmes à Court			DC Thompson
Austria	— Kronen Zeitung			Granada Group
				ITN
Belgium	— Groupe Bruxelles Lambert			Ladbroke
	Audiopresse			London Weekend TV
France	— Bouygues			Maxwell
	Chargeurs			Parallel Media
	Editions Mondiale			Pearson
	Générale Des Eaux			Rank
	Hachette			Thames TV
	Havas			TVS
	Hersant			Virgin
	Lyonnaise des Eaux			Visnews (Reuters)
				Yorkshire TV
FR of Germany	— Axel Springer			W.H. Smith Television
	Bertelsmann			
	Beta-Taurus		USA	— ABC
Ireland	— INI			Cablevision
				Cannon
Italy	— Berlusconi			CBS
Japan	— Dentsu			CNN (TBS)
				Disney
Luxembourg	— CLT			ESPN
Spain	— Grupo 16			Hughes Communications
	Grupo Zeta			Lorimar Telepictures
	Prisa (El País)			Murdoch
				NBC
Sweden	— Bonniergroup			Samuel Broadcast
	Esselte			UIP
	Kinnevik			Viacom
	VIP Media			Worldvision

Source : Logica.

others were active in the field of transport (Seydoux) or stationery production (Esselte) or, again, consumer electronics (Thorn-EMI).

Publishing companies have at least one good reason for investing in the audiovisual sector : the justified fear that advertising revenue will be diverted from the press to television.

Publishers were involved with British ITV companies as early as 1955. The success of Home Box Office, the first great cable television company controlled by Time Inc., also served as a model for diversification. Robert Maxwell's group represented the most astounding example in this, although it now seems to be considering concentrating again on publishing following difficulty with its audiovisual enterprises.

The concentration of broadcasting and publishing activity in the hands of single operators is not viewed favourably. Regulation against it prevented, for example, the French TF1 from being acquired at the time of its privatization by the Hachette/Havas alliance, and it is the reason for the absence of Fiat (the Turin car manufacturer controlling the major Italian publishing group Rizzoli) from the audiovisual arena. Finally, the use of Rupert Murdoch's press to campaign in favour of his television channels on Astra is the object of repeated complaints on the part of competitors BSB and W.H. Smith, who call for intervention by the British Merger and Monopolies Commission.

The threat of such regulation can be the impulse for the pre-emptive internationalization of activity in cases such as Bertelsmann's, a group that reacted precociously to impending saturation on the domestic German market.

Havas is an advertising company, and so is Publicis. The former has held a share in CLT since the 1950s, while the latter was involved with the French TV6. Saatchi & Saatchi, the world's largest advertising group, was associated in 1986 in a study for the launching of two European television channels on Astra, a project that never saw the light of day. Finally, the Japanese advertising giant Dentsu is now investing in German regional stations.

Banks are beginning to show an interest in the sector. The Italian Banca Nazionale del Lavoro was probably the first to create a special section for cinematographic loans which was a crucial support to the Italian cinema in the hardest years of its crisis during the 1970s.

In Belgium, the Groupe Bruxelles Lambert is heavily involved in CLT, while the Société Générale was the main investor in cable networks. The German Deutsche Bank and Dresdner Bank are involved in SES.

The French Compagnie Financière de Suez directly holds 1.6 % of TF1 as well as 5 % of the Bouygues group, the main TF1 shareholder. The Banque Nationale de Paris is present in Canal Plus and Havas, while the Lyonnaise des Eaux is heavily involved in cabling.

However, some of the new audiovisual investors have been active in the field since the beginning (Beta Taurus, Granada, Virgin, etc.). It is remarkable that the great majority of them are European, with the important exception of Rupert Murdoch.

Alliances and concentration

Alliances tend to develop horizontally in the market occupation phase.

They can form on specific issues and occasions, for example pre-emptively in view of a change in regulation.

Bonds between broadcasters and satellite or hardware companies, such as the Murdoch — SES and BSB — Philips alliances, are also frequent.

Steady co-production agreements, such as the formation in July 1989 of the Association of Commercial Television for the common production of programmes, occurred occasionally.

Just as an example, somewhat steady alliances seemed at the beginning of 1989 to be the following:

Time Inc. — Warner
News International (Murdoch) — Walt Disney
Havas — CLT — Bertelsmann — Canal Plus — TVS
Fininvest — Bouygues — Kirch — Pathe — Maxwell
W.H. Smith — Compagnie Générale des Eaux.

All these alliances are liable to change very rapidly.

Concentration will appear in connection with a consolidated and autonomously regulated sector. It will necessarily be vertical: investment in the audiovisual field will have to cover the whole chain leading from programme production through differentiated diffusion (theatres, home video) to broadcasting.

The broadcasters will be the starting point for this process. This is a major difference from evolution in America, where the production majors concentrated on the distribution infrastructure. In Europe production is marginal in scale, and the market is conquered by investors in the broadcasting segment of the industry.

The groups

A portrait of the main groups active in the audiovisual media is very hard to draw. These groups are hardly ever involved exclusively in the film and television business, and the degree of their involvement changes constantly; it will keep doing so as long as verticalization does not impose definite borders on the sector.

The five groups listed here should be taken as examples for possible development in audiovisual case records.

(i) *Bertelsmann*

The Bertelsmann group registered in 1987 a turnover of ECU 5 243 million. Until the Time-Warner merge, it was the primary media group in the world.

Its revenues come from various media sectors in the following proportion:

Books (35 publishing companies)	50%
Press (395 daily newspapers, 1 131 magazines)	40%
AV and other media	10%.

Its principal activity remains book club publishing, and the acquisition of Doubleday Publishing in the USA represented its main investment in recent years, along with the purchase of the RCA Records Department.

Bertelsmann is a 38.5% shareholder in RTL Plus. Together with the French Canal Plus, it plans the launch of Canal Plus Deutschland by means of one TDF1 transponder.

In 1988, Bertelsmann acquired diffusion rights for the German football league and for the Wimbledon tennis tournament. These rights represent a major score for the group and should extend over five years.

Other investment in electronic media concerns UFA film, Universum Film, Stern TV, GEO Films, Grüner + Jahr Film, UFA Radio, DFS Hamburg, Radio Hamburg, Radio 1 Munich, Rheinland Pfälzischer Rundfunk. Sonapress, also a Bertelsmann company, is a leading developer of digital technology.

58% of the group's turnover originates outside its home country, the FR of Germany; 29% of it comes from activity in the United States and Canada.

(ii) *News Corporation Worldwide (Rupert Murdoch)*

Rupert Murdoch has the fourth largest share of the US television sector. He controls two-thirds of the Australian press. In Britain he controls *The Times* and *The Sun*. His ECU 3 956 million turnover in 1987 was divided as follows:

Daily newspapers	38%
Cinema	26%
Television	13%
Magazines	11%
Printing	3%
Other sectors	9%.

In 1986 Murdoch bought Metromedia TV for USD 1 700 million and 20th Century Fox for nearly USD 900 million. Metromedia, renamed Fox Broadcasting, reaches — directly or through arrangements with other independent stations — around 80% of the US population. The acquisition of the Fox studio capacity provided the group with production potential to match its broadcasting space, along with the enormous capital of classic films in the Fox library.

Murdoch's American performance dwarfs the losses of Sky Channel, his first European television station.

The European branch of the group, News International, hired six transponders on Astra. Four channels were launched in March 1989: Sky Television, Eurosport, Sky Movies and Sky News. The remaining two transponders should carry Disney Channel, a 50-50 Disney — Murdoch venture, and a culture channel. Of all these only Eurosport is European in vocation, the others being conceived for the British and Irish public.

Murdoch holds a 9.5% share in Reuters and is trying to gain more influence within it in connection with the operation of Sky News.

News Corporation is a giant which is certainly among the fastest groups in asserting a vertical, all-round presence in the European media and audiovisual sector.

(iii) *Compagnie luxembourgeoise de télédiffusion (CLT)*

CLT is the oldest commercial television company in Europe. In 1987 its turnover amounted to ECU 299 million.

CLT did the opposite of Bertelsmann: it began with television and started diversifying its activity later on. Shareholders in CLT are the Groupe Bruxelles Lambert, holding the majority, the French Havas, the Fratel, Audiofina and Audiolux groups and Paribas.

The governments of Belgium, Luxembourg and France have an interest and a word to say in the administration of the group via the national companies and groups holding shares. RTL terrestrial broadcasting covers the whole of Luxembourg, 73% of Belgian TV homes, as well as eastern France. Through a TDF1 transponder, it is capable of reaching most of the French- and German-speaking markets. In Germany, CLT holds a 46% share in RTL Plus, together with Bertelsmann which, in turn, controls around 15% of the Fratel group, a 27.6% shareholder in CLT. In 1982 the Groupe Bruxelles Lambert began gaining active control of CLT policy as the main shareholder. This caused reaction on the part of the French and Luxembourgish Governments, now represented respectively by Havas and Audiolux.

CLT started to diversify investment as early as 1973. Now it is present in the sixth French channel M 6 (25%), in RTL Plus (48%), in the Italian Compagnia di Distribuzione Cinematografica (80%), in Stand'Art Production (100%) as well as in at least four more cinema distribution companies in France; in television production companies (Cristal Image, DIS, World Entertainment Group Luxembourg, a company co-producing TV programmes with American partners, Cerise, a firm created to develop synthetic TV and participating in a Eureka project); finally, in publishing, with 51% of the Editions Robert Laffont and 65% of RTL Edition, and advertising. Future plans include the creation of a private station in Spain, running for a Channel 3 franchise in the United Kingdom in 1992 and launching a commercial station in the Netherlands in cooperation with Veronique.

CLT took one of the Astra transponders, but the use it will make of it is still uncertain.

Its aim seems now to be that of concentrating on production. In autumn 1988 talks were started with Robert Maxwell about a possible collaboration. At the same time the International Film Production was created in Luxembourg.

(iv) *Maxwell Communications Corporation*

Robert Maxwell seemed, until a year ago, to be the leading figure in the British audiovisual scene. His background is that of a huge publishing group. In November 1988 he acquired the American Macmillan publishing group: his became the second printing group in the United States, the first being R.R. Donnelley & Sons. His debt also soared to around USD 2 000 million. In the audiovisual field, however, the group recently registered some setbacks. The cable stations Première, MTV and Children's Channel, in which it is involved, did not develop as desired. In 1987 Maxwell failed to be included in the British DBS venture, BSB. Attempts to increase his weight within the Havas and Société Générale de Belgique groups also failed, as well as the effort to gain more influence within TF1, of which he holds a 12% share. In the privatized French channel he remains, however, the main shareholder after Bouygues. The acquisition of British Cable Service, with a potential network of over a million homes, gives him good chances following the dispute between BSB and Murdoch resulting in two different transmission standards for the British satellite channels. This increased the convenience of cabling to avoid double equipment expenses.

The group is also in contact with Portuguese and Spanish authorities. The possibility for new commercial channels in those countries is being discussed.

From the point of view of production, Maxwell took a 20% share in Select TV, a group controlling Witzend Productions, a major British independent production company. He also signed an agreement with Japan's NHK for the supply of European current affairs programmes. Finally, he is involved in the Media investment club for advanced technologies applied to audiovisual production, an organization created within the framework of the Media 92 programme of the European Commission. Together with Leo Kirch, Silvio Berlusconi and a Spanish media company, Maxwell is a member of the European Satellite TV Broadcast Consortium (ESTBC) formed in 1985 and planning originally some 170 hours of joint TV production. ESTBC is one example of vertical integration in the audiovisual field.

(v) *Fininvest (Silvio Berlusconi)*

Fininvest is the main southern European actor on the continental scene. In 1987 it was the 14th media group in the world with assets of ECU 2 917. 72% of this came from audiovisual media and advertising.

With three of Italy's six national television stations (the rest being the three RAI — State television — channels), Fininvest holds a major share of the Italian television market. Apart from investment in sectors totally different from the media (acquisition of the Italian chain of supermarkets Standa), Berlusconi's strategy registered two main features in recent months; involvement in cinema and programme production and a consistent international policy.

Fininvest represents a rather extraordinary case. In the absence of consistent and binding national regulations, commercial television developed in Italy much earlier and faster than anywhere else. Concentration began almost immediately in a chaotic environment and focused on the domestic market, the only one presenting such favourable regulatory conditions.

Berlusconi's strategy developed, therefore, independently from new technological assets such as satellites or cable.

In a very traditional fashion, internationalization followed until now the pattern of financial participation in foreign enterprises.

Fininvest manages programme sales in Spain through its company Redespana and negotiates with Grupo Zeta, a commercial audiovisual group. It shares Tele Fünf with Tele München and has an agreement on the management of advertising for Soviet television. The group has good prospects for expansion in Portugal and Greece, and could join, or trade places with, Robert Maxwell in TF1.

Public-service television

The role of public-service television in Europe has begun to change in the last few years and will keep evolving dramatically in the foreseeable future.

Public-service monopoly on broadcasting depended on frequency scarcity and on tradition. Broadcasting was viewed in Europe very much as a public service until a very short time ago. When private stations started swarming in Italy in the mid-1970s, people were disconcerted to discover that there was no law against it or about it.

Public-service television cannot match quantitatively the growth of commercial stations. The available air-time cannot and should not be filled exclusively by public-service broadcasting. The proliferation of channels is such that it inevitably calls for specialization. Single-theme channels will arguably become the best outlet for investment in broadcasting, with single general channels serving as show-windows for a certain group of channels.

Interaction within cable networks will associate broadcasting with other functions subject to subscription fees, such as teletext and data transmission.

In short, television will become something very similar to the publishing market. Just as there are only a few general magazines while the majority deals with specific topics, such as fishing, numismatics, economics or sports, and is aimed at a specific portion of the public, there will be a few general channels and a large number of movie, news, sports or cultural channels. In America the term 'narrowcasting' already defines the practice.

Narrowcasting will be delivered to the home on a subscription basis. Through encryption techniques, which encode a signal so as to make it impossible to receive it without installing a decoder in the TV set, DBS pay-TV is perfectly practical. What is the role of public-service television in this landscape? The first consideration concerns its survival. Public-service broadcasting is determined to stay alive. It will also retain its two fundamental functions:

(1) representing a vehicle for social communication; and

(2) providing a model for quality broadcasting.

In a situation of monopoly, these two were merged in a single effect that we could describe as educational. The term should not be confused with an appreciation for merit. It only involves the notion of centralized choice in the distribution and organization of programming in the hands of administrations where the proportion in each country's social composition is reproduced.

Service v business

A symposium organized in Brussels by the European Film and Television Year in March 1989 offered representatives of European public-television stations the occasion to assess their accomplishments and perspectives.

Broadcasting quality certainly benefited in a certain measure from competition. The necessity to satisfy so as to receive an immediate response in terms of audience had a vivifying effect on public-broadcaster programming.

In the long run, however, quality decreases as only the immediately profitable programmes, which are not necessarily the best, allow public broadcasters to compete with commercial stations for advertising revenue and, what is more important, for audiences.

The Brussels symposium quite reasonably identified three main problems for European public-service television:

(i) defining its necessity and its new role;

(ii) developing national strategies; and

(iii) creating a public broadcasting service at European level.

(a) *A new role*

Public broadcasting cannot be defined exclusively by the public source of its revenue. Very few public broadcasters derive their income exclusively from State sources and licence fees.

The need for public-service broadcasting is traditionally felt quite strongly in Europe. 'Public' information is fundamental to European politics. Besides, even in countries where commercial television spread irresistibly, as in Italy, public broadcasters managed to retain a higher prestige in spite of a dramatic fall in audiences.

The role of television services as opposed to that of broadcasting business could become that of providing a parameter for programming. 'Quality' here should not be read as an equivalent of culture or élite programmes. Public-service broadcasting, if adequately independent in administration and financing, will be able to supply quality programmes of all kinds: from entertainment to sports, games, documentaries, movies and information.

In order to do that, public broadcasters will have to retain minimum guarantees of survival independently of the audience-hunt in competition with commercial television.

(b) *National strategy*

The strategy of a public-television service relies upon the national markets and audiences. Public broadcasters are national broadcasters.

First of all, public stations must confirm their presence and attractiveness for their national audience in the face of competition. Programming and management will assume, even in public broadcasting institutions, more flexible and entrepreneurial features.

A large percentage of in-house production will distinguish public broadcasters from commercial television for a while. Structures and management strategies will have to become more supple.

A vital point is diversification in financing: 'More money coming from more sources', as Mr Robert Stephane put it at the Brussels symposium. An adequate proportion of public funding evidently remains the cornerstone of public broadcasting. However, a higher percentage of revenue originating in advertising and other forms of effect-dependent financing, apart from being necessary because of the growing need for financial resources, will act as a healthy stimulus for dynamic programming.

Finally, resources must be invested in technological research and upgrading as technological choices become fundamental in strategy.

(c) *The European battle*

Various forms of cooperation were undertaken by European public-service broadcasters notably in the field of production.

The European Co-production Association (ECA) is a successful enterprise started by six major European stations: Antenne 2, Channel 4, ORF, RAI, SRG/SSR and ZDF. ECA was created in 1985 for the co-production of series and serials. Its first output was seven episodes of 'Eurocops', a series which will eventually total 41. They were broadcast to 85% of western European TV homes.

ECA normally pools resources for productions carried on by the proposing member or members. 'Eurocops' represents an exception, as each member produces seven episodes and broadcasts the whole series.

In general, a European strategy for public-service broadcasting includes certain cultural objectives:

(i)   the quick establishment of a regulatory framework as a guarantee for fair competition;

(ii) encouraging European programme production and reserving the majority of air-time to its diffusion; and

(iii) preserving cultural and language diversity.

4. Advertising

Advertising is the main source of revenue for commercial television. Public-service broadcasters derive from it increasing percentages of their income. An understanding of its importance and working mechanism is essential for progress evaluation in the audiovisual field.

Appendix I contains data on advertising expenditure in the individual EC countries as well as in the USA and Japan over the period 1980-87 (see also Tables III.4.1 to III.4.12).

Table III.4.1

Percentage change 1987/1980: Advertising v GDP at constant prices

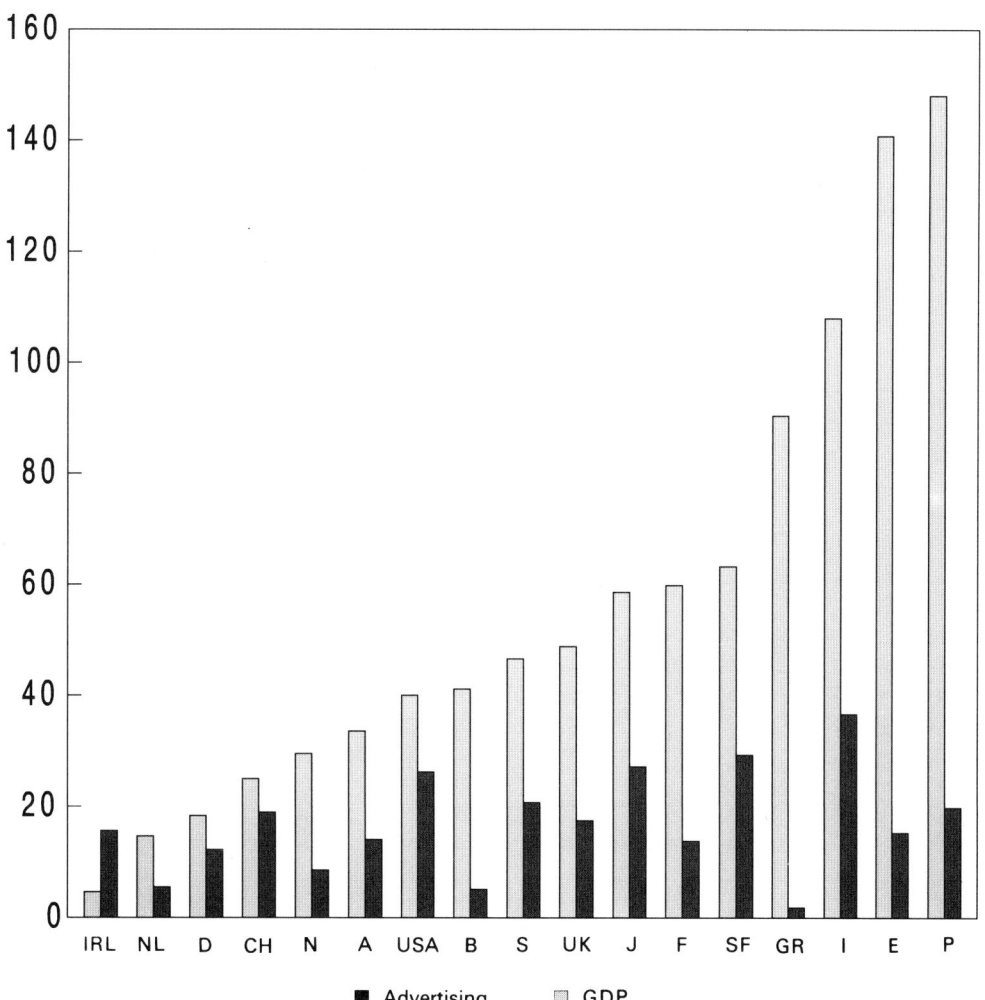

Source: EAT. *International advertising expenditure trends and forecasts to 1992,* December 1988.

Evolution in advertising investment is crucial for developments in commercial television, most private stations depending for survival exclusively on this source of revenue. For the European television industry as a whole, the part of income covered by advertising goes from around 0% in Sweden and Norway to 100% in Greece, the average being 46.3% (Table III.4.13).

European advertising expenditure as a whole soared between 1980 and 1987 and registered a 103% growth. Television advertising grew by 181%.

The question is often posed whether capital is available in advertising to finance the development of commercial television and the growing thirst for advertising revenue on the part of public-service broadcasters.

Table III.4.2

Advertising expenditure
at current prices and exchange rates

(million ECU)

	1980	1981	1982	1983	1984	1985	1986	1987	1988
Austria	260	254	301	360	408	448	512	567	646
Belgium	405	400	404	465	516	569	633	748	813
Denmark	365	390	411	446	491	542	594	635	670
Finland	409	534	627	722	885	990	1 017	1 088	1 279
France	2 273	2 517	2 792	3 198	3 485	3 965	4 539	5 163	5 872
FR of Germany	4 386	4 441	5 032	5 549	5 992	6 490	7 029	7 579	7 976
Greece	73	109	138	136	145	152	169	194	253
Ireland	92	96	102	99	113	132	158	181	198
Italy	1 036	1 264	1 571	2 004	2 367	2 717	3 351	3 615	4 277
Netherlands	1 232	1 202	1 320	1 385	1 495	1 599	1 838	1 996	2 169
Norway	319	382	449	458	549	609	639	656	645
Portugal	38	51	56	66	64	78	99	147	204
Spain	833	999	1 319	1 309	1 572	1 858	2 304	2 904	3 794
Sweden	569	630	663	678	826	924	980	1 075	1 264
Switzerland	747	855	922	1 048	1 117	1 236	1 407	1 594	1 671
UK	4 269	5 095	5 578	6 097	6 872	7 540	7 620	8 204	10 203
Europe	17 303	19 217	21 684	24 020	26 897	29 850	32 888	36 346	41 933
EC	15 000	16 562	18 722	20 754	23 112	25 642	28 334	31 366	36 429
Japan	5 529	7 611	8 164	10 008	11 830	15 023	16 994	18 235	22 619
USA	25 494	35 625	44 355	55 864	72 801	80 388	66 753	60 499	63 107

Source: EAT. *International advertising expenditure*, December 1989.

Note: These figures have not been adjusted to account for different methods of compilation and are therefore not fully comparable.

Once more the Italian case can be quoted. Although the global advertising expenditure in that country followed the general trend, the television portion of it increased over the 1980-87 period by 307%, passing from 26 to 51% of the total. This was the result of total deregulation, or non-regulation, which enabled nearly 1 000 television stations to emerge and survive on advertising revenue since the mid 1970s.

In general, the television portion of advertising investment grew over the last few years all over the world (see Tables III.4.14 to III.4.20).

It is evident, therefore, that growth in one sector brings about a similar trend in the other. As a European Advertising Tripartite (EAT) report puts it: 'the television sector ... will undoubtedly be the main engine of growth for European advertising expenditure over the next few years'. (*International advertising expenditure trends and forecasts to 1992*—December 1988).

Table III.4.3

Rank order of 1988 advertising expenditure by country at current prices and exchange rates

Country	Expenditure (million ECU)	% share
USA	60 734	48.36
Japan	22 619	18.01
UK	10 203	8.12
FR of Germany	8 078	6.43
France	5 872	4.68
Italy	4 277	3.41
Spain	3 794	3.02
Netherlands	2 169	1.73
Switzerland	1 671	1.33
Sweden	1 471	1.17
Finland	1 279	1.02
Belgium	813	0.65
Denmark	676	0.54
Austria	646	0.51
Norway	645	0.51
Greece	253	0.20
Ireland	198	0.16
Portugal	193	0.15
Total	120 973	100.00

Source: EAT. *International advertising expenditure*, December 1989.

Note: These figures have not been adjusted to account for different methods of compilation and are therefore not fully comparable.

Forecasts for advertising expenditure in Europe are optimistic. In the European Community, investment is estimated to grow by 46.2% in four years, passing from ECU 36 213 million in 1988 to ECU 52 956 million in 1992 (Tables III.4.21 and III.4.22).

Moreover, in 1992 the EC is likely to represent 67% of the US advertising market, as compared to the present 57%.

Advertising investment should therefore be available for funding private television stations. Such forecasts do not take into account the acceleration that deregulation in broadcasting will certainly involve. The Italian example is indicative in this respect.

In Europe, however, the per capita investment in advertising remains much lower than in the United States or in Japan. Compared to an average ECU 260.34 per year per person spent in the USA and the Japanese figure of ECU 151.45, Europe spends only

Table III.4.4

Gross domestic product at current prices and exchange rates

(1 000 million USD)

	1980	1981	1982	1983	1984	1985	1986	1987	1988
Austria	76.88	66.48	64.64	67.17	63.81	65.16	93.21	117.19	126.90
Belgium	118.02	95.86	84.46	80.22	76.59	79.60	111.53	138.85	148.70
Denmark	66.32	57.64	55.74	56.11	54.58	58.05	82.02	101.21	107.60
Finland	51.69	49.12	50.86	49.27	51.51	54.34	71.08	89.52	104.80
France	664.59	571.54	542.75	516.32	499.13	522.52	726.95	879.88	947.00
FR of Germany	813.65	682.56	658.50	654.43	616.96	621.78	889.36	1 117.78	1 201.40
Greece	40.15	36.88	38.21	34.66	33.75	33.42	39.60	47.18	52.80
Ireland	19.23	17.02	18.82	18.19	17.87	18.63	24.95	29.39	30.90
Italy	452.65	353.02	347.86	355.43	414.24	427.16	601.23	755.88	828.30
Netherlands	169.38	141.58	138.14	132.59	124.74	125.90	175.46	213.17	227.90
Norway	57.71	57.24	56.13	55.00	55.44	58.18	69.59	82.66	90.30
Portugal	25.09	23.81	23.29	20.67	19.23	20.68	29.55	36.83	41.80
Spain	212.12	187.65	180.87	158.15	156.20	164.01	228.12	289.24	339.90
Sweden	124.15	112.85	99.91	92.00	95.45	100.06	130.80	158.54	178.50
Switzerland	101.65	94.06	96.53	97.12	90.75	92.77	135.28	171.09	184.80
UK	534.89	500.83	482.02	454.16	428.75	452.46	553.54	675.30	812.50
Europe	3 528.17	3 048.14	2 938.73	2 841.49	2 799.00	2 894.72	3 962.27	4 903.71	5 424.10
EC	3 116.09	2 668.39	2 570.66	2 480.93	2 442.04	2 524.21	3 462.31	4 284.71	4 738.80
Japan	1 059.26	1 141.77	1 082.50	1 179.98	1 254.41	1 326.00	1 958.37	2 373.05	2 842.70
USA	2 688.47	2 923.77	3 045.28	3 275.73	3 722.34	3 967.47	4 191.46	4 472.91	4 806.60

Source: EAT. *International advertising expenditure*, December 1989.

ECU 117.4 per year per person on advertising. In the whole of Europe, Finland leads in per capita investment while, in the EC, only the United Kingdom invests more than Japan (ECU 182) (Tables III.4.23 and III.4.24).

Economic factors are evidently crucial to advertising investment. However, regulation and taste also play important roles in its development.

Table III.4.25 gives an overview of regulations on advertising in European countries. These differ greatly and urgently call for some sort of harmonization. As advertising becomes more and more integrated in programming, quality in production and discretion in use are increasingly necessary. 'The effect of popularity of advertising can have crucial effects on trends in advertising expenditure' (EAT—*International advertising expenditure*). Wild developments, as in the case of Italy, bring about a saturation

Table III.4.5

Advertising as a percentage of GDP

(at market prices)

	1980	1981	1982	1983	1984	1985	1986	1987	1988
Austria	0.55	0.49	0.53	0.55	0.58	0.61	0.62	0.64	0.70
Belgium	0.48	0.47	0.47	0.51	0.53	0.54	0.56	0.62	0.65
Denmark	0.95	0.94	0.90	0.88	0.88	0.88	0.88	0.90	0.91
Finland	1.10	1.21	1.21	1.30	1.35	1.38	1.40	1.40	1.44
France	0.48	0.50	0.51	0.56	0.56	0.58	0.62	0.68	0.74
FR of Germany	0.88	0.86	0.88	0.89	0.90	0.93	0.91	0.92	0.93
Greece	0.30	0.39	0.41	0.41	0.39	0.40	0.48	0.55	0.66
Ireland	0.78	0.74	0.62	0.56	0.57	0.61	0.72	0.82	0.88
Italy	0.37	0.47	0.52	0.58	0.52	0.56	0.64	0.64	0.71
Netherlands	1.01	0.95	0.94	0.93	0.94	0.96	1.03	1.08	1.12
Norway	0.96	0.93	0.97	0.92	0.97	0.99	1.12	1.14	1.04
Portugal	0.22	0.26	0.25	0.30	0.27	0.30	0.35	0.49	0.61
Spain	0.63	0.69	0.83	0.85	0.92	1.00	1.15	1.35	1.54
Sweden	0.67	0.65	0.68	0.69	0.71	0.73	0.77	0.82	0.88
Switzerland	1.08	1.07	0.98	1.01	1.02	1.06	1.07	1.13	1.12
UK	1.11	1.14	1.13	1.19	1.26	1.26	1.35	1.40	1.48
Europe	0.74	0.76	0.78	0.81	0.82	0.84	0.88	0.93	0.99
EC	0.73	0.75	0.77	0.81	0.81	0.83	0.87	0.92	0.99
Japan	0.73	0.74	0.74	0.75	0.74	0.86	0.85	0.89	0.94
USA	1.32	1.36	1.43	1.52	1.54	1.55	1.57	1.56	1.55

Source: EAT. *International advertising expenditure*, December 1989.

Note: This table has added in estimates of production costs, classified advertising and commission for those countries which exclude these factors from their advertising statistics.

Table III.4.6
Index of advertising as a percentage of GDP

Country	1980	1981	1982	1983	1984	1985	1986	1987
Austria	100.0	90.4	96.1	101.1	106.6	110.1	112.1	116.3
Belgium	100.0	96.7	96.9	106.6	110.0	112.0	114.5	133.9
Denmark	100.0	99.5	94.3	92.4	93.1	92.4	92.1	94.1
Finland	100.0	107.0	110.4	118.7	124.1	126.0	128.6	130.2
France	100.0	101.9	104.3	114.1	113.8	118.7	126.0	139.5
FR of Germany	100.0	97.0	99.8	100.6	101.9	100.3	103.9	105.3
Greece	100.0	129.0	138.3	137.3	132.2	129.7	162.6	184.2
Ireland	100.0	87.8	80.8	72.7	74.2	81.0	93.5	93.5
Italy	100.0	110.3	120.8	136.1	123.1	132.4	148.7	150.0
Netherlands	100.0	93.8	92.4	91.8	93.3	94.3	102.8	108.5
Norway	100.0	97.1	101.8	96.2	101.1	102.9	117.0	118.8
Portugal	100.0	114.4	110.8	135.8	123.8	135.0	157.0	213.2
Spain	100.0	109.0	129.6	133.3	143.5	156.0	179.5	211.0
Sweden	100.0	97.8	101.6	103.0	116.5	117.3	115.2	121.3
Switzerland	100.0	99.3	91.0	93.3	94.3	97.8	99.3	104.9
UK	100.0	100.9	101.7	107.2	114.1	113.3	122.6	128.0

Source: EAT. *International advertising expenditure.*

Table III.4.7
Advertising as a percentage of GDP

(at market prices, ranked by 1988 percentage)

Spain	1.54
USA	1.49
UK	1.48
Finland	1.44
Netherlands	1.12
Switzerland	1.12
Norway	1.04
Sweden	1.02
Japan	0.94
FR of Germany	0.94
Denmark	0.92
Ireland	0.88
France	0.74
Italy	0.71
Austria	0.70
Greece	0.66
Belgium	0.65
Portugal	0.58

Source: EAT. *International advertising expenditure,* December 1989.

and resentment toward advertising breaks and inserts on television that affect legislation. After using barbaric techniques in the first expansion phase (such as, for example, increasing the sound volume during commercials), advertisers seem to be becoming increasingly conscious of the need for moderation in the very interest of advertising quality and effectiveness.

It is certain, however, that advertising will generate sufficient investment for a full-scale development of the commercial television sector.

Table III.4.8

Advertising expenditure per capita at current prices and exchange rates

(ECU)

	1980	1981	1982	1983	1984	1985	1986	1987	1988
Austria	34.5	33.6	39.7	47.7	54.0	59.3	67.7	74.8	85.0
Belgium	41.1	40.6	41.0	47.1	52.4	57.7	64.2	75.8	82.2
Denmark	71.2	76.1	80.2	87.2	96.1	106.1	116.0	123.7	130.4
Finland	85.5	111.3	129.9	148.7	181.3	202.0	206.8	220.6	258.6
France	42.2	46.4	51.2	58.4	63.4	71.9	81.9	92.8	105.1
FR of Germany	71.2	72.0	81.6	90.3	97.9	106.4	115.1	123.8	130.0
Greece	7.5	11.2	14.1	13.8	14.7	15.3	16.9	19.4	25.3
Ireland	27.0	27.7	29.4	28.3	32.0	37.2	44.7	51.0	55.9
Italy	18.4	22.4	27.7	35.3	41.5	47.6	58.6	63.1	74.5
Netherlands	87.1	84.4	92.2	96.4	103.6	110.4	126.1	136.0	146.9
Norway	78.0	93.2	109.1	110.8	132.6	146.7	153.3	156.8	153.1
Portugal	3.9	5.2	5.6	6.6	6.3	7.6	9.7	14.3	19.8
Spain	22.3	26.5	34.7	34.3	41.0	48.3	59.6	74.8	97.3
Sweden	68.4	75.6	79.6	81.5	99.1	110.6	117.1	128.0	149.8
Switzerland	117.0	132.9	142.5	161.7	171.7	189.2	214.0	240.8	250.9
UK	75.8	90.4	99.0	108.1	121.7	133.2	134.2	144.1	178.7
Europe	49.6	54.9	61.8	68.3	76.3	84.5	92.9	102.3	117.7
EC	47.2	52.0	58.6	64.8	72.0	79.7	87.9	97.0	112.3
Japan	47.3	64.7	68.9	83.9	98.6	124.4	139.9	149.4	184.5
USA	111.9	154.8	190.8	237.9	307.2	336.0	276.3	248.0	256.2

Source: EAT. *International advertising expenditure*, December 1989.

Note: These figures have not been adjusted to account for different methods of compilation and are therefore not fully comparable.

Table III.4.9

**Rank order of 1988 per capita advertising expenditure by country
at current prices and exchange rates**

(ECU)

Country	Expenditure	UK = 100
Finland	258.6	145
Switzerland	250.9	140
USA	246.6	138
Japan	184.5	103
UK	178.7	100
Sweden	174.4	98
Norway	153.1	86
Netherlands	146.9	82
FR of Germany	131.6	74
Denmark	131.6	74
France	105.1	59
Spain	97.3	54
Austria	85.0	48
Belgium	82.2	46
Italy	74.5	42
Ireland	55.9	31
Greece	25.3	14
Portugal	18.7	10
Total	2 322.1	

Source: EAT. *International advertising expenditure*, December 1989.

Note: These figures have not been adjusted to account for different methods of compilation and are therefore not fully comparable.

Table III.4.10

Television advertising expenditure at current prices and exchange rates

(million ECU)

	1980	1981	1982	1983	1984	1985	1986	1987	1988	% of total media, 1988
Austria	78.8	79.8	94.9	110.3	110.3	122.4	145.0	164.2	170.8	26.5
Belgium	33.2	39.2	41.9	53.2	60.1	70.1	85.2	110.8	105.4	13.0
Denmark	0.0	0.0	0.0	0.0	0.0	0.0	0.0	1.3	10.1	1.5
Finland	53.2	70.3	83.0	92.4	109.9	122.5	124.9	126.9	147.3	11.5
France	324.6	369.0	449.8	531.7	537.7	680.6	866.2	1 154.7	1 443.9	24.6
FR of Germany	443.3	463.4	524.8	565.9	606.0	656.2	702.9	780.9	884.2	11.1
Greece	36.1	55.2	73.8	66.0	72.4	75.3	84.2	94.6	112.3	44.4
Ireland	26.6	28.9	34.9	35.7	42.7	53.0	58.2	59.7	61.8	31.2
Italy	268.3	382.9	571.6	865.5	1 131.6	1 336.7	1 591.8	1 840.2	2 045.8	47.8
Netherlands	83.3	88.3	99.1	113.1	118.5	130.6	153.3	191.1	218.0	10.0
Norway	0.0	0.0	0.0	0.0	0.0	0.0	0.0	0.0	6.5	1.0
Portugal	16.6	23.5	24.4	29.0	31.4	40.7	53.0	75.9	101.6	49.8
Spain	274.3	330.8	421.7	410.1	501.2	577.5	732.6	913.5	1 177.3	31.0
Sweden	0.0	0.0	0.0	0.0	0.0	0.0	0.0	0.0	0.0	0.0
Switzerland	59.7	59.9	57.9	68.0	76.3	80.8	99.4	103.6	111.1	6.7
UK	1 156.2	1 462.6	1 655.8	1 889.2	2 114.7	2 336.3	2 494.3	2 656.5	3 201.2	31.4
Japan	2 502.2	3 418.8	3 718.0	4 551.6	5 509.1	5 888.9	6 611.0	7 049.7	8 689.5	38.4
USA	8 237.3	11 506.1	14 939.1	18 825.7	25 154.8	27 548.6	23 249.1	20 716.4	21 722.1	34.4

Source: EAT. *International advertising expenditure*, December 1989.

Note: These figures have not been adjusted for different methods of compilation and are therefore not fully comparable.

Table III.4.11

Television advertising expenditure at current prices and exchange rates

(million USD)

	1980	1981	1982	1983	1984	1985	1986	1987	1988	% of total media, 1988
Austria	109.6	89.1	93.0	98.1	86.7	92.6	141.9	189.0	201.9	26.5
Belgium	46.5	43.8	41.0	47.3	47.3	53.0	83.4	127.7	124.5	13.0
Denmark	0.0	0.0	0.0	0.0	0.0	0.0	0.0	1.5	11.9	1.5
Finland	73.8	78.3	81.2	82.2	86.5	92.8	122.5	146.3	174.0	11.5
France	451.4	410.3	440.3	472.5	422.9	514.9	849.3	1 331.2	1 706.3	24.6
FR of Germany	616.7	517.5	514.0	503.3	476.6	496.4	687.9	900.2	1 044.8	11.1
Greece	50.8	61.7	72.2	58.7	56.8	57.6	82.7	109.0	132.7	44.4
Ireland	37.0	32.3	34.2	31.7	33.6	40.1	57.1	68.8	73.0	31.2
Italy	373.2	430.5	559.5	769.3	890.0	1 014.5	1 558.6	2 122.1	2 417.3	47.8
Netherlands	115.9	98.7	97.0	100.6	93.4	98.8	150.0	220.2	257.6	10.0
Norway	0.0	0.0	0.0	0.0	0.0	0.0	0.0	0.0	7.7	1.0
Portugal	23.1	26.3	23.8	25.9	24.7	30.9	52.0	87.5	120.1	49.8
Spain	382.3	369.6	412.9	364.4	394.5	438.7	718.1	1 052.4	1 391.4	31.0
Sweden	0.0	0.0	0.0	0.0	0.0	0.0	0.0	0.0	0.0	0.0
Switzerland	83.1	67.0	56.7	60.5	60.0	61.1	97.2	119.4	131.3	6.7
UK	1 609.8	1 640.6	1 621.4	1 681.1	1 661.7	1 760.2	2 451.3	3 060.5	3 784.1	31.4
Japan	3 492.2	3 817.0	3 639.7	4 051.1	4 340.2	4 460.0	6 465.3	8 124.1	10 272.2	38.4
USA	11 469.0	12 846.0	14 636.0	16 759.0	19 848.0	21 022.0	22 881.0	23 904.0	25 686.0	34.4

Source: EAT. *International advertising expenditure*, December 1989.

Note: These figures have not been adjusted for different methods of compilation and are therefore not fully comparable.

Table III.4.12

Television advertising revenue as a percentage of GDP

Country	1980	1981	1982	1983	1984	1985	1986	1987	% change 1987 v 1980
Austria	0.14	0.13	0.14	0.15	0.14	0.14	0.15	0.16	14.3
Belgium	0.04	0.05	0.05	0.06	0.06	0.07	0.07	0.09	125.0
Denmark	0.00	0.00	0.00	0.00	0.00	0.00	0.00	0.00	0.0
Finland	0.13	0.14	0.15	0.16	0.17	0.17	0.16	0.17	30.8
France	0.07	0.07	0.08	0.09	0.08	0.10	0.11	0.15	114.3
FR of Germany	0.08	0.08	0.08	0.08	0.08	0.08	0.08	0.08	0.9
Greece	0.13	0.17	0.19	0.17	0.17	0.17	0.21	0.23	76.0
Ireland	0.19	0.18	0.20	0.17	0.19	0.22	0.23	0.24	26.3
Italy	0.09	0.12	0.16	0.22	0.22	0.24	0.26	0.28	211.1
Netherlands	0.07	0.07	0.07	0.08	0.07	0.08	0.10	0.12	71.4
Norway	0.00	0.00	0.00	0.00	0.00	0.00	0.00	0.00	0.0
Portugal	0.09	0.11	0.10	0.13	0.13	0.15	0.18	0.24	166.7
Spain	0.19	0.20	0.23	0.23	0.25	0.27	0.31	0.36	89.5
Sweden	0.00	0.00	0.00	0.00	0.00	0.00	0.00	0.00	0.0
Switzerland	0.08	0.07	0.06	0.06	0.07	0.07	0.07	0.07	− 12.5
UK	0.30	0.32	0.34	0.37	0.39	0.39	0.45	0.46	53.3
Turkey	0.04	0.10	0.10	0.06	0.08	0.13	0.11	0.11	175.0

Source: EAT. *International advertising expenditure.*

Table III.4.13

Advertising revenue as a percentage of total income for European television industries (1987)

(%)

Country	1987
Greece	100.0
Spain	93.9
Turkey	66.4
Portugal	66.2
Italy	60.3
UK	60.0
Austria	50.7
Ireland	50.0
Belgium	49.6
France	43.7
Finland	42.0
Switzerland	36.3
Netherlands	35.1
FR of Germany	32.0
Denmark	0.9
Sweden	0.0
Norway	0.0
	Average : 46.3

Source : EAT.

Table III.4.14

**All Europe, USA and Japan combined media split
at current prices and exchange rates**

(million ECU)

	News-papers	Magazines	TV	Radio	Cinema	Outdoor/Transport
1980	18 450	7 644	10 826	3 310	152	1 386
1981	23 280	9 394	14 581	4 512	170	1 649
1982	27 339	10 908	18 505	5 619	187	1 919
1983	33 160	12 803	22 796	6 771	188	2 175
1984	40 962	15 703	29 543	8 395	209	2 532
1985	45 321	17 047	32 502	9 604	224	2 840
1986	40 532	15 562	28 857	8 327	235	2 799
1987	39 882	15 427	27 159	7 638	248	2 897
1988	42 694	16 914	29 484	8 291	274	3 132

Table III.4.15

All Europe, USA and Japan combined media split
at current prices and exchange rates

(million USD)

	News-papers	Magazines	TV	Radio	Cinema	Outdoor/Transport
1980	25 688	10 643	15 073	4 609	211	1 930
1981	25 991	10 488	16 279	5 038	190	1 841
1982	26 784	10 686	18 130	5 505	183	1 880
1983	29 519	11 397	20 293	6 028	168	1 936
1984	32 321	12 390	23 310	6 624	165	1 998
1985	34 584	13 008	24 802	7 329	171	2 167
1986	39 890	15 315	28 400	8 195	231	2 754
1987	46 018	17 801	31 338	8 813	286	3 343
1988	50 485	20 001	34 865	9 804	324	3 703

Table III.4.16

All Europe, USA and Japan combined media split

(%)

	News-papers	Magazines	TV	Radio	Cinema	Outdoor/Transport
1980	44.2	18.3	25.9	7.9	0.4	3.3
1981	43.4	17.5	27.2	8.4	0.3	3.1
1982	42.4	16.9	28.7	8.7	0.3	3.0
1983	42.6	16.4	29.3	8.7	0.2	2.8
1984	42.1	16.1	30.3	8.6	0.2	2.6
1985	42.1	15.9	30.2	8.9	0.2	2.6
1986	42.1	16.2	30.0	8.6	0.2	2.9
1987	42.8	16.5	29.1	8.2	0.3	3.1
1988	42.4	16.8	29.3	8.2	0.3	3.1

Source: EAT. *International advertising expenditure*, December 1989.

Table III.4.17

EC combined media split
at current prices and exchange rates

(million ECU)

	News-papers	Magazines	TV	Radio	Cinema	Outdoor/Transport
1980	6 251	3 692	2 395	620	134	874
1981	6 650	3 994	2 862	690	148	955
1982	7 248	4 566	3 327	813	165	1 034
1983	7 815	5 093	3 695	873	165	1 112
1984	8 537	5 746	4 086	964	184	1 230
1985	9 406	6 292	4 622	1 031	196	1 382
1986	10 017	6 810	5 231	1 175	204	1 548
1987	11 007	7 496	6 041	1 279	213	1 719
1988	12 580	8 550	7 318	1 559	236	1 913

Table III.4.18

EC combined media split
at current prices and exchange rates

(million USD)

	News-papers	Magazines	TV	Radio	Cinema	Outdoor/Transport
1980	8 704	5 140	3 334	863	187	1 218
1981	7 424	4 459	3 195	771	166	1 067
1982	7 101	4 474	3 259	796	162	1 013
1983	6 957	4 534	3 289	777	147	990
1984	6 736	4 533	3 224	761	145	970
1985	7 177	4 801	3 527	787	150	1 055
1986	9 858	6 702	5 149	1 157	201	1 524
1987	12 700	8 649	6 970	1 476	246	1 983
1988	14 875	10 110	8 653	1 844	280	2 262

Table III.4.19
EC combined media split

(%)

	News-papers	Magazines	TV	Radio	Cinema	Outdoor/Transport
1980	44.8	26.4	17.1	4.4	1.0	6.3
1981	43.5	26.1	18.7	4.5	1.0	6.2
1982	42.3	26.6	19.4	4.7	1.0	6.0
1983	41.7	27.2	19.7	4.7	0.9	5.9
1984	41.2	27.7	19.7	4.6	0.9	5.9
1985	41.0	27.4	20.2	4.5	0.9	6.0
1986	40.1	27.3	20.9	4.7	0.8	6.2
1987	39.7	27.0	21.8	4.6	0.8	6.2
1988	39.1	26.6	22.8	4.8	0.7	5.9

Source: EAT. *International advertising expenditure*, December 1989.

Table III.4.20
International advertising expenditure by media, 1987 (ranked by TV)

(%)

	Press	TV	Others
Portugal	29.9	53.6	16.5
Italy	39.8	50.9	9.3
Greece	39.3	48.9	11.8
Japan	48.0	45.3	6.7
Ireland	41.9	37.1	21.0
USA	53.7	34.1	12.2
UK	61.6	32.4	6.0
Spain	51.5	30.9	17.6
Austria	50.3	29.3	20.4
France	57.4	22.0	20.6
Belgium	68.1	14.0	17.8
Finland	85.1	11.7	3.2
Netherlands	76.5	11.1	12.4
FR of Germany	81.4	10.2	8.4
Switzerland	80.2	6.5	13.3
Denmark	95.1	0.2	4.7
Norway	96.8	0.0	3.2
Sweden	95.7	0.0	4.3

Source: EAT.

Table III.4.21

Advertising investment forecasts (European Community) [1]

(million ECU at 1.1.1989 rates)

European Community	1988	1992	1992/1988
Belgium/Luxembourg	825	1 137	+ 37.8%
Denmark	659	904	+ 37.2%
France	5 696	8 045	+ 41.2%
FR of Germany	7 989	9 663	+ 21.0%
Greece	233	501	+115.0%
Ireland	177	225	+ 27.1%
Italy	4 202	6 843	+ 62.8%
Netherlands	2 038	2 317	+ 13.7%
Portugal	183	366	+100.0%
Spain	3 862	8 283	+114.5%
UK	10 349	14 672	+ 41.8%
Total EC	36 213	52 956	+ 46.2%
Japan	18 491	22 600	+ 22.2%
USA	63 463	79 386	+ 25.1%

Source: European Association of Advertising Agencies.

[1] Press, TV, radio, cinema, outdoor/transit.

Table III.4.22

Advertising investment forecasts (European Economic Space) [1]

(million ECU at 1.1.1989 rates)

European Free Trade Association	1988	1992	1992/1988
Austria	597	840	+40.7%
Finland	1 238	1 653	+33.5%
Iceland [3]	—	—	—
Norway	664	788	+18.7%
Sweden	1 339	1 759 [2]	+31.3%
Switzerland	1 633	2 089	+27.9%
Total EFTA	5 471	7 129	+30.3%
Total EC	36 213	52 956	+46.2%
Total European Economic Space	41 684	60 085	+44.1%
Japan	18 491	22 600	+22.2%
USA	63 463	79 386	+25.1%

Source: European Association of Advertising Agencies.

[1] Press, TV, radio, cinema, outdoor/transit.
[2] No forecast for television and radio in Sweden.
[3] Figures for Iceland not available.

Table III.4.23

Advertising investments per capita in the EC

	Advertising, 1988 (million ECU)	Population (1 000)	Per capita (ECU)
Belgium/Luxembourg	825	9 862	83.65
Denmark	659	5 130	128.46
France	5 696	55 627	102.39
FR of Germany	7 989	61 149	130.65
Greece	233	10 000	23.30
Ireland	177	3 560	49.72
Italy	4 202	57 331	73.29
Netherlands	2 038	14 671	138.91
Portugal	183	10 305	17.76
Spain	3 862	38 888	99.31
UK	10 349	56 863	182.00
Total EC	36 213	323 386	111.98

Source: EAT.

Table III.4.24

Rank order of 1987 per capita advertising expenditure by country at current prices and exchange rates

(ECU)

Country	Expenditure	UK = 100
USA	249.1	172.87
Switzerland	240.8	167.09
Finland	220.3	152.89
Norway	156.8	108.81
UK	144.1	100.00
Netherlands	139.4	96.74
Japan	127.5	88.46
Sweden	127.4	88.39
FR of Germany	125.3	86.92
Denmark	123.7	85.87
France	92.4	64.11
Belgium	78.7	54.63
Spain	74.7	51.86
Austria	74.0	51.36
Italy	63.1	43.76
Ireland	45.1	31.33
Greece	19.4	13.43
Portugal	13.6	9.45
Total	156.4	

Source: EAT. *International advertising expenditure statistics*, March 1989.

Table III.4.25

Current regulations on TV advertising in Europe

Country	TV households (million)	Number of channels accepting advertising	Total ad. mins. p/week	Specific features/comments	Restrictions
Austria	2.78	2.00	280	Limits on number of spots for a brand p/mth. Bookings taken in October for the following year	Tobacco and spririts banned. Beer, wines and pharmaceuticals restricted
Belgium	3.50	3.00	926	Channels broadcast in Flemish and French in the two regions	Tobacco banned. State-TV only carries non-commercial spots
Denmark	2.20	1.00	105[1]	New advertising channel launched in October 1988	
Finland	1.80	3.00	310	Booking period three months ahead	Political parties, religious groups, alcohol, undertakers, slimming drugs and tobacco banned
France	20.50	6.00	1 194	All channels accept advertising	Alcohol, tobacco, press, cinema, shows and retailers banned
FR of Germany	25.34	4.00	451	Demand high, bookings made in September for following year	Tobacco and prescription drugs banned
Greece	3.00	2.00	399	Two State-owned stations providing national commercial coverage	Pharmaceutical products and cigarettes banned
Ireland	0.92	2.00	882	National TV broadcast on two channels. 59% of homes receive BBC/ITV from the UK	Cigarettes and spirits banned
Italy	18.53	350+	7 189	Three State-owned channels. Over 350 commercial channels	Tobacco only is banned on independent TV
Netherlands	5.32	3.00	246	Advertising is managed by an independent company STER	Tobacco is banned
Norway	1.55	—	—	Commercials not allowed	All TV advertising
Portugal	2.42	2.00	608	Both State-run channels funded by advertising	Tobacco banned. Alcohol allowed after 22.00 hrs
Spain	10.33	2.00	704	Only two State-run channels offer national coverage although four regionals accept advertising	Tobacco and alcohol banned

Table **III.4.25** *(continued)*
Current regulations on TV advertising in Europe

Country	TV households (million)	Number of channels accepting advertising	Total ad. mins. p/week	Specific features/comments	Restrictions
Sweden	3.33	—	—	Commercials not allowed	All TV advertising
Switzerland	2.49	1.00	150	One State-owned station consisting of three regionals serving the three major language groups	Alcohol, medicine, tobacco, religion and politics banned
UK	20.60	3.00	1354	Three majors of ITV, Channel 4	Tobacco and spirits banned

Source: EAT. 'International advertising expenditure'.
¹ This includes five minutes per day permitted on eight regional TV channels to be launched over the next two years.

5. *International organizations*

The last group of actors is the one that should provide the framework for all the developments wrought by the others. As in all changes so rapid as to be defined as revolutions, they are unprepared and badly equipped.

The European organizations influencing the evolution in the audiovisual sector are:

(i)   the European Community, in particular the Commission;

(ii) the European Broadcasting Union (EBU);

(iii) the Council of Europe; and

(iv) Eutelsat.

Among the extra-European organizations, Intelsat and the International Telecommunications Union (ITU) must be recalled.

The European Community

The weakness of Europe's most effective regulatory institution is the second 'e' in 'EEC'. While Community regulation is the closest that international law comes to law without adjectives, its competences are limited to the realm of economic activity. Cinema and television can therefore only be handled as economic activities.

However, the Commission has made a serious effort to minimize the damage of this partial approach. In particular, since January 1989 audiovisual affairs have been the object of special concern on the part of the whole Commission and of its President in particular.

Three Commission departments (or Directorates-General) are primarily involved in the development of the European Commission's audiovisual policy:

DG III—Internal Market and Industrial Affairs;

DG X—Information, Communication and Culture; and

DG XIII—Telecommunications, Information Industries and Innovation.

The three Directorates represent the three aspects of the Commission's policy:

(1) regulatory;

(2) cultural; and

(3) technological.

The first of the three is the one for which the Commission arguably has best defined competence.

The main product of EC efforts in providing a legal framework for transborder broadcasting within the Community is the draft Directive 'Television without frontiers'. The principal department involved in its drafting is DG III.

Its outcome is now jeopardized by division caused precisely by the 'cultural' provisions within it (see Chapter 1, section 4).

In fact, the Directorate for culture, DG X, is in charge of action co-ordination. Paradoxically, as culture is a province to which European institutions juridically have no access, its impulse is also the most fragile in the face of opposition. A number of EC Member States are in fact hostile to any kind of Community action in the field of culture.

The Media 92 programme (see Chapter 2) is an offspring of DG X and represents the main Community action in support of software production to date.

Finally, DG XIII deals with the industrial aspects of broadcasting, the whole high-definition television file lies under its principal responsibility (see Chapter 4).

Among the adversaries of cultural action at Community level, the United Kingdom, Denmark and Germany remain the most pugnacious.

As in other issues, integration in Europe strenuously endeavours to remain partial and economic. The result is the mutilation of efforts in all fields that cannot be regarded as purely economic. Film and television are among the clearest examples. While the draft Directive is in danger of annihilation after years of work, the Media programme is forced to struggle for survival in a fight put up, in spite of patent success, by the very institutions of which it is an emanation.

The European Broadcasting Union (EBU)

The EBU was founded in 1950 as the successor to the International Broadcasting Union. It gathers European public-service broadcasters as well as broadcasters from the United States, Japan and other extra-European countries.

It is managed by a General Assembly and a 15-member executive. Its main committees are the Radio Programme Committee, the Television Programme Committee, the Legal Committee and the Technical Committee. EBU's best known activity is the exchange of news material among its members. Its practically exclusive rights on the retransmission of all major sports events must also be recalled. It was the object of recent recrimination on the part of commercial broadcasters (see Chapter II).

The EBU is in fact a major gathering and represents an impressive number of important broadcasters. Its influence goes beyond its nominal functions.

In the past, the EBU and the European Commission disagreed on EC broadcasting regulation, notably on quotas. The EBU represents European as well as extra-European broadcasters, and the EC Directive provisions on the minimum percentages of broadcasting time reserved to European productions were not viewed favourably. This also led the EBU to support more actively the efforts for the drafting of a European Convention on Broadcasting within the Council of Europe, as the Convention would have less binding effects than an EC Directive.

In February 1988, the EBU modified its statute and opened access to the organization to broadcasters addressing 'individual or common reception, regardless of the technical means used for transmission'. This represents an effort to include some of the new broadcasting market operators. The effort is indeed so cautious that doubts remain as to the EBU's representativity in the future. With an increasing number of commercial broadcasters excluded from the organization, the EBU's influence is likely to be eroded. Ultimately, it is even conceivable that a rival organization might appear.

The Council of Europe

The Council of Europe elaborates measures in the audiovisual field through its Steering Committee on mass communication (Comité directeur des moyens de communication de masse — CDMM). The Committee was in charge of the drafting of a European Convention on transborder broadcasting (see Chapter 1, section 4).

The framework of the Council of Europe is weak as compared to the stronger Community institutions. Within it only conventions and agreements of a traditional, international kind can be stipulated.

On the other hand, its competence is geographically more extended.

The support fund for European co-productions, Eurimages, also developed as a partial agreement within the Council of Europe. It offers an example of the organization's structural flexibility as opposed to EC institutions. Its members are all the EC Member States except the Netherlands and the United Kingdom, plus Austria, Sweden and Switzerland. Half of its ECU 4.35 million budget will probably be supplied by France, which inspired the initiative.

Eutelsat

The European telecommunications satellite organization (Eutelsat) was founded in 1977 as a regional equivalent of the global international Intelsat organization. Its members are 26 PTTs that are also members of the Conference of European Postal and Telecommunications Administrations (CEPT). They are the authorized carriers: frequencies and satellite transponders are assigned to them exclusively. Users have to deal with national PTTs regarding the leasing of channels.

We already noted that this working mechanism brings about paradoxical situations (see Chapter 1, section 1). In the face of commercial television stations swarming the European landscape, it is a wholly anachronistic method of operation. Its original mission was similar to that of Intelsat: planning and launching telecommunications satellites.

However, since the appearance of medium-power and DBS satellites, Eutelsat has become increasingly involved in the conception of broadcasting satellites. The second generation of Eutelsat spacecraft, ECS 1 and ECS 2, will be medium-powered satellites on the Astra model carrying 16 television channels each.

Within Eutelsat, plans for a joint European medium-power broadcasting satellite (Europesat) are also being devised in collaboration with the European Commission.

As in the case of EBU, Eutelsat risks being by-passed by competing ventures or organizations, as in the case of Astra, unless it reconsiders its function in the new audiovisual environment.

While its monopoly on telecommunication satellites is hardly at stake, broadcasting by satellite will be increasingly independent of deliberation within Eutelsat.

The organization will certainly retain an important role even as a satellite broadcasting organization if it evolves from its present function of a defence fortress for national PTTs. In a time of transborder broadcasting, end-users must be allowed to deal directly with Eutelsat without having to pass the filter of national administrations.

Association of Commercial Television in Europe (ACT)

ACT is a European Economic Interest Group (EEIG) formed in the Summer of 1989 by five European commercial broadcasters: CLT/RTL, Fininvest, ITV (Independent Television Association), SAT-1 and TF1. The Chairman is Silvio Berlusconi of Fininvest. Its seat is in Brussels.

ACT is the first organization representing commercial TV stations on a European scale. Its aim seems to be that of defending the interests and principles of commercial broadcasting. Apart from collaboration among its members to improve their production capacity and their activity in general, its Charter declares the intention to promote a balance in regulatory activity between the private and public sector, acting thus as a pressure group or a lobby.

Other international organizations

The International Telecommunications Union (ITU) is the most important United Nations agency for telecommunications. It is also the world's oldest international organization (it was founded in 1865 as the International Telegraph Union).

The ITU has an International Frequency Registration Board (IFRB), an International Consultative Committee on Radio (CCIR) and an International Telegraph and Telephone consultative committee (CCITT)

Telecommunications is defined by ITU as: 'any transmission, emission or reception of signs, signals, writing, images and sounds or intelligence of any nature by wire, radio, optical or other electromagnetic systems'. (ITU Convention, Nairobi, 1982, ITU, Geneva, 1983, Annex 2, paragraph 2015).

Its competence is therefore quite extended. The CCIR has, as will be shown in Chapter 4, direct responsibility for the high-definition television file.

Intelsat was mentioned in Chapter I, section 1. It is the global satellite organization of which Eutelsat is the European regional equivalent. It gathers 114 member states. Its USSR-based Eastern-bloc equivalent is Intersputnik, with 14 full members. Finally, maritime communications via satellite fall under the competence of Inmarsat.

Chapter IV

The technological challenge

Technological developments are ambiguous. Every new opportunity cannot help implying a new danger. Developments in satellite technology, along with new opportunities for the quantity and quality of services available to individuals, carry the risk of indiscriminate and 'wild' broadcasting, and therefore the danger of a trend precisely to the opposite: loss of quality in services; loss of cultural identity for entire continents. VCRs and digital recording can signify an enormous chance for fiction distribution and, indirectly, production; piracy can turn this chance into jeopardy for those same sectors.

In the absence of an effective over-all philosophy, it is unthinkable to retain control on the fast-changing reality of the audiovisual industry.

Among all technologies, high-definition television (HDTV) represents undoubtedly the biggest challenge at present. It is also the issue about which the most consistent common European policy could be developed up to this moment. Above all, it has by now become a battle no one can afford to lose.

High-definition television (HDTV)

We pointed out the closeness of cinema and television from the point of view of software production. Competition exists only as far as the mode of diffusion is concerned. The nature of production, of the main single kind of production for television as well as of the only product in the film industry, is similar.

Differences are especially relevant in relation to the material and its cost. Ever since the Lumière brothers, films have been produced much in the same way. Voluminous, expensive and relatively fragile rolls of celluloid have been manually shuttled and screened around the world for almost 100 years.

Television uses magnetic tape. Tape sensibly lowers production costs; since it is cheaper than film, it can be used more than once and, especially, it makes immediate viewing of production possible, as it does not need developing or printing.

At present, however, there is still a large quality gap between pictures delivered by magnetic tape on a television set and those projected through film onto a large cloth screen. Recent developments in film production have relied heavily on image quality to face competition coming from television, concentrating on big costly productions rich in effects that are inevitably lost on a small screen.

High-definition television will bring about a revolution in this balance.

HDTV produces images on magnetic tape of a definition nearly as good as that of film pictures. While traditional television uses 625 lines for picture definition. HDTV pictures will be formed of over 1 000 lines. HDTV will use monitors the size of film screens, bringing film quality to television broadcasts.

At the same time, HDTV will be used for feature film production, providing it with all the economic and technical advantages of electronic recording.

The very distribution of films to theatres will take place via broadcasting of a single original copy. Deterioration and transport will become a memory, and production for theatres will be from the start identical with production for television. HDTV also represents a vast potential market. Among the most impressive figures:

(i) TV reception equipment had in 1986 a market of USD 70 000 million worldwide. It should attain USD 103 000 million in 1991;

Table IV.1

The world market for professional broadcasting equipment

	1987	1990
Europe	25%	27.5%
Rest of world	20%	19%
USA	55%	53.5%
Total market	USD 1 570 million	USD 2 220 million

Source: Commission of the European Communities.

Table IV.2

EC market shares of broadcasting VTR/VCRs, 1976/1986

Manufacturers	1976	1986
Japanese	25%	60%
European	35%	20%
Others, mainly US	40%	20%

Source: Commission of the European Communities.

(ii) in 1995 there should be 1 000 million TV sets in the whole world; and

(iii) the professional TV equipment business had a volume of USD 1 600 million in 1987, and should grow to USD 2 200 million by the end of 1990.

Tables IV.1 to IV.11 provide details on market volume and forecasts.

Table IV.3
Product shares of the broadcasting-equipment market-place

	1987	1990
Audio synthesizers	2.2%	5.0%
Audio processors	8.3%	10.1%
Image synthesizers	2.2%	4.1%
Image processors	16.3%	19.5%
VTRs	17.5%	14.0%
Audio tape recorders/editors	29.0%	26.0%
Video editors	4.5%	4.1%
Cameras	20.0%	17.0%
Total market	USD 1 500 million	USD 2 200 million

Source: Commission of the European Communities.
1987 = traditional broadcasting equipment.
1990 = new broadcasting equipment.

Table IV.4
Japan — Hardware market volumes

(1 000 units)

	1981	1986	1991
Colour television	6 565	8 270	8 650
Video tape recorders	1 550	4 850	6 500
Home audio systems	2 410	2 120	2 600
Compact disc players	[1]	1 940	5 950
Portable personal audio equipment	12 360	11 225	10 100
Video camcorders	[1]	650	1 750
DAT players and decks	[1]	[1]	3 975
Electronic still cameras	[1]	[1]	300
Home computers	289	800	1 000

Source: Commission of the European Communities.
[1] Not yet developed.

Historical background

HDTV technology was first developed in Japan in the 1960s. Since the development of European direct broadcasting satellite (DBS) programmes, however, industrial groups in the old continent have been working on their own HDTV system.

Table IV.5
Japan — Hardware market volumes (retail value at 1986 prices)

(million USD)

	1981	1986	1991
Colour television	3 289	4 145	4 334
Video tape recorders	922	2 886	3 868
Home audio systems	3 164	2 784	3 414
Compact disc players	1	389	1 310
Portable personal audio equipment	1 224	1 112	1 000
Video camcorders	1	900	2 424
DAT players and decks	1	1	2 385
Electronic still cameras	1	1	240
Home computers	91	364	455
Total value (SM)	8 690	12 580	19 430

Source: Commission of the European Communities.

[1] Not yet developed.

Table IV.6
USA — Hardware market volumes

(1 000 units)

	1981	1986	1991
Colour television	11 380	18 530	23 700
Video tape recorders	1 330	12 005	15 000
Home audio systems	5 410	4 715	6 200
Compact disc players	1	2 675	13 400
Portable personal audio equipment	63 110	67 635	68 200
Video camcorders	1	1 170	2 850
DAT players and decks	1	1	4 420
Electronic still cameras	1	1	200
Home computers	500	4 500	5 000

Source: Commission of the European Communities.

[1] Not yet developed.

The European system produces pictures defined in 1 250 lines, as opposed to the Japanese standard's 1 125.

There is, however, another major difference between the two systems. While the Japanese standard uses a 60 Hz frequency, the European signal travels on a frequency of 50 Hz. The two systems were consequently labelled 1125/60 and 1250/50.

Table IV.7

USA — Hardware market volumes (retail value at 1986 prices)

(million USD)

	1981	1986	1991
Colour television	5 440	8 852	11 329
Video tape recorders	333	3 001	3 750
Home audio systems	2 299	2 006	2 635
Compact disc players	[1]	604	3 440
Portable personal audio equipment	2 714	2 894	2 933
Video camcorders	[1]	1 209	2 944
DAT players and decks	[1]	[1]	2 652
Electronic still cameras	[1]	[1]	160
Home computers	170	1 520	2 000
Total value	10 956	20 086	31 843

Source: Commission of the European Communities.

[1] Not yet developed.

Table IV.8

EC — Hardware market volumes

(1 000 units)

	1981	1986	1991
Colour television	9 660	14 250	15 425
Video tape recorders	2 515	6 535	8 550
Home audio systems	8 235	6 315	6 800
Compact disc players	[1]	1 635	7 880
Portable personal audio equipment	36 915	35 630	33 555
Video camcorders	[1]	435	995
DAT players and decks	[1]	[1]	1 650
Electronic still cameras	[1]	[1]	100
Home computers	400	2 475	2 590

Source: Commission of the European Communities.

[1] Not yet developed.

Table IV.9
EC — Hardware market volumes (retail value at 1986 prices)

(million USD)

	1981	1986	1991
Colour television	5 458	8 044	8 715
Video tape recorders	1 627	4 229	5 332
Home audio systems	4 340	3 329	3 800
Compact disc players	[1]	599	3 021
Portable personal audio equipment	2 585	2 456	2 350
Video camcorders	[1]	708	1 622
DAT players and decks	[1]	[1]	990
Electronic still cameras	[1]	[1]	80
Home computers	115	718	872
Total value	14 126	20 083	25 782

Source : Commission of the European Communities.

[1] Not yet developed.

Table IV.10
Television penetration in 1995

(million units)

Total	Colour		Black and white	
	Pal/Secam	NTSC	625 lines	525 lines
Japan		100		3
Asia	69	27	59.5	6
Western Europe	177		37	
Middle East	30		9	
Africa	11		10	
North America		184		47
Central/South America	35	17	16	12
Oceania	10		1.4	
Eastern Europe	79		68	
World total	412	328	200	68
	740		268	
	1 008			
NTSC world	396.5		40 %	
PAL/Secam world	612.0		60 %	
	1 008		100 %	

Source : Commission of the European Communities, June 1988.

Table IV.11

Forecast of colour-television demand in 1995

(million units)

	NTSC	PAL/Secam
Japan	11.5	
Asia	4	10.8
Western Europe		20.9
Middle East		4.9
Africa		2.012
North America	22.02	
Central/South America	2.69	4.65
Oceania		1.19
Eastern Europe		8.89
World total	40.21	53.3
World total	93.7	
NTSC	43%	
PAL/Secam	57%	

Source: Commission of the European Communities, June 1988.

This latter difference is substantial. During talks within the International Consultative Committee for Radio (CCIR), it led to the formation of antagonistic fronts in the attempt to fix a single common world production standard for the new broadcasting technique.

Production and transmission standards are not the same. While the first affects the manufacturing of studio equipment (cameras, recorders, etc.), transmission is relevant to the much larger market for receivers (TV sets, aerials, etc.). CCIR discussions focus at the moment on production standards.

Originally most extra-European countries, and the United States in the first place, supported the adoption of the Japanese system as a world standard, mainly because of the advance it had on any other. The European Commission, however, succeeded in coordinating the diplomatic efforts of the member countries during CCIR discussions, and the united opposition on the part of the Europeans, who claimed they could produce in a short time a better HDTV system than the Japanese, prevented the Committee from adopting the Japanese system as a world standard in 1986.

On that occasion Europe won four years in which to develop its own HDTV system, before a decision on world standards is reached in May 1990 at the new CCIR meeting on the issue.

CCIR Study Group 11

Standards are an issue of vital importance to the future of broadcasting and production. The aim of debates on a world standard is to avoid reproducing the situation of a chaotic colour broadcasting system, with various incompatible standards (PAL, Secam and NTSC) and all the consequent economic and technical disadvantages for programme circulation.

All the opportunities HDTV could bring about in the field of film distribution and the unification of production techniques would be lost in a world environment which involved different and incompatible recording and broadcasting standards. As for consumer electronic products, marketing for software (films and television programmes) will be conducted more and more on a global, worldwide scale. Technical gaps between markets would negate much of the technological accomplishment of HDTV.

The group responsible for the drafting of a recommendation to be adopted in 1990 (CCIR Study Group 11) is chaired by Professor Krivocheev of the Soviet Ministry of Posts and Telecommunications and counts a number of interim working parties (IWP), of which IWP 11/6 is the most important.

The SG11 and IWP 11/6 meetings in May 1989 produced a draft recommendation that identified parameters for a worldwide HDTV standard to be found both in the European and the Japanese proposals.

Europe registered significant successes as:

(i) the United States stopped supporting the adoption of the 1125/60 system as a world standard and proposed to prolong the study period until 1994;

(ii) coordination among the EC delegations during the meeting was successful; and

(iii) the delegations of EFTA countries confirmed their support for the European proposal.

Evolution v revolution

The European system is developed within the framework of Eureka. A group of big manufacturers led by France's Thomson, Germany's Bosch and the Netherlands' Philips initiated Eureka project No 95, known as EU-95, which, in September 1988, produced a public demonstration of a complete HDTV production chain (from cameras to broadcasting, receiving and recording equipment) in Brighton, England.

The European system is described as evolutionary as opposed to a revolutionary Japanese HDTV system.

European HDTV is conceived for direct broadcasting by satellite (DBS) on a MAC 50 Hz signal. MAC stands for multiplex analogue component. It is a new standard for television transmission that encompasses digital sound channels. Ideally suited for satellite broadcasting, it can carry both PAL/Secam and high-definition

Table IV.12

Comparison between different MAC standards

Transmission format	C-MAC	D-MAC	D2-MAC
Video	Identical MAC video signal format in all three systems: — standard 4:3 aspect ratio — 16:9 wide aspect ratio — compatible 4:3 out of 16:9 transmission — HDTV		
Audio channel [1] Mono: Stereo: Other option:	8 × 15 KHz 4 × 15 KHz 2 × 15 KHz stereo with eight commentary channels	6 × 15 KHz 2 × 15 KHz 2 × 15 KHz stereo with four commentary channels	4 × 15 KHz 2 × 15 KHz 1 × 15 KHz stereo with four commentary channels
Applications	Satellite only	Cable and satellite	Narrowband and broadband cable and satellite and (later) video recording

Source: Logica.

[1] Sound comparison is complicated by relative ruggedness of signal standards:
  D2-MAC – assumes NICAM, Level 1 protection,
  C-MAC – assumes ideal receiver, NICAM, Level 1 protection,
  D-MAC – assumes companded, Level 2 protection.

transmission on a 50 Hz frequency, the same used in present-day broadcasts. The MAC-based broadcasting system is therefore called 'compatible', since it simply requires a special adaptor to be received by normal television sets (details on the MAC signal are given in Table IV.12). Even high-definition pictures can be received with existing equipment, although they are evidently reproduced with the available 625 lines. The European system's compatibility will make it possible to receive HDTV channels from the commencement of broadcasting, even if only in the traditional 625 line definition mode. In a situation similar to the transition from black and white to colour television, consumers could choose when to buy high-definition receiving equipment without losing programme choice at any moment, provided they get the adaptor needed for the reception of HD-MAC signals.

The Japanese HD system includes a production system, called 'Hi-vision', as well as the MUSE transmission system. Both were developed by broadcaster NHK in close collaboration with Sony.

The Japanese system uses a 60 Hz frequency. No commercialized TV set can be modified to receive a 60 Hz signal. To receive broadcasts on that frequency, in high definition or not, a completely new receiving equipment would be required from the start. The Japanese system is hence incompatible with existing TV sets: it calls for a 'revolution' in consumer habits and the immediate diffusion of HD consumer hardware.

In this respect, the Japanese proposal violates CCIR Recommendation 601, which requires that the parameters of two different TV standards bear a certain relationship with one another to allow the manufacture of equipment capable of handling both without difficulty.

The Japanese case for their system maintains that a 60 Hz frequency gives much better picture quality. At the second meeting of the EC-Japan working group on HDTV in September 1988, they claimed that the ideal frequency would have been 59.94 Hz, and that they had already made an effort to facilitate conversion of filmed material to HDTV electronic bringing that figure up to 60.

The conversion of film material into HDTV is also a crucial point. The frequency of 50 Hz (European system), being the one used until now, has traditionally been used in converting 24-25 picture/second films (i.e. normal films) into electronic recording. Although the Japanese insist that they never experienced any problems in converting film into 60 Hz frequency HD pictures, the European system has on its side a proven and diffused compatibility with all existing equipment. Considering the amount of film material broadcast on television, convertibility is, of course, a major factor.

The international situation and the possible outcomes

In the diplomatic and technological race to HDTV, factors are reshuffling. Special attention must be devoted to developments in the United States, since that country represents the major factor of uncertainty for the final outcome on the HDTV issue. The US position is also a determinant factor in the attitude of countries heavily dependent on its market choices, such as Canada and Brazil. These were both supporting, until now, the adoption of the Japanese standard.

(a) *United States of America*

The American position has evolved considerably. Initially, the United States actively supported the adoption of the Japanese system as a world standard. The relevance of HDTV technology for fields of application other than broadcasting (information, telecommunications, defence), and the foreseen volume of business for HDTV equipment, generated growing worries in American electronic consumer industries about being cut off from a potentially large and technologically crucial market. At the same time, European success in developing an alternative HDTV system to the Japanese showed that it was not too late to enter the race.

A symptom of the new American attitude was the decision of the US Federal Communications Commission that, as far as terrestrial HDTV transmission is concerned,

(i)   there has to be, in the United States, one system for all media;

(ii) that this system has to be of a high quality; and

(iii) that it must be compatible with the existing spectrum allocation and installed base of TV sets.

The FCC has jurisdiction over the HDTV terrestrial broadcasting standard. The immediate effect of its decision (announced in September 1988) was to reinforce the position of the American television companies by blocking the Japanese system for the time being in the USA. The decision marks, therefore, a major point in favour of the European system. However, the FCC is not involved in any activity relating to DBS, cable, video or other media.

It must also be noted that, as broadcasting standards are different in the USA and in Europe (the American system is called NTSC, as opposed to the European Pal and Secam), it also implies that it is almost unavoidable that transmission standards will be different. The production issue, however, remains open.

There are only two important US corporations involved in television equipment manufacturing: Zenith (specialized in TV sets) and Ampex (studio equipment). Alone, these two do not have the dimensions needed to represent the driving force for a US HDTV solution. Moreover, while Zenith is in search of cooperation with AT & T, Ampex expressed interest in collaborating with Eureka on the development of HDTV studio equipment.

There seems to be, in fact, a fairly substantial disposition on the part of some US circles to seek cooperation with Europe provided it leads, of course, to active participation of US industry in the Eureka initiatives.

It is possible that the Americans will show more flexibility on HDTV in exchange for reassurance on the regulatory issue, which is a renowned source of preoccupation for the US Administration. The section of the Administration that has adopted, until now, the highest profile in HDTV discussions is the Department of Commerce, led by Secretary Mosbacher, who claims administrative leadership on the matter.

Finally, the private sector is far from constituting a unanimous front.

Film producers and terrestrial broadcasters (these latter virtually represented by the FCC) are taken to be evaluating the matter, now that the adoption of the Japanese system as a world standard does not appear as imminent as it did before the 1986 CCIR meeting.

Both the American Electronics Association and the semiconductor industry in the SIA do not exclude, in their call for US industry to join this sector of production, cooperation with Europe, while the Electronics Industry Association, which includes the principal Japanese companies operating in the USA, obviously took a more pro-Japanese stance.

The last known official position adopted by the USA included the proposal for a postponement of a decision on the production standard to 1994. While this would give European industry time to improve, it is also likely to represent a good occasion for the Japanese to establish a sort of *de facto* world standard before official decisions are taken. Considering the pros and cons, the European Commission seems to consider the adoption of a recommendation for 1992 as an ideal solution.

(b) *Other countries*

The USSR has the chairmanship of CCIR Study Group 11. It will therefore play a coordinating role in the decision-making process.

At a recent meeting in Moscow involving representatives of the Soviet Union, Japan, the United States and Europe, the Soviets said that they are also working on their own HDTV system based on a 1350/50 parameter set. During a recent visit by Germany's Chancellor Kohl to Moscow, the Soviets had specifically required the HDTV issue to be put on the agenda, and German experts in Mr Kohl's staff had been approached with proposals for cooperation between Western Europe and the USSR.

Indeed, the Soviets show a certain propensity to supporting the European proposal within the CCIR, but they make their final position depend on direct involvement in Eureka. In a note of 3 April 1989, the USSR also proposed to organize European HDTV demonstrations in East European countries.

Difficulties in dealing with the Soviets stem from the fact that, among other things, because of its potential defence applications, digital and progressive scan HDTV technology has not yet been cleared for export to Eastern-bloc countries.

The Japanese concede, in very private conversations, that they made mistakes in timing and/or in their strategy toward the USA, and they are certainly likely to reshape it. What is not likely at all is that they abandon their stand for the 1250/60 standard, their MUSE system.

Everything considered, the chances are that in 1990 the CCIR will not be in a position to adopt any system as a world standard for HDTV.

European policy

(a) *Diplomatic action*

The European Commission displayed an impressive activity in support of the Eureka HDTV system. The results up to now have been positive especially in the field of standards.

(i) Europe

A first large-scale diplomatic effort was conducted in order to form a compact front at the 1986 Dubrovnik meeting of the CCIR, when the adoption, strongly supported by the USA, of the Japanese system as a world standard was avoided. Regulation coordination resulted in November 1986 in a Directive that prescribes the MAC broadcasting parameter for all direct broadcasting by satellite in Europe. The Directive prevents future inconsistency in broadcasting parameters within the Community and sets an example for harmonization elsewhere.

In 1986 the European HDTV Forum was also created. Chaired by the Commission, the Forum gathers manufacturers, broadcasters, film producers, the national administrations involved, representatives of the EBU, the CEPT, the FERA as well as of the Eureka Secretariat. It meets on a flexible basis, sometimes with only some of the represented categories attending, more often in plenary session. All its members agree that it is an extremely useful instrument for coordination and information exchange.

The most recent accomplishment in EC action on HDTV was the creation of the Media Investment Club. A pilot project within the framework of the Media programme of the Commission, the Club promotes and supports productions involving the use of advanced technologies, including, of course, HDTV. Among its members, apart from the Commission, there are the French INA (Institut National de l'Audiovisuel), Thomson, Ian Maxwell and the RAI.

A crucial factor in the commercial launch of HDTV European services will be, of course, support on the part of broadcasters.

Significant difficulties have arisen in the past in relations between the broadcasters (with their umbrella institution, the EBU) and the Commission of the European Communities. The EBU initially supported quite strongly the Japanese system, while various broadcasters took a practical stand in favour of the Japanese system by using it for productions in HDTV.

RAI produced a feature film in HDTV, 'Julia and Julia', using Sony 1125/60 equipment. The BBC, normally very supportive of the European standard, nevertheless decided to produce a series in four parts using Japanese standard HDTV equipment. The motive is evident: the Japanese will lend the equipment and offer a financial contribution of UKL 1 million (the cost of one of the four parts).

From the initial EBU standpoint in outright support of the Japanese system there has been, however, a substantial evolution. Although it never issued a public statement in favour of the European proposal, the organization has now been persuaded that the 1125/60 parameter will not be adopted as a world standard, and this has induced greater flexibility in its position.

(ii) External relations

The proposed guidelines for EC action outside Europe include a series of diplomatic initiatives directed toward the main actors involved.

In the United States there is scope for relevant diplomatic pressure. The Commission seems anxious to put something in writing and to come to some form of formal agreement for common action. Of course, such an agreement should include the possibility for US industries to join EC-sponsored initiatives in the field of HDTV: we are thinking of Eureka 95, certainly, but also of those provided for in the Esprit or RACE programmes.

We mentioned the changes in the American attitude which have already occurred within the CCIR. Few of the original supporters of the Japanese position are still at the State Department after the last presidential elections. Full adoption of a new formal US position, whichever this may be, might take some time.

Tokyo's position of strength on HDTV will hardly bring Japan to concede anything. In the foreseeable future the European and Japanese positions will probably remain opposed to one another, and the tone of discussion within the Japan-EC working group on HDTV mentioned above is evidence for this. The group might meet again before the October session of the CCIR Study Group 11 and state again the difference between the European and the Japanese positions.

The Commission will certainly devote a special effort to prevent the Japanese standard from obtaining the status of a *de facto* world parameter before a decision is taken within the CCIR.

As soon as the standard issue is settled, however, there will certainly be scope for cooperation, and the European position, although uncompromising (and the more so since it is defensive), will certainly take this into account.

(b) *Policy*

The future EC strategy on HDTV provides for the launching of HDTV services on a commercial basis in the course of the 1990s. This strategy is sketched in the four points of a Council Resolution adopted on 27 April 1989:

(1) ensuring that the European industry develops the necessary technology, components and equipment required for the progressive launching of HDTV services throughout the 1990s;

(2) ensuring that the European parameter 1250/50 for HDTV is adopted as the single world production standard, and to ensure that broadcast standards are consistent with CCIR Recommendation 601 and are thus easily convertible into each other;

(3) ensuring the widest use of the European HDTV system throughout the world and the most favourable environment for the sale of European HDTV equipment and programmes throughout the world; and

(4) developing a strategy and action plan for the progressive launch of HDTV services in Europe throughout the 1990s.

Before commenting on these four general objectives of the future EC strategy, two elements must be recalled. The first is the advantage of the Japanese, not so much in the know-how as in the commercialization of their equipment. Commission officials admit informally that, although the technology available in Europe is virtually at a par with the Japanese system, the Japanese manufacturers will make competitively equipment to any specification, regardless of what standards are adopted by the CCIR. Among other things, the Japanese broadcaster NHK began broadcasting an hour of programmes in HDTV by satellite in May 1989. Although the broadcast has a demonstrative value since HDTV receiving equipment is not yet available, it represents substantial progress.

The second important element is the relevance of satellite programmes, notably of DBS, to the development of HDTV. The MAC signal is particularly suited for satellite broadcasting. What is more, satellite broadcast HDTV would render equipment for individual satellite signal reception more appealing for the public. Since the profitability of medium- and high-power satellite programmes depends on the marketing and diffusion of receiving equipment, it is clear that DBS through MAC signal and MAC-based HDTV should be the object of complementary promotion strategies.

The four EC objectives for HDTV

(1) From the point of view of technology, the European Commission is ready to undertake a reorientation within specialized aspects of its technology initiatives, notably in the Esprit and RACE programmes.

Among all the aspects that call for further development, we will mention a few:

(i) Technology for the terrestrial broadcasting of HDTV must still be developed. It is needed for obvious purposes, and especially to render European HDTV less exclusively dependent on satellite programmes.

(ii) Following the decision of France and Germany to use D2 MAC and Germany's decision to use a D MAC signal, dual D+D2 MAC decoders will be needed at acceptable costs to avoid negative consequences on the receiver market.

In general, the Commission's policy will be aimed at accelerating the development into commercial products of all the prototype equipment available.

(2) In the field of standards, the European Community attained a major positive result in coordinating Member States action within the CCIR and avoiding the adoption of the Japanese NHK production and MUSE transmission systems as a world parameter. As noted before, the Japanese system is inconsistent with CCIR Recommendation 601, and the Europeans did not fail to make the point strongly in the various working groups of the CCIR involved.

Commission officials have been persuaded that the Japanese will not abandon their proposal and that the European system has therefore no chance of being adopted as a single world standard as far as production is concerned.

For transmission, the incompatibility of the Japanese 60 Hz parameter with all existing equipment gives Europe hope for worldwide adoption of the European system.

The Commission has observer status in the CCIR, and its main effort will be aimed at coordinating the position of Member States on the occasion of meetings as well as keeping up regular contacts on the issue with other European countries (EFTA).

Diplomatic action toward the main countries involved has been described above. In general, Community representatives throughout the world will do all they can to facilitate the penetration of the European HDTV system in each country. In spite of the difficulties mentioned above, Eastern Europe and the USSR are likely to receive special attention.

(3) The third objective includes the effort to inform the public of the benefits of HDTV; in other words, an audience for HDTV must be created.

The point is not subsidiary. Some even protest that HDTV broadcasting services are premature and that it would have been better to wait for full development of digital technology and aim at systems providing for a much higher picture definition than high definition offers. Such statements imply that the demand for HDTV, especially in the province of private reception, is not exactly pressing, if it exists at all.

We are therefore likely to witness, in the next few years, an impressive 'propaganda' activity, including demonstrations, literature production, exhibitions as well as lobbying.

The most concrete impending European initiative is the creation of a European Economic Interest Group (EEIG) with the purpose of promoting the European HDTV. In particular, the group would:

(i) put Eureka HDTV facilities at the disposal of Community professionals for demonstration and training purposes; and

(ii) carry out demonstrations worldwide.

The EEIG, called 'Vision 1250', will be based in Brussels. It will be formed by manufacturers (among which the principal are Philips, Thomson and Bosch), broadcasters and film producers, as well as the European Community itself, represented by the Commission.

EC sources evaluate the cost of the initiative at ECU 45 million over a period of four years (1989-92), ECU 15 million of which would be brought in by the Commission.

Consultations are under way between the Commission and the three main industrial groups involved. Apart from the broadcasters, whose form of representation within the group (individual or collective) is still discussed, some Member State administrations might be interested in becoming members of the group (notably, the German, French, Dutch and UK Governments).

(4) The fourth objective starts from the evident consideration that a global strategic alliance and coordination of all relevant agents in the audiovisual sector is needed for the launch of HDTV services, during the 1990s as at any other time.

Manufacturers, software producers and distributors (i.e. public and commercial broadcasters, distribution companies) must all agree on it. If any one of them does not, an essential link will be missing in the chain leading to an HDTV audiovisual environment.

A global action plan will eventually have to be conceived. The basis for it should be a series of pilot initiatives that will be the object of comprehensive study in the coming months. Such initiatives could include the broadcasting of a number of hours per week, on the model of the NHK present activity. This could take place using DBS satellite channels or, when available, terrestrial frequencies and should necessarily be of an attractive nature (sports events or films particularly suitable for HDTV transmission).

Even such a pilot phase would require the full cooperation of manufacturers, broadcasters and software producers. The question of 'attractive' programming is particularly delicate since film-makers tend to be conservative in relation to technology.

A particular emphasis will fall on the circulation of training and experience with the new techniques, and resources will have to be devoted to the establishment of HDTV facilities in professional training centres and to the encouragement of production in HDTV through the institution of prizes or other means.

Conclusions

The stakes of HDTV are enormous. It is no wonder that its history unfolds with a dramatic element to it.

HDTV will bring about a revolution. The signs of this revolution are not yet evident. In spite of all the advantages it could not fail to bring to every sector in audiovisual production, some developments in the ways and timing of its adoption could result in a situation where:

(i) differences in production and transmission systems throughout the world negate the unification and rationalizing potential of HDTV; and/or

(ii) the monopoly of one country, or group of countries, in technology and manufacture renders the rest of the world dependent on the commercial and industrial choices in that country for developments in every sector of their own audiovisual environment.

Indeed, the technical quality of the issue should not make anyone forget the relevance of outcomes on HDTV for the culture of nations. Once again the dual nature of the audiovisual business reaffirms itself: an industry that has culture for trade. One does not go without the other.

Conclusion

Elements of an audiovisual policy

The European audiovisual single market cannot wait until 1993. Progress unfolds itself with the blind inertia and the speed of an avalanche. Unless choices are formulated and followed up quickly, there will be no choice left, only *de facto* winners and losers.

The French Government took the initiative, in December 1987, of a policy proposal in support of the European audiovisual industry. The model for this proposal is the technological Eureka; accordingly, it was christened 'Audiovisual Eureka'.

Its basic principles were laid down at a conference in Paris at the end of September 1989.

The initiative's scope will cover the technological as well as the software-related aspects of production. As in the technological Eureka, single projects may include only some of the EC countries (i.e. not necessarily all of them all the time), and substantial openings could be made to non-EC States. Moreover, support could be given to single production projects.

The Media 92 programme is likely to represent the main model for action in the field of software. Its philosophy proved highly effective in the course of its pilot phase, and the Media projects cover most aspects of the industry. The programme's fate could conceivably be that of becoming the Community's arm in the global, pan-European Eureka support initiative.

The structure devised for the implementation of Eureka consists of:

(i)   a Committee of Coordinators (Comité des Coordonnateurs) formed by one representative for each of the 26 participating countries and institutions (the EC and Council of Europe Member States and the European Community represented by the Commission);

(ii) a Secretariat, provided by the European Commission; and

(iii) the so-called 'Observatory'. This should become the main source of data on the audiovisual market and industry. The details for its administration and functioning will be worked out by the Committee of Coordinators.

The audiovisual Eureka has only just been born and it is impossible to assess its performance. Pros and cons come to mind only in relation to past experience.

131

Consistently with what was maintained in preceding sections of this book, it must be noted that Eureka is a coming together of national efforts within a rather loose framework. The Coordinators will presumably work in close connection with their own national environment and act, therefore, as the representatives of national interests, albeit expressed by professionally competent milieux. As Eureka becomes the main action in support of the European audiovisual production, i.e. the main act in European audiovisual policy, this policy will remain essentially national or, at best international; it will hardly become supranational, or European. Furthermore, being the initiative of a single State, and one very keen on taking and keeping the main role in the audiovisual field, unless its administrators use extraordinary care and balance Eureka risks giving rise to jealousy and suspicion among the other Community Member States.

On the other hand, the development of the audiovisual 'Assises' honoured the results and philosophy of the Media programme, and that initiative's main priorities also rate first and second among the Eureka objectives. We are talking about the distribution and financing of audiovisual productions, the first two titles of Annex 1 to the joint statement issued at the end of the Paris conference.

If even a breath of Media's soul remains to inspire Eureka, some positive results in the way of a genuinely common European policy, a cultural policy, will be seen.

The President of the European Commission, Jacques Delors, spoke at the 'Assises' of the peculiarity of audiovisual products and of their specific, cultural nature: 'I refuse to talk about the free circulation of productions, I want to speak of organizing the audiovisual space', a sentence that was applauded at the Conference. Mr Delors intended to ask the European Council at Strasbourg in December to give a mandate to the Commission for the allocation of some ECU 250 million to action in the audiovisual field. Audiovisual policy would thus become a major EC issue and grant the Commission an important influence on European initiatives, and on Eureka first of all.

The European audiovisual policy remains, however, the priority of providing both regulation and support. A list of specific topics in urgent need of regulation consideration includes:

(i)   the structure of multi-media groups, through effective anti-trust provisions;

(ii) copyright;

(iii) public subsidies to audiovisual production; and

(iv) the free circulation of persons and equipment.

Support will follow the principles set in the past. Financing can only be conceived as 'seed-money'; a financial participation in schemes equally supported by private or public institutions, in which the Community will bring a decreasing quota of the needed capital and eventually cease to support.

Eureka will, on the contrary, provide financing for single productions and other individual projects.

In spite of the EC's weak role in cultural affairs, its institutions seem to be the most convenient framework for the development of an audiovisual policy. It has been proven that broadcasting will not spare the borders of the Community any more than those of nations. However, the regulatory and political instruments of the EC are the most effective among the most geographically extended. The Community cannot renounce a role in the definition of an audiovisual policy, and its effectiveness is, in the long run, the best bet for all Europeans.

The future audiovisual scene will be radically different from what it is today. The easiest comparison is that with printing and the press. As for general affairs and specialized magazines, and as for encyclopedias and books, eventually there will be a few general television channels and a plethora of single-theme stations, transmitting only news or documentaries, films, games, etc. While commercial general channels will have the role of showcase for the single-theme stations, public-service broadcasting should become a parameter for quality.

As printing used to be, audiovisual means will become the principal form of expression for private and public communication.

The history of audiovisual production in the age of information industry, of satellites and cables, does not, as yet, yield patterns for wisdom, for the 'knowledge of the future' which, today as in pre-Socratic Greece, is the only useful kind. The sense of an enormous revolution in social communication remains the strongest impression. The depth of change, its speed and the stakes involved should dissolve trivial preoccupations for the preservation of autonomy and induce an urge for common, genuinely common, action.

Appendix I

**Advertising expenditure in EC Member States,
the United States of America and Japan**

The source for statistics in this section is the European Advertising Tripartite (EAT), particularly S. Haq/M. Waterson, 'International advertising expenditure statistics', March 1989.

The sourcing given in the original tables has been retained as it provides essential information on data composition.

Belgium

Data sources

1. Advertising data source   Conseil de la Publicité et Chambre des Agences Conseils en Publicité

2. Method of compilation   Survey data/trade association

3. Coverage
   Includes agency commission
   Includes production costs
   Includes classified advertising
   Directories not included
   Imperfect radio coverage
   Outdoor and transport includes light-up advertisements
   Discounts deducted

4. Economic data source   OECD main economic indicators

5. Currency data source   Eurostat money and finance

	Advertising expenditure as % of GDP	Per capita advertising expenditure at constant 1985 prices
1980	0.48	2 344
1981	0.47	2 188
1982	0.47	2 200
1983	0.51	2 389
1984	0.53	2 495
1985	0.54	2 590
1986	0.56	2 776
1987	0.65	3 293

Belgium
Advertising expenditure at constant prices

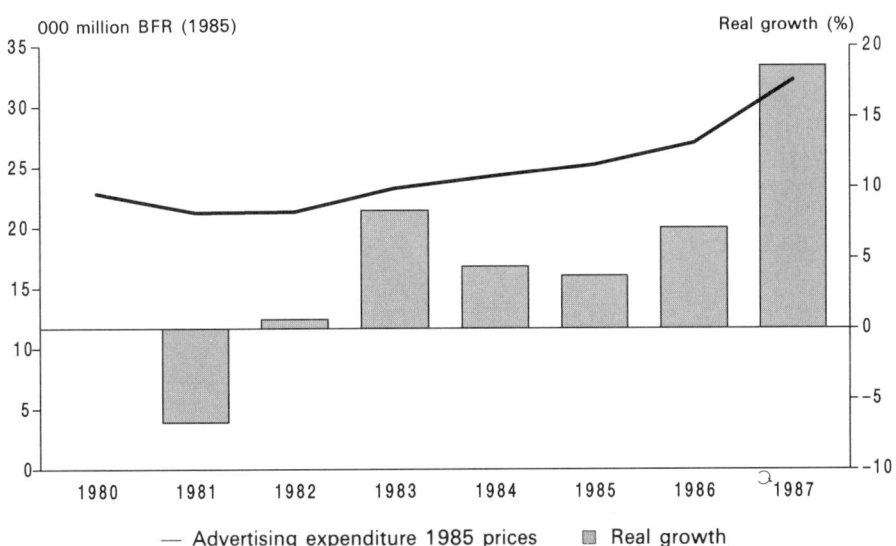

000 million BFR (1985)
Real growth (%)

— Advertising expenditure 1985 prices ▨ Real growth

Expenditure as a percentage of European total

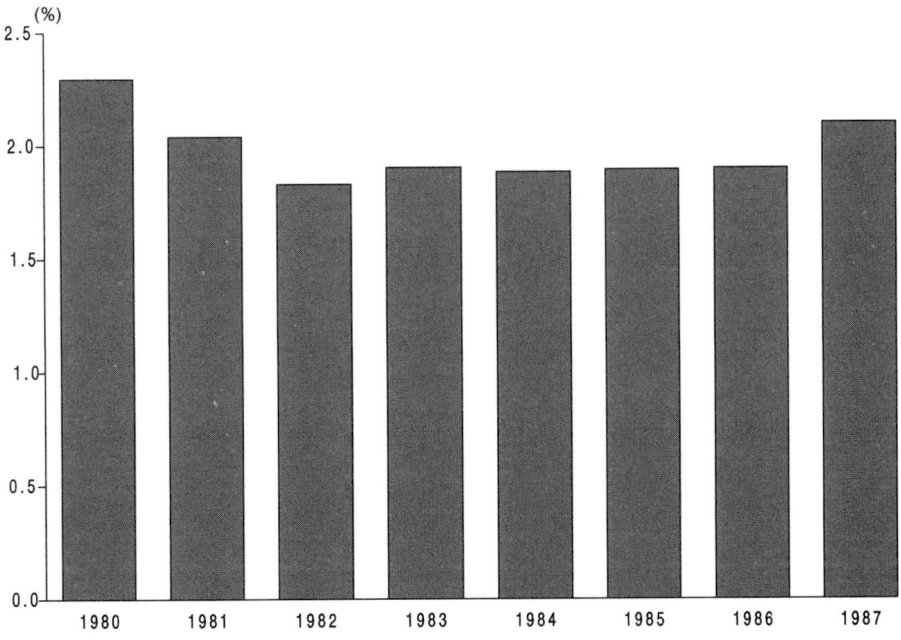

(%)

Denmark

Data sources

1. Advertising data source   Innovation

2. Method of compilation   Survey data/trade association

3. Coverage   Includes agency commission
                           Excludes production costs
                           Excludes classified advertising
                           NB Commercial TV & radio introduced in 1988

4. Economic data source   OECD main economic indicators

5. Currency data source   Eurostat money and finance

	Advertising expenditure as % of GDP	Per capita advertising expenditure at constant 1985 prices
1980	0.77	801
1981	0.76	794
1982	0.72	784
1983	0.71	793
1984	0.71	820
1985	0.71	851
1986	0.71	890
1987	0.72	909

Note: The advertising data have not been adjusted to compensate for the exclusion of production costs etc.

Denmark
Advertising expenditure at constant prices

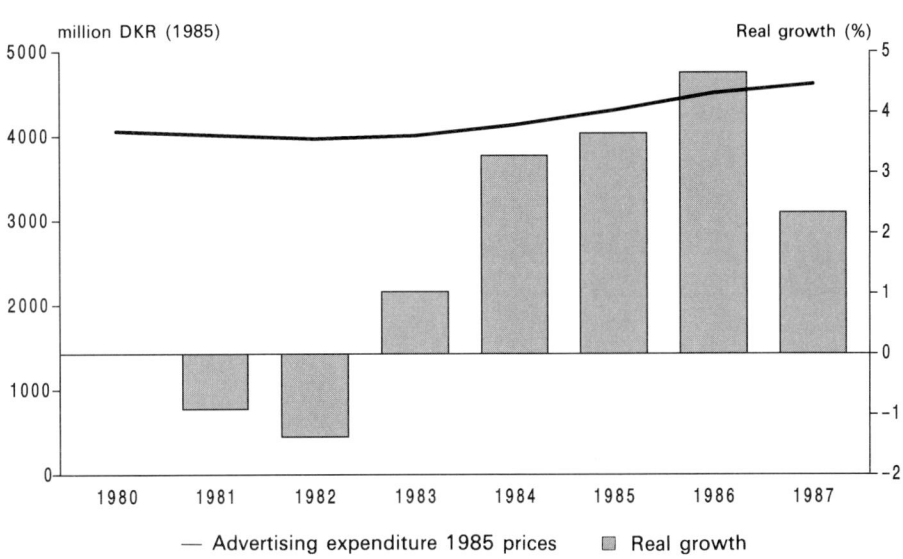

Expenditure as a percentage of European total

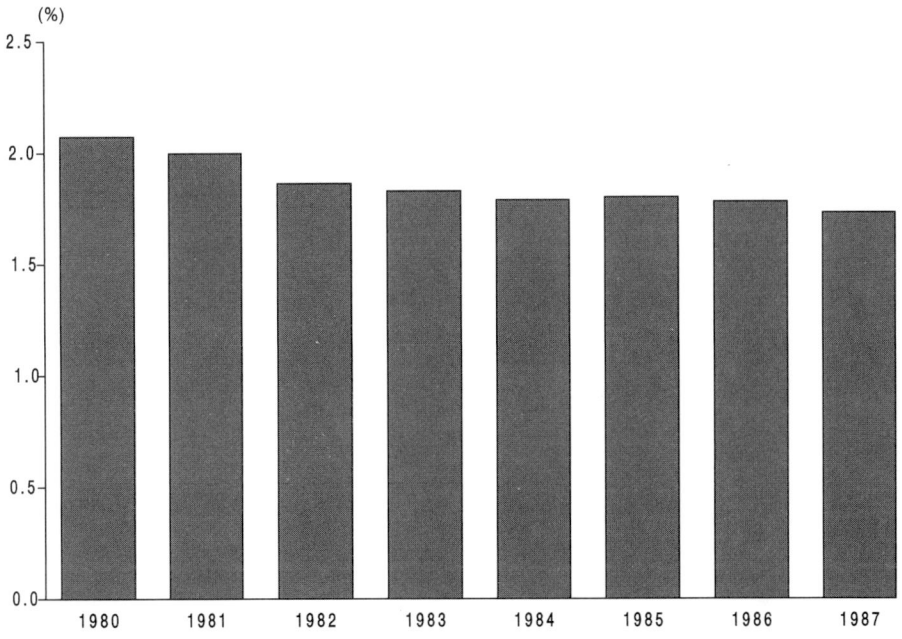

France

Data sources

1. Advertising data source   IREP
2. Method of compilation   Survey data/trade association
3. Coverage   Includes agency commission
                                  Includes production costs
                                  Excludes classified advertising
                                  Discounts deducted
4. Economic data source   OECD main economic indicators
5. Currency data source   Eurostat money and finance

	Advertising expenditure as % of GDP	Per capita advertising expenditure at constant 1985 prices
1980	0.48	391
1981	0.49	391
1982	0.50	411
1983	0.55	450
1984	0.55	461
1985	0.57	487
1986	0.61	539
1987	0.67	604

France
Advertising expenditure at constant prices

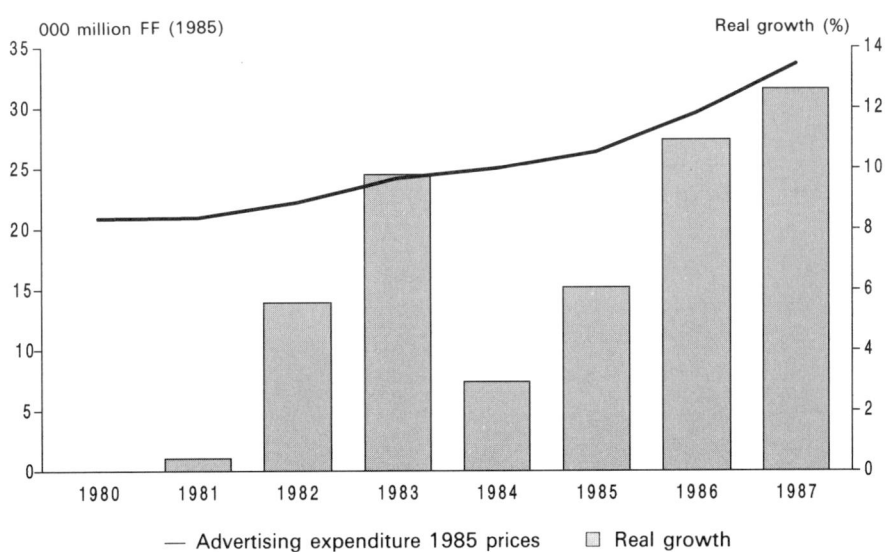

000 million FF (1985)

Real growth (%)

— Advertising expenditure 1985 prices ☐ Real growth

Expenditure as a percentage of European total

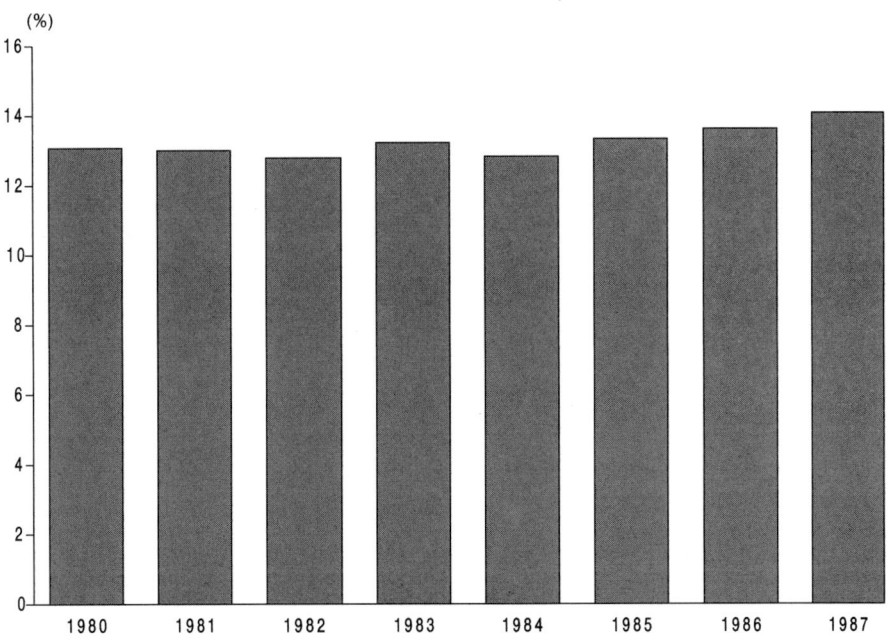

(%)

Federal Republic of Germany

Data sources

1. Advertising data source   ZAW
2. Method of compilation   Survey data/trade association
3. Coverage   Excludes agency commission
   Excludes production costs
   Includes classified advertising
   Free newspapers included in 1986 for the first time
   Magazine data includes trade magazines and directories
   Discounts deducted
4. Economic data source   OECD main economic indicators
5. Currency data source   Eurostat money and finance

	Advertising expenditure as % of GDP	Per capita advertising expenditure at constant 1985 prices
1980	0.75	218
1981	0.73	206
1982	0.75	210
1983	0.75	215
1984	0.76	224
1985	0.75	226
1986	0.78	248
1987	0.79	259

Note: The advertising data have not been adjusted to compensate for the exclusion of production costs etc.

Federal Republic of Germany
Advertising expenditure at constant prices

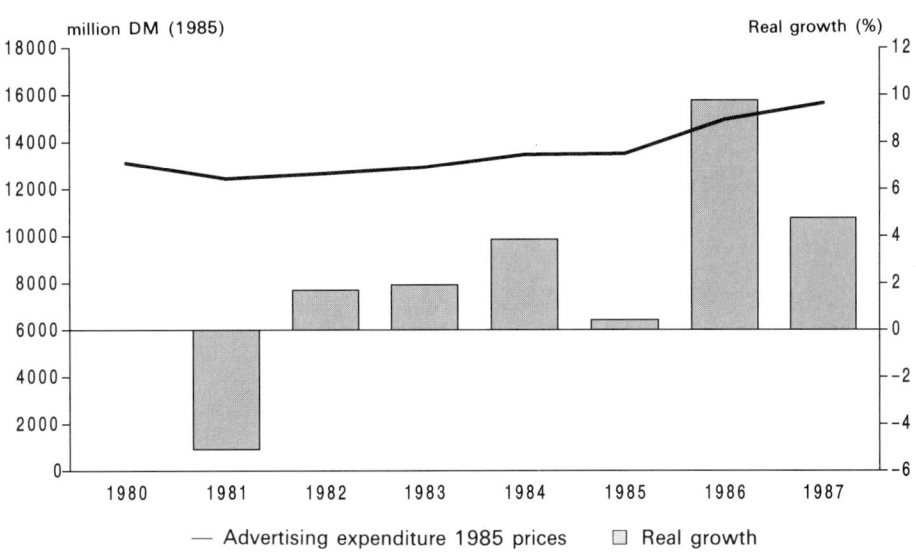

— Advertising expenditure 1985 prices   ☐ Real growth

Expenditure as a percentage of European total

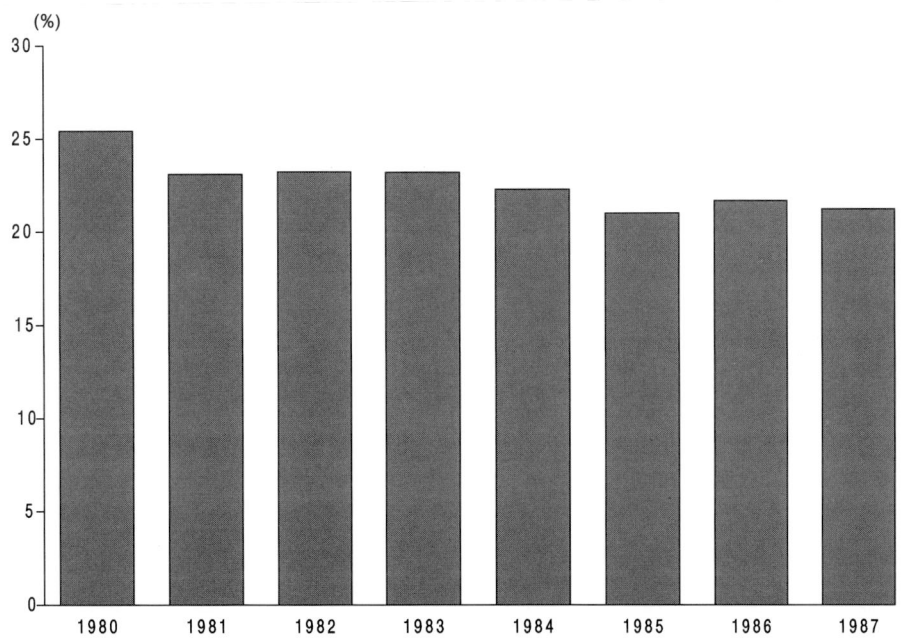

Greece

Data sources

1. Advertising data source   1980-84 Adel Compton/A.C. Nielsen/Metrix/EMRB Hellas
                                        1985-87 Greek Advertising Agencies Association

2. Method of compilation   Volume/rate card

3. Coverage   Includes agency commission
                     Excludes production costs
                     Excludes classified advertising
                     Cinema expenditure data only available for 1986-87
                     Discounts not deducted

4. Economic data source   OECD main economic indicators

5. Currency data source   Eurostat money and finance

	Advertising expenditure as % of GDP	Per capita advertising expenditure at constant 1985 prices
1980	0.25	1 154
1981	0.33	1 414
1982	0.35	1 567
1983	0.35	1 526
1984	0.34	1 545
1985	0.33	1 542
1986	0.42	1 908
1987	0.47	2 111

Note: The advertising data have not been adjusted to compensate for the exclusion of production costs etc.

Greece
Advertising expenditure at constant prices

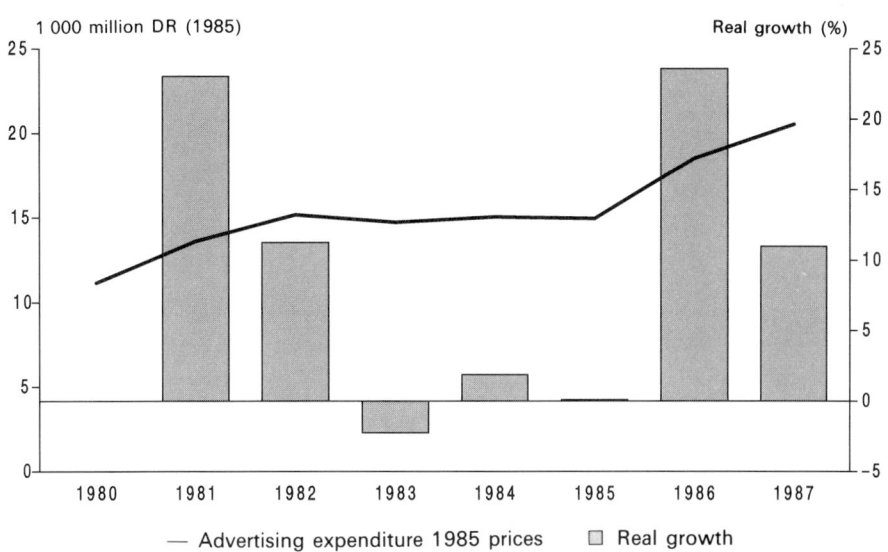

Expenditure as a percentage of European total

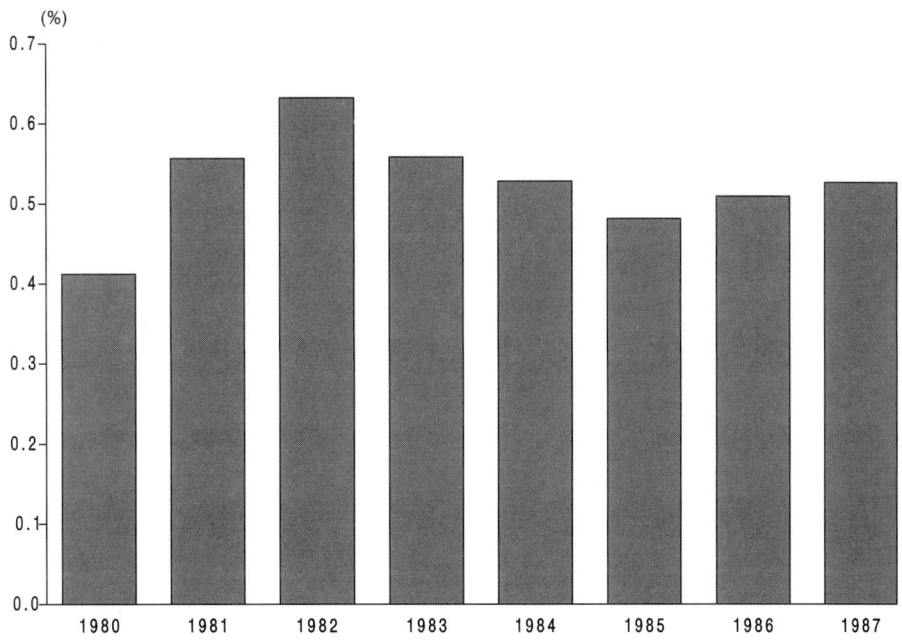

Ireland

Data sources

1. Advertising data source   1980-83 Central Statistics Office
   1984-87 Advertising Statistics Ireland

2. Method of compilation   Volume/rate card

3. Coverage
   Includes agency commission
   Excludes production costs
   Excludes classified advertising
   1980-85 data only approximate and subject to significant rounding errors
   Press data exclude trade press
   Cinema not available from 1980-87
   Discounts not deducted

4. Economic data source   OECD main economic indicators

5. Currency data source   Eurostat money and finance

	Advertising expenditure as % of GDP	Per capita advertising expenditure at constant 1985 prices
1980	0.66	33
1981	0.63	28
1982	0.54	26
1983	0.49	24
1984	0.50	24
1985	0.54	27
1986	0.62	32
1987	0.63	33

Note: The advertising data have not been adjusted to compensate for the exclusion of production costs etc.

Ireland
Advertising expenditure at constant prices

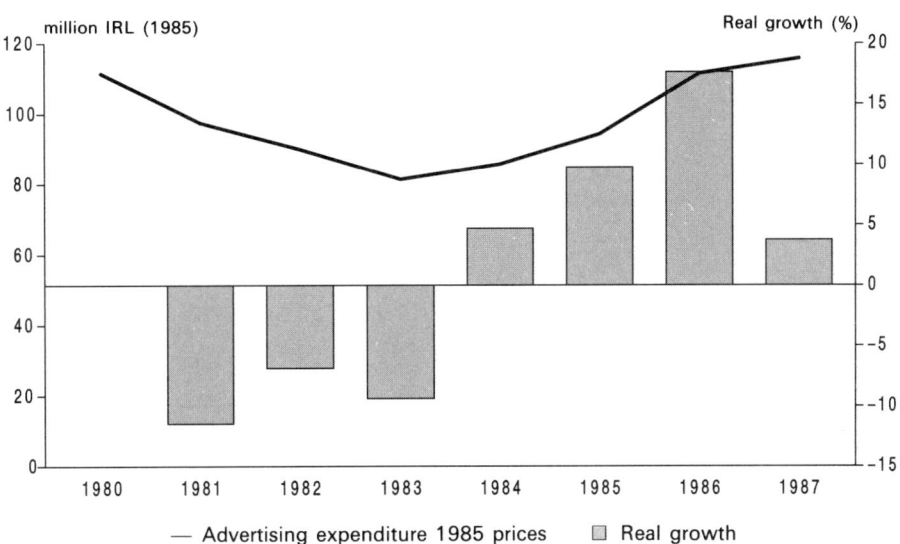

— Advertising expenditure 1985 prices   ☐ Real growth

Expenditure as a percentage of European total

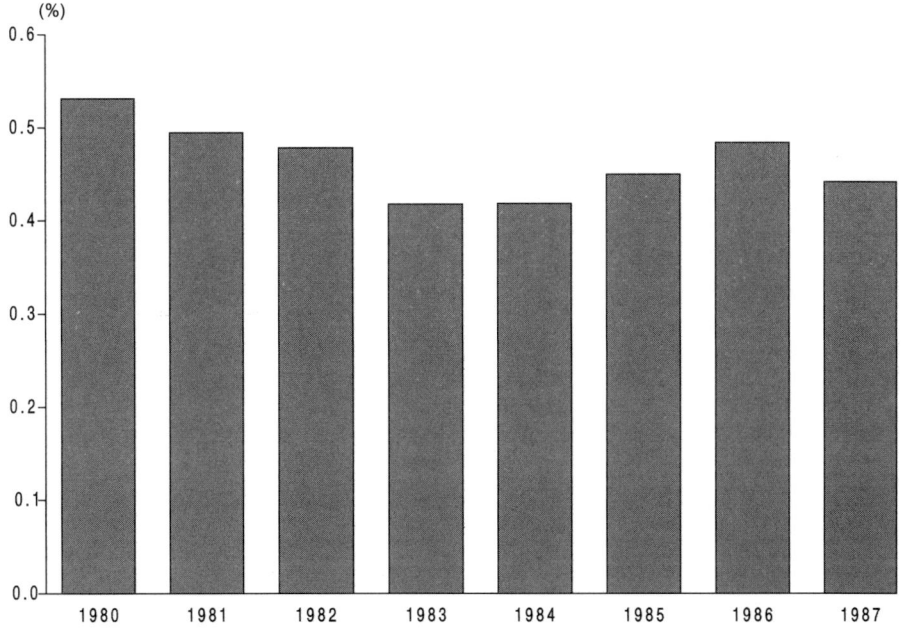

147

Italy

Data sources

1. Advertising data source   UPA/IL millimetro[1]
2. Method of compilation   Volume/rate card
3. Coverage   Includes agency commission
   Excludes production costs
   Excludes classified advertising
   Discounts deducted
4. Economic data source   OECD main economic indicators
5. Currency data source   Eurostat money and finance

---

[1] IL millimetro data are Nielsen data with estimated discounts deducted.

	Advertising expenditure as % of GDP	Per capita advertising expenditure at constant 1985 prices
1980	0.32	41 635
1981	0.40	45 388
1982	0.44	50 695
1983	0.50	57 156
1984	0.45	62 326
1985	0.48	68 861
1986	0.54	80 706
1987	0.55	84 909

Note: The advertising data have not been adjusted to compensate for the exclusion of production costs etc.

Italy
Advertising expenditure at constant prices

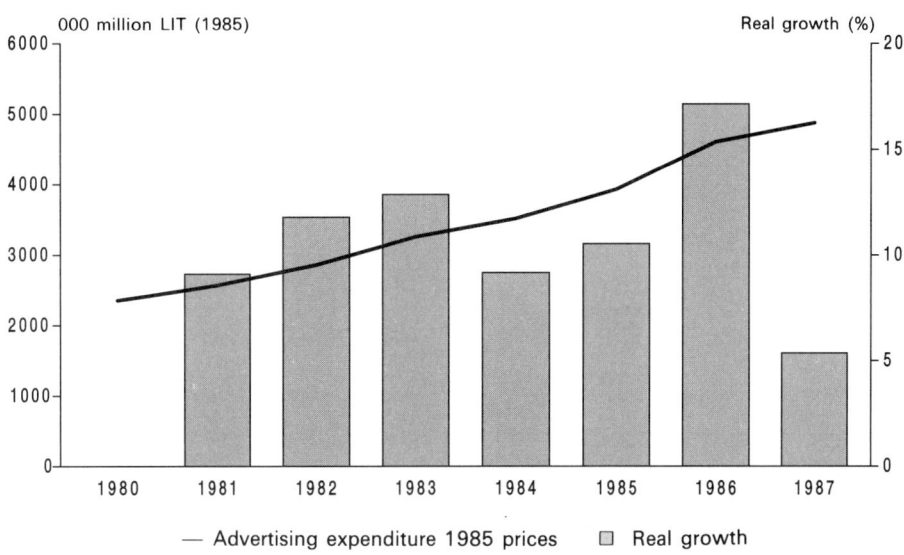

000 million LIT (1985)

Real growth (%)

— Advertising expenditure 1985 prices ☐ Real growth

Expenditure as a percentage of European total

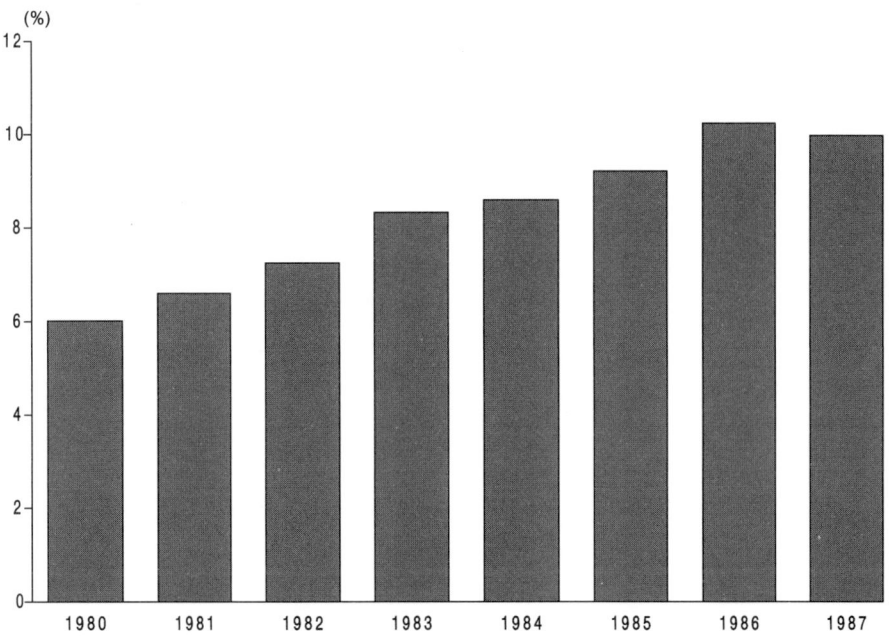

(%)

The Netherlands

Data sources

1. Advertising data source   VEA

2. Method of compilation   Survey data/trade association

3. Coverage

       Includes agency commission
       Includes production costs
       Includes classified advertising
       Sportsground advertising counted as
       sponsorship and therefore excluded from outdoor
       Production costs estimated across TV and radio on pro-rata basis
       1986 TV figure includes Sky Channel
       Discounts deducted

4. Economic data source   OECD main economic indicators

5. Currency data source   Eurostat money and finance

	Advertising expenditure as % of GDP	Per capita advertising expenditure at constant 1985 prices
1980	1.01	295
1981	0.95	269
1982	0.94	261
1983	0.93	258
1984	0.94	267
1985	0.95	274
1986	1.04	307
1987	1.11	327

The Netherlands
Advertising expenditure at constant prices

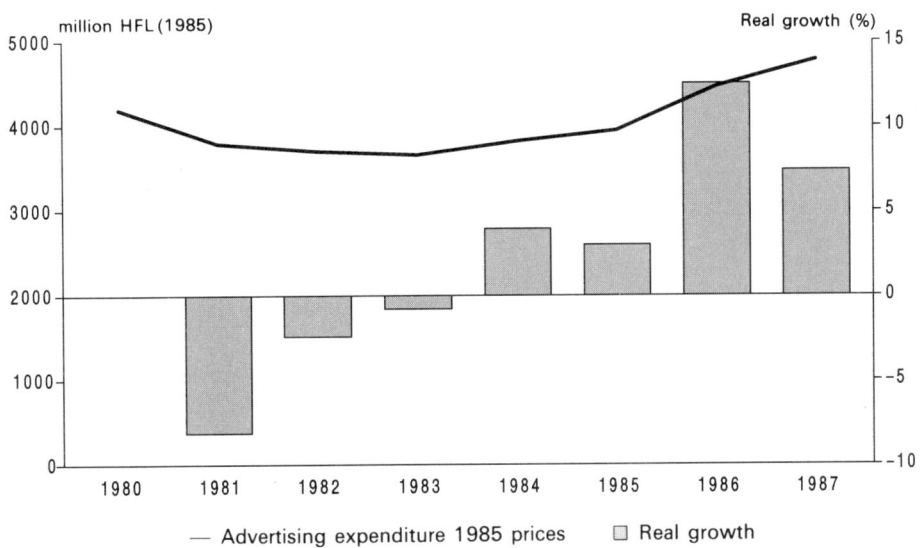

— Advertising expenditure 1985 prices   ☐ Real growth

Expenditure as a percentage of European total

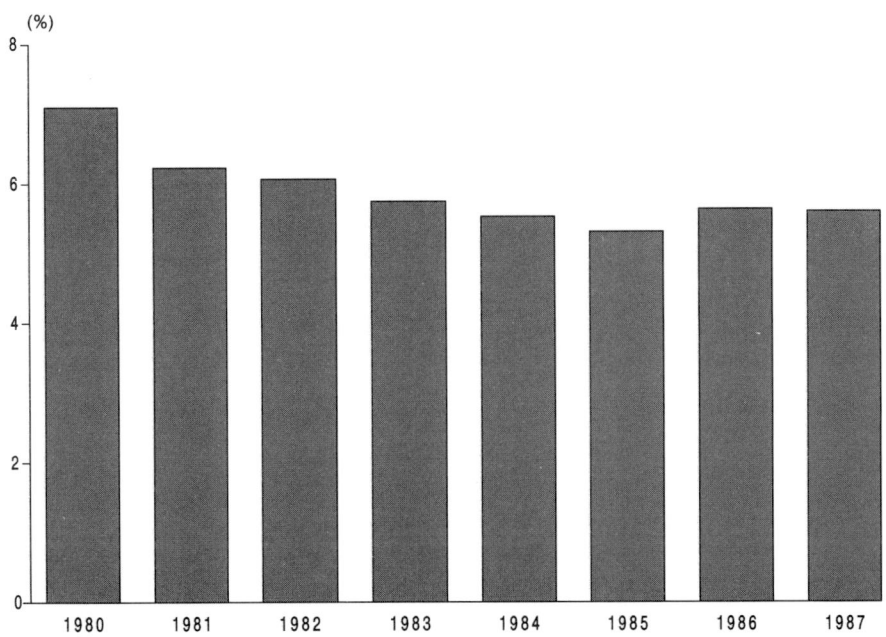

Portugal

Data sources

1. Advertising data source   James Rogerson Williamson, Lintas
2. Method of compilation   Volume/rate card
3. Coverage   Includes agency commission
   Excludes production costs
   Excludes classified advertising
   1980-85 magazine data included with newspapers
   Cinema data not available for 1986-87
   Transport not included with transport/outdoor in 1986
   Outdoor/transport not available for 1987
   All expenditure in magazines is included in consumer magazines
   Discounts deducted
4. Economic data source   OECD main economic indicators
5. Currency data source   Eurostat money and finance

Because of the change in coverage in 1986, this year is not comparable with the previous data.

	Advertising expenditure as % of GDP	Per capita advertising expenditure at constant 1985 prices
1980	0.21	764
1981	0.24	845
1982	0.23	843
1983	0.29	1 004
1984	0.26	865
1985	0.29	995
1986	0.33	1 262
1987	0.44	1 812

Note: The advertising data have not been adjusted to compensate for the exclusion of production costs etc.

Portugal
Advertising expenditure at constant prices

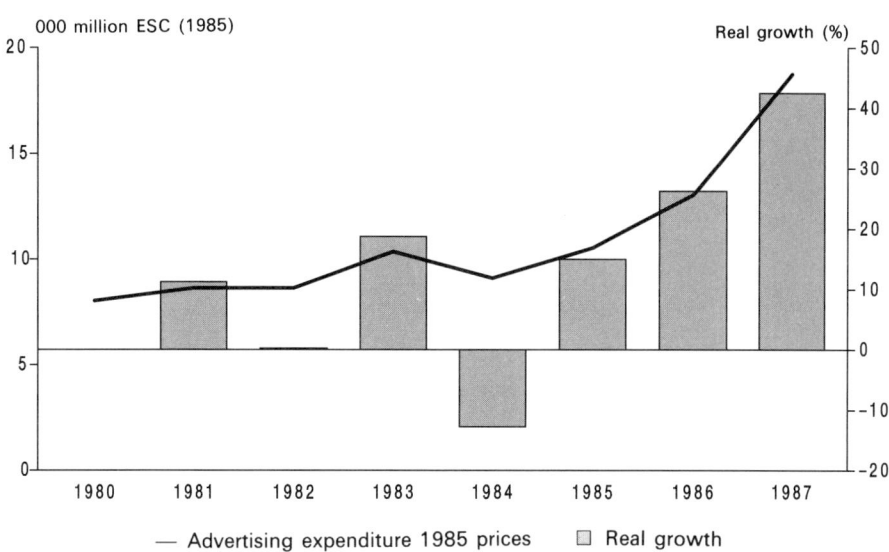

— Advertising expenditure 1985 prices ☐ Real growth

Expenditure as a percentage of European total

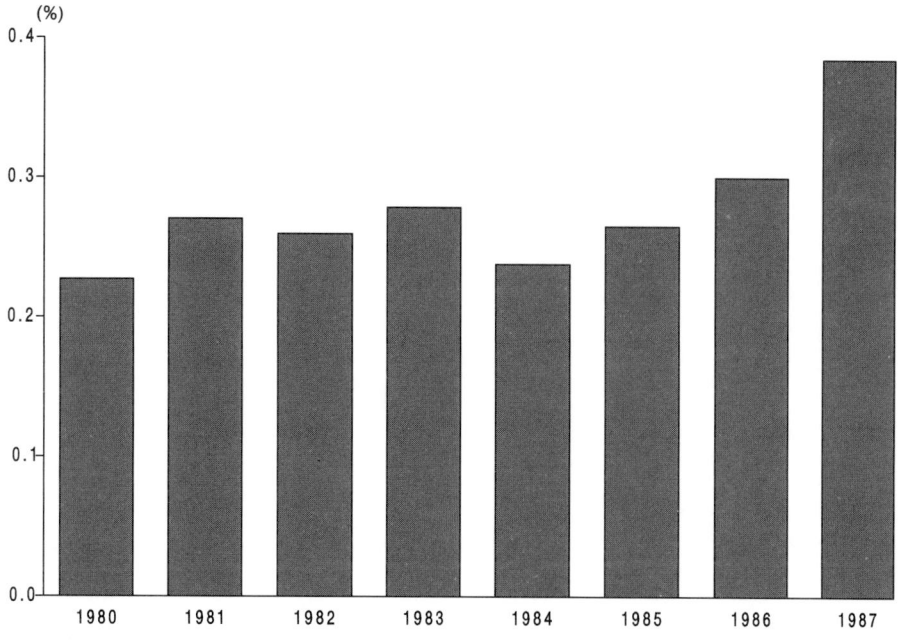

153

Spain

Data sources

1. Advertising data source   JWT/Spain, Repress/Nielsen
2. Method of compilation   Volume/rate card
3. Coverage   Includes agency commission
   Excludes production costs
   Excludes classified advertising
   Excludes Directories
   Discounts not deducted
4. Economic data source   OECD main economic indicators
5. Currency data source   Eurostat money and finance

	Advertising expenditure as % of GDP	Per capita advertising expenditure at constant 1985 prices
1980	0.55	3 999
1981	0.60	4 271
1982	0.72	5 086
1983	0.74	5 296
1984	0.79	5 647
1985	0.86	6 233
1986	0.99	7 530
1987	1.16	9 280

Note: The advertising data have not been adjusted to compensate for the exclusion of production costs etc.

Spain
Advertising expenditure at constant prices

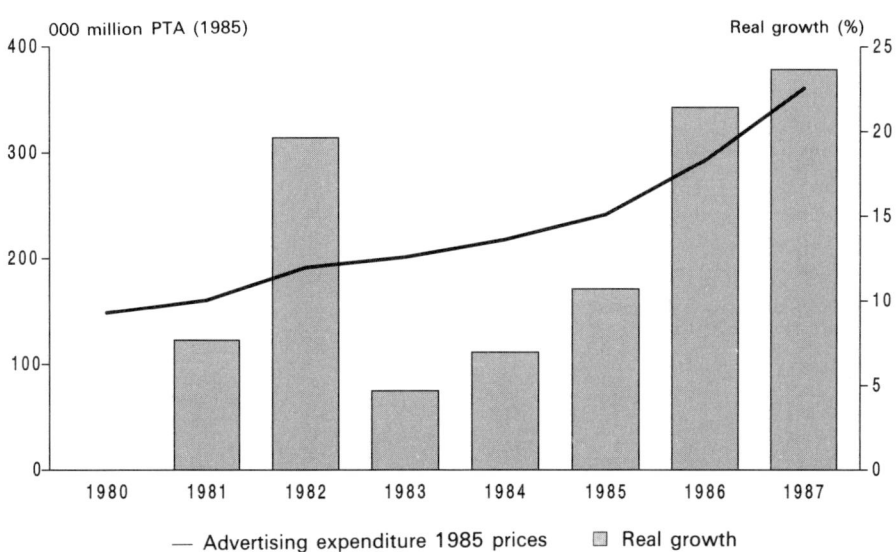

000 million PTA (1985)

Real growth (%)

— Advertising expenditure 1985 prices   ▨ Real growth

Expenditure as a percentage of European total

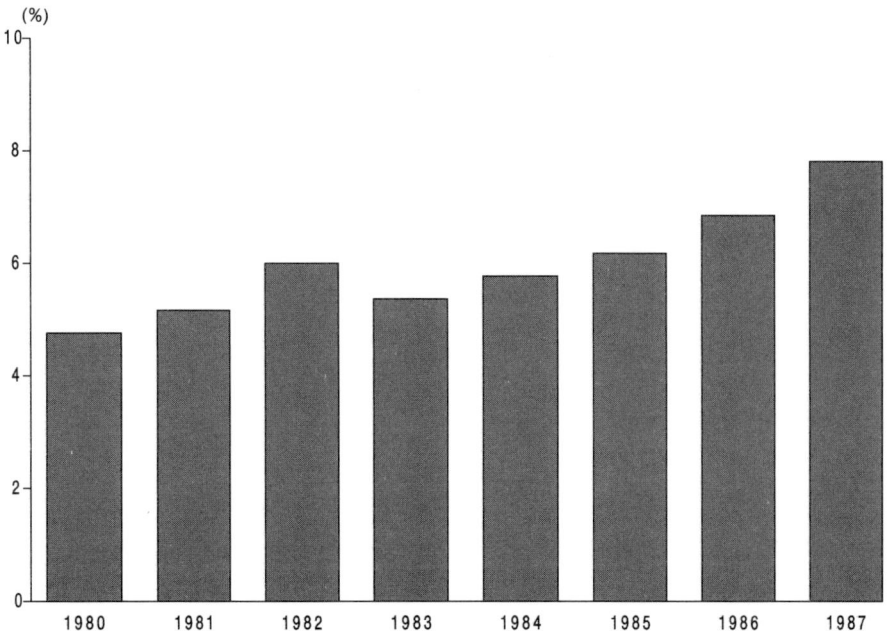

(%)

United Kingdom

Data sources

1. Advertising data source   Advertising Association, London
2. Method of compilation   Survey data/trade association
3. Coverage   Includes agency commission
   Includes production costs
   Includes classified advertising
   Includes directories
   Discounts deducted
4. Economic data source   OECD main economic indicators
5. Currency data source   Eurostat money and finance

	Advertising expenditure as % of GDP	Per capita advertising expenditure at constant 1985 prices
1980	1.11	64
1981	1.14	63
1982	1.13	65
1983	1.19	71
1984	1.26	76
1985	1.26	78
1986	1.36	87
1987	1.41	94

United Kingdom
Advertising expenditure at constant prices

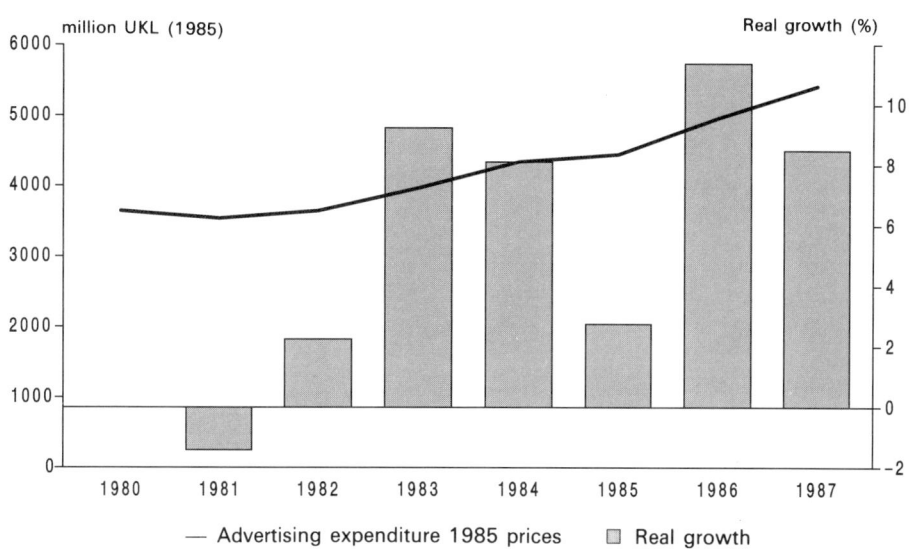

Expenditure as a percentage of European total

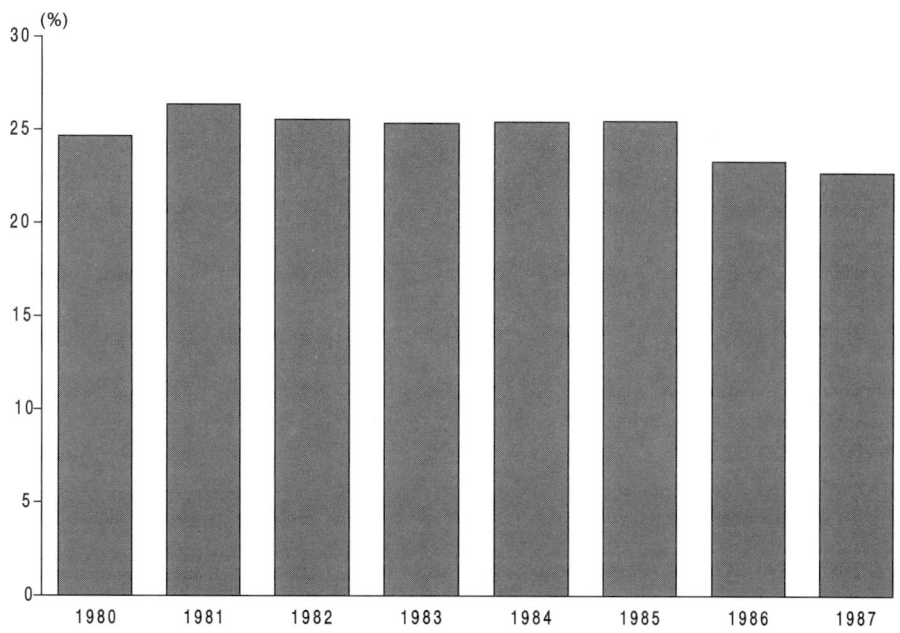

Japan

Data sources

1. Advertising data source   Dentsu
2. Method of compilation   Survey data/trade association
3. Coverage   Includes agency commission
   Includes production costs
   Includes classified advertising
   Cinema data not available
   Outdoor/transport data unavailable
   Discounts not deducted
4. Economic data source   OECD main economic indicators
5. Currency data source   Eurostat money and finance

	Advertising expenditure as % of GDP	Per capita advertising expenditure at constant 1985 prices
1980	0.73	17 091
1981	0.74	17 341
1982	0.74	17 845
1983	0.75	18 512
1984	0.74	18 819
1985	0.71	18 696
1986	0.73	19 698
1987	0.75	21 091

Note: Cinema and outdoor expenditure data not available.

Japan
Advertising expenditure at constant prices

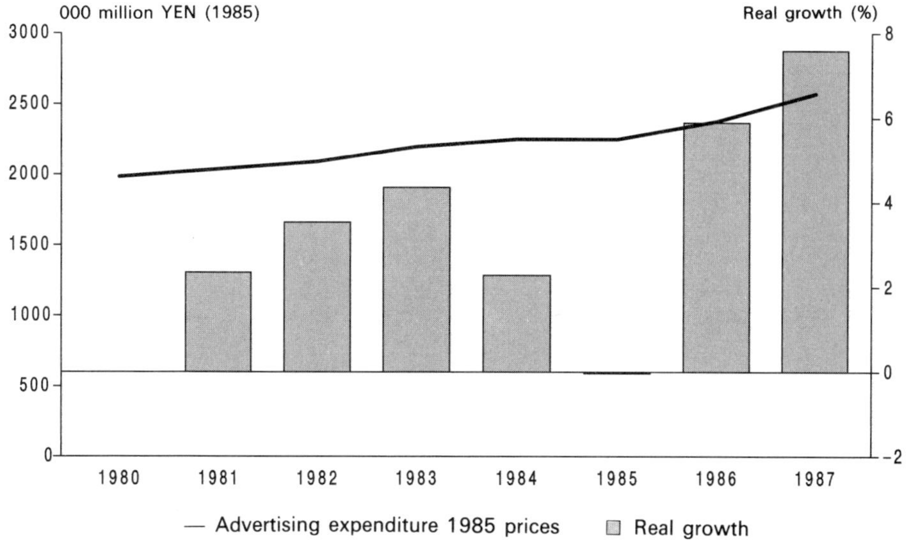
000 million YEN (1985)
Real growth (%)
3000
2500
2000
1500
1000
500
0
8
6
4
2
0
-2
1980
1981
1982
1983
1984
1985
1986
1987
— Advertising expenditure 1985 prices
Real growth

USA

Data sources

1. Advertising data source   Robert J Coen, McCann-Eriksen Inc/SSCW

2. Method of compilation   Survey data/trade association

3. Coverage   Includes agency commission
   Includes production costs
   Includes classified advertising
   Cinema data not available
   Magazines exclude farm publications and business publications
   Television figures include barter syndication
   Discounts deducted

4. Economic data source   OECD main economic indicators

5. Currency data source   Eurostat money and finance

	Advertising expenditure as % of GDP	Per capita advertising expenditure at constant 1985 prices
1980	1.32	201
1981	1.36	202
1982	1.43	207
1983	1.52	227
1984	1.54	251
1985	1.54	255
1986	1.57	268
1987	1.57	273

Note: Cinema data not available. Magazine data exclude farm and business publications.

USA
Advertising expenditure at constant prices

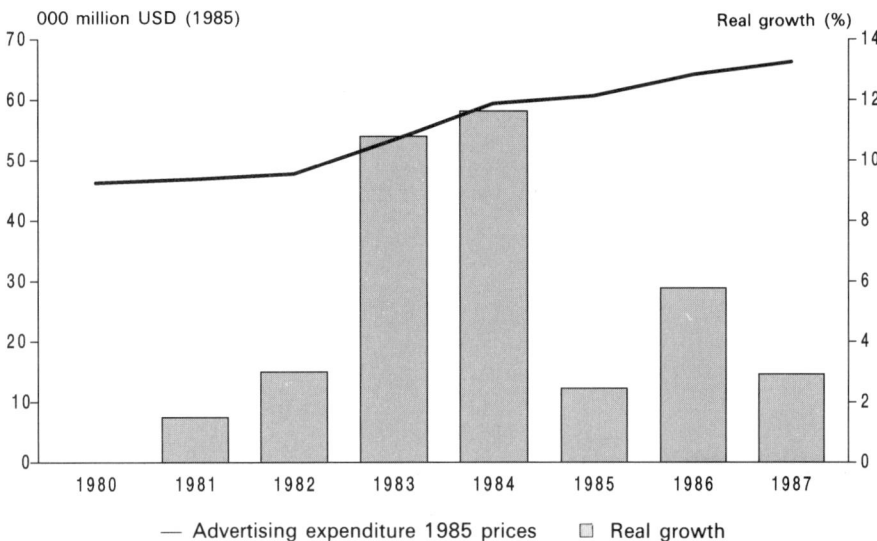

000 million USD (1985)   Real growth (%)

— Advertising expenditure 1985 prices   ☐ Real growth

Appendix II

EC Directive on broadcasting

Council Directive

of 3 October 1989

on the coordination of certain provisions laid down by law, regulation or administrative action in Member States concerning the pursuit of television broadcasting activities

(89/552/EEC)

THE COUNCIL OF THE EUROPEAN COMMUNITIES,

Having regard to the Treaty establishing the European Economic Community, and in particular Articles 57 (2) and 66 thereof,

Having regard to the proposal from the Commission ([1]),

In cooperation with the European Parliament ([2]),

Having regard to the opinion of the Economic and Social Committee ([3]),

Whereas the objectives of the Community as laid down in the Treaty include establishing an even closer union among the peoples of Europe, fostering closer relations between the States belonging to the Community, ensuring the economic and social progress of its countries by common action to eliminate the barriers which divide Europe, encouraging the constant improvement of the living conditions of its peoples as well as ensuring the preservation and strengthening of peace and liberty;

Whereas the Treaty provides for the establishment of a common market, including the abolition, as between Member States, of obstacles to freedom of movement for services and the institution of a system ensuring that competition in the common market is not distorted;

Whereas broadcasts transmitted across frontiers by means of various technologies are one of the ways of pursuing the objectives of the Community; whereas measures should be adopted to permit and ensure the transition from national markets to a common programme production and distribution market and to establish conditions of fair competition without prejudice to the public interest role to be discharged by the television broadcasting services;

Whereas the Council of Europe has adopted the European Convention on Transfrontier Television;

---

(1) OJ No C 179, 17.7.1986, p. 4.
(2) OJ No C 49, 22.2.1988 p. 53, and OJ No C 158, 26.6.1989.
(3) OJ No C 232, 31.8.1987, p. 29.

Whereas the Treaty provides for the issuing of directives for the coordination of provisions to facilitate the taking up of activities as self-employed persons;

Whereas television broadcasting constitutes, in normal circumstances, a service within the meaning of the Treaty;

Whereas the Treaty provides for free movement of all services normally provided against payment, without exclusion on grounds of their cultural or other content and without restriction of nationals of Member States established in a Community country other than that of the person for whom the services are intended;

Whereas this right as applied to the broadcasting and distribution of television services is also a specific manifestation in Community law of a more general principle, namely the freedom of expression as enshrined in Article 10 (1) of the Convention for the Protection of Human Rights and Fundamental Freedoms ratified by all Member States; whereas for this reason the issuing of directives on the broadcasting and distribution of television programmes must ensure their free movement in the light of the said Article and subject only to the limits set by paragraph 2 of that Article and by Article 56 (1) of the Treaty;

Whereas the laws, regulations and administrative measures in Member States concerning the pursuit of activities as television broadcasters and cable operators contain disparities, some of which may impede the free movement of broadcasts within the Community and may distort competition within the common market;

Whereas all such restrictions on freedom to provide broadcasting services within the Community must be abolished under the Treaty;

Whereas such abolition must go hand in hand with coordination of the applicable laws; whereas this coordination must be aimed at facilitating the pursuit of the professional activities concerned and, more generally, the free movement of information and ideas within the Community;

Whereas it is consequently necessary and sufficient that all broadcasts comply with the law of the Member State from which they emanate;

Whereas this Directive lays down the minimum rules needed to guarantee freedom of transmission in broadcasting; whereas, therefore, it does not affect the responsibility of the Member States and their authorities with regard to the organization — including the systems of licensing, administrative authorization or taxation — financing and the content of programmes; whereas the independence of cultural developments in the Member States and the preservation of cultural diversity in the Community therefore remain unaffected;

Whereas it is necessary, in the common market, that all broadcasts emanating from and intended for reception within the Community and in particular those intended for reception in another Member State, should respect the law of the originating Member State applicable to broadcasts intended for reception by the public in that Member State and the provisions of this Directive;

Whereas the requirement that the originating Member State should verify that broadcasts comply with national law as coordinated by this Directive is sufficient under Community law to ensure free movement of broadcasts without secondary control on the same grounds in the receiving Member States; whereas, however, the receiving Member State may, exceptionally and under specific conditions provisionally suspend the retransmission of televised broadcasts;

Whereas it is essential for the Member States to ensure the prevention of any acts which may prove detrimental to freedom of movement and trade in television programmes or which may promote the creation of dominant positions which would lead to restrictions on pluralism and freedom of televised information and of the information sector as a whole;

Whereas this Directive, being confined specifically to television broadcasting rules, is without prejudice to existing or future Community acts of harmonization, in particular to satisfy mandatory requirements concerning the protection of consumers and the fairness of commercial transactions and competition;

Whereas coordination is nevertheless needed to make it easier for persons and industries producing programmes having a cultural objective to take up and pursue their activities;

Whereas minimum requirements in respect of all public or private Community television programmes for European audiovisual productions have been a means of promoting production, independent production and distribution in the abovementioned industries and are complementary to other instruments which are already or will be proposed to favour the same objective;

Whereas it is therefore necessary to promote markets of sufficient size for television productions in the Member States to recover necessary investments not only by establishing common rules opening up national markets but also by envisaging for European productions where practicable and by appropriate means a majority proportion in television programmes of all Member States; whereas, in order to allow the monitoring of the application of the rules and the pursuit of the objectives, Member States will provide the Commission with a report on the application of the proportions reserved for European works and independent productions in this Directive; whereas for the calculation of such proportions account should be taken of the specific situation of the Hellenic Republic and the Portuguese Republic; whereas the Commission must inform the other Member States of these reports accompanied, where appropriate by an opinion taking account of, in particular, progress achieved in relation to previous years, the share of first broadcasts in the programming, the particular circumstances of new television broadcasters and the specific situation of countries with a low audiovisual production capacity or restricted language area;

Whereas for these purposes 'European works' should be defined without prejudice to the possibility of Member States laying down a more detailed definition as regards television broadcasters under their jurisdiction in accordance with Article 3 (1) in compliance with Community law and account being taken of the objectives of this Directive;

Whereas it is important to seek appropriate instruments and procedures in accordance with Community law in order to promote the implementation of these objectives with a view to adopting suitable measures to encourage the activity and development of European audiovisual production and distribution, particularly in countries with a low production capacity or restricted language area;

Whereas national schemes for the development of European production may be applied in so far as they comply with Community law;

Whereas a commitment, where practicable, to a certain proportion of broadcasts for independent productions, created by producers who are independent of broadcasters, will stimulate new sources of television production, especially the creation of small and medium-sized enterprises; whereas it will offer new opportunities and outlets to the marketing of creative talents of employment of cultural professions and employees in the cultural field; whereas the definition of the concept of independent producer by the Member States should take account of that objective by giving due consideration to small and medium-sized producers and making it possible to authorize financial participation by the co-production subsidiaries of television organizations;

Whereas measures are necessary for Member States to ensure that a certain period elapses between the first cinema showing of a work and the first television showing;

Whereas in order to allow for an active policy in favour of a specific language, Member States remain free to lay down more detailed or stricter rules in particular on the basis of language criteria, as long as these rules are in conformity with Community law, and in particular are not applicable to the retransmission of broadcasts originating in other Member States;

Whereas in order to ensure that the interests of consumers as television viewers are fully and properly protected, it is essential for television advertising to be subject to a certain number of minimum rules and standards and that the Member States must maintain the right to set more detailed or stricter rules and in certain circumstances to lay down different conditions for television broadcasters under their jurisdiction;

Whereas Member States, with due regard to Community law and in relation to broadcasts intended solely for the national territory which may not be received, directly or indirectly, in one or more Member States, must be able to lay down different conditions for the insertion of advertising and different limits for the volume of advertising in order to facilitate these particular broadcasts;

Whereas it is necessary to prohibit all television advertising promoting cigarettes and other tobacco products including indirect forms of advertising which, whilst not directly mentioning the tobacco product, seek to circumvent the ban on advertising by using brand names, symbols or other distinctive features of tobacco products or of undertakings whose known or main activities include the production or sale of such products;

Whereas it is equally necessary to prohibit all television advertising for medicinal products and medical treatment available only on prescription in the Member State within whose jurisdiction the broadcaster falls and to introduce strict criteria relating to the television advertising of alcoholic products;

Whereas in view of the growing importance of sponsorship in the financing of programmes, appropriate rules should be laid down;

Whereas it is, furthermore, necessary to introduce rules to protect the physical, mental and moral development of minors in programmes and in television advertising;

Whereas although television broadcasters are normally bound to ensure that programmes present facts and events fairly, it is nevertheless important that they should be subject to specific obligations with respect to the right of reply or equivalent remedies so that any person whose legitimate interests have been damaged by an assertion made in the course of a broadcast television programme may effectively exercise such right or remedy.

HAS ADOPTED THIS DIRECTIVE:

CHAPTER I

Definitions

Article 1

For the purpose of this Directive:

(a) 'television broadcasting' means the initial transmission by wire or over the air, including that by satellite, in unencoded or encoded form, of television programmes intended for reception by the public. It includes the communication of programmes between undertakings with a view to their being relayed to the public. It does not include communication services providing items of information or other messages on individual demand such as telecopying, electronic data banks and other similar services;

(b) 'television advertising' means any form of announcement broadcast in return for payment or for similar consideration by a public or private undertaking in connection with a trade, business, craft or profession in order to promote the supply of goods or services, including immovable property, or rights and obligations, in return for payment.

Except for the purposes of Article 18, this does not include direct offers to the public for the sale, purchase or rental of products or for the provision of services in return for payment;

(c) 'surreptitious advertising' means the representation in words or pictures of goods, services, the name, the trade mark or the activities of a producer of goods or a provider of services in programmes when such representation is intended by the broadcaster to serve as advertising and might mislead the public as to its nature. Such representation is considered to be intentional in particular if it is done in return for payment or for similar consideration;

(d) 'sponsorship' means any contribution made by a public or private undertaking not engaged in television broadcasting activities or in the production of audiovisual works, to the financing of television programmes with a view to promoting its name, its trade mark, its image, its activities or its products.

CHAPTER II

General provisions

Article 2

1. Each Member State shall ensure that all television broadcasts transmitted
— by broadcasters under its jurisdiction, or
— by broadcasters who, while not being under the jurisdiction of any Member State, make use of a frequency or a satellite capacity granted by, or a satellite up-link situated in, that Member State,
comply with the law applicable to broadcasts intended for the public in that Member State.

2. Member States shall ensure freedom of reception and shall not restrict retransmission on their territory of television broadcasts from other Member States for reasons which fall within the fields coordinated by this Directive. Member States may provisionally suspend retransmissions of television broadcasts if the following conditions are fulfilled:

(a) a television broadcast coming from another Member State manifestly, seriously and gravely infringes Article 22;

(b) during the previous 12 months, the broadcaster has infringed the same provision on at least two prior occasions;

(c) the Member State concerned has notified the broadcaster and the Commission in writing of the alleged infringements and of its intention to restrict retransmission should any such infringement occur again;

(d) consultations with the transmitting State and the Commission have not produced an amicable settlement within 15 days of the notification provided for in point (c), and the alleged infringement persists.

The Commission shall ensure that the suspension is compatible with Community law. It may ask the Member State concerned to put an end to a suspension which is contrary to Community law, as a matter of urgency. This provision is without prejudice to the application of any procedure, remedy or sanction to the infringements in question in the Member State which has jurisdiction over the broadcaster concerned.

3. This Directive shall not apply to broadcasts intended exclusively for reception in States other than Member States, and which are not received directly or indirectly in one or more Member States.

Article 3

1. Member States shall remain free to require television broadcasters under their jurisdiction to lay down more detailed or stricter rules in the areas covered by this Directive.

2. Member States shall, by appropriate means, ensure, within the framework of their legislation, that television broadcasters under their jurisdiction comply with the provisions of this Directive.

CHAPTER III

Promotion of distribution and production
of television programmes

Article 4

1. Member States shall ensure where practicable and by appropriate means, that broadcasters reserve for European works, within the meaning of Article 6, a majority proportion of their transmission time, excluding the time appointed to news, sports events, games, advertising and teletext services. This proportion, having regard to the broadcasters' informational, educational, cultural and entertainment responsibilities to its viewing public, should be achieved progressively, on the basis of suitable criteria.

2. Where the proportion laid down in paragraph 1 cannot be attained, it must not be lower than the average for 1988 in the Member State concerned.

However, in respect of the Hellenic Republic and the Portuguese Republic, the year 1988 shall be replaced by the year 1990.

3. From 3 October 1991, the Member States shall provide the Commission every two years with a report on the application of this Article and Article 5.

The report shall in particular include a statistical statement on the achievement of the proportion referred to in this Article and Article 5 for each of the television programmes falling within the jurisdiction of the Member State concerned, the reasons, in each case, for the failure to attain that proportion and the measures adopted or envisaged in order to achieve it.

The Commission shall inform the other Member States and the European Parliament of the reports, which shall be accompanied, where appropriate, by an opinion. The Commission shall ensure the application of this Article and Article 5 in accordance with the provisions of the Treaty. The Commission may take account in its opinion, in particular, of progress achieved in relation to previous years, the share of first broadcast works in the programming, the particular circumstances of new television broadcasters and the specific situation of countries with a low audiovisual production capacity or restricted language area.

4. The Council shall review the implementation of this Article on the basis of a report from the Commission accompanied by any proposals for revision that it may deem appropriate no later than the end of the fifth year from the adoption of the Directive.

To that end, the Commission report shall, on the basis of the information provided by Member States under paragraph 3, take account in particular of developments in the Community market and of the international context.

Article 5

Member States shall ensure, where practical and by appropriate means, that broadcasters reserve at least 10% of their transmission time, excluding the time appointed to news, sports events, games, advertising and teletext services, or alternately, at the discretion of the Member State, at least 10% of their programming budget, for European works created by producers who are independent of broadcasters. This proportion, having regard to broadcasters' informational, educational, cultural and entertainment responsibilities to its viewing public, should be achieved progressively, on the basis of suitable criteria; it must be achieved by earmarking an adequate proportion for recent works, that is to say works transmitted within five years of their production.

Article 6

1. Within the meaning of this chapter, 'European works' means the following:

(a) works originating from Member States of the Community and, as regard television broadcasters falling within the jurisdiction of the Federal Republic of Germany, works from German territories where the Basic Law does not apply and fulfilling the conditions of paragraph 2;

(b) works originating from European third States party to the European Convention on Transfrontier Television of the Council of Europe and fulfilling the conditions of paragraph 2;

(c) works originating from other European third countries and fulfilling the conditions of paragraph 3.

2. The works referred to in paragraph 1 (a) and (b) are works mainly made with authors and workers residing in one or more States referred to in paragraph 1 (a) and (b) provided that they comply with one of the following three conditions:

(a) they are made by one or more producers established in one or more of those States; or

(b) production of the works is supervised and actually controlled by one or more producers established in one or more of those States; or

(c) the contribution of co-producers of those States to the total co-production costs is preponderant and the co-production is not controlled by one or more producers established outside those States.

3. The works referred to in paragraph 1 (c) are works made exclusively or in co-production with producers established in one or more Member States by producers established, in one or more European third countries with which the Community will conclude agreements in accordance with the producers of the Treaty, if those works are mainly made with authors and workers residing in one or more European States.

4. Works which are not European works within the meaning of paragraph 1, but made mainly with authors and workers residing in one or more Member States, shall be considered to be European works to an extent corresponding to the proportion of the contribution of Community co-producers to the total production costs.

Article 7

Member States shall ensure that the television broadcasters under their jurisdiction do not broadcast any cinematographic work, unless otherwise agreed between its rights holders and the broadcaster, until two years have elapsed since the work was first shown in cinemas in one of the Member States of the Community; in the case of cinematographic works co-produced by the broadcaster, this period shall be one year.

Article 8

Where they consider it necessary for purposes of language policy, the Member States, whilst observing Community law, may as regards some or all programmes of television broadcasters under their jurisdiction, lay down more detailed or stricter rules in particular on the basis of language criteria.

Article 9

This chapter shall not apply to local television broadcasts not forming part of a national network.

CHAPTER IV

Television advertising and sponsorship

Article 10

1. Television advertising shall be readily recognizable as such and kept quite separate from other parts of the programme service by optical and/or acoustic means.

2. Isolated advertising spots shall remain the exception.

3. Advertising shall not use subliminal techniques

4. Surreptitious advertising shall be prohibited.

Article 11

1. Advertisements shall be inserted between programmes. Provided the conditions contained in paragraphs 2 to 5 of this Article are fulfilled, advertisements may also be inserted during programmes in such a way that the integrity and value of the programme, taking into account natural breaks in and the duration and nature of the programme, and the rights of the rights holders are not prejudiced.

2. In programmes consisting of autonomous parts, or in sports programmes and similarly structured events and performances comprising intervals, advertisements shall only be inserted between the parts or in the intervals.

3. The transmission of audiovisual works such as feature films and films made for television (excluding series, serials, light entertainment programmes and documentaries), provided their programmed duration is more than 45 minutes, may be interrupted once for each complete period of 45 minutes. A further interruption is allowed if their programmed duration is at least 20 minutes longer than two or more complete periods of 45 minutes.

4. Where programmes, other than those covered by paragraph 2, are interrupted by advertisements, a period of at least 20 minutes should elapse between each successive advertising break within the programme.

5. Advertisements shall not be inserted in any broadcast of a religious service. News and current affairs programmes, documentaries, religious programmes, and children's programmes, when their programmed duration is less than 30 minutes shall not be interrupted by advertisements. If their programmed duration is of 30 minutes or longer, the provision of the previous paragraphs shall apply.

Article 12

Television advertising shall not:

(a) prejudice respect for human dignity:

(b) include any discrimination on grounds of race, sex or nationality;

(c) be offensive to religious or political beliefs;

(d) encourage behaviour prejudicial to health or to safety;

(e) encourage behaviour prejudicial to the protection of the environment.

Article 13

All forms of television advertising for cigarettes and other tobacco products shall be prohibited.

Article 14

Television advertising for medicinal products and medical treatment available only on prescription in the Member State within whose jurisdiction the broadcaster falls shall be prohibited.

Article 15

Television advertising for alcoholic beverages shall comply with the following criteria:

(a) it may not be aimed specifically at minors or, in particular, depict minors consuming these beverages;

(b) it shall not link the consumption of alcohol to enhanced physical performance or to driving;

(c) it shall not create the impression that the consumption of alcohol contributes towards social or sexual success;

(d) it shall not claim that alcohol has therapeutic qualities or that it is a stimulant, a sedative or a means of resolving personal conflicts;

(e) is shall not encourage immoderate consumption of alcohol or present abstinence or moderation in a negative light;

(f) it shall not place emphasis on high alcoholic content as being a positive quality of the beverages.

Article 16

Television advertising shall not cause moral or physical detriment to minors, and shall therefore comply with the following criteria for their protection:

(a) it shall not directly exhort minors to buy a product or a service by exploiting their inexperience or credulity;

(b) it shall not directly encourage minors to persuade their parents or others to purchase the goods or services being advertised;

(c) it shall not exploit the special trust minors place in parents, teachers or other persons;

(d) it shall not unreasonably show minors in dangerous situations.

Article 17

1. Sponsored television programmes shall meet the following requirements:

(a) the content and scheduling of sponsored programmes may in no circumstances be influenced by the sponsor in such a way as to affect the responsibility and editorial independence of the broadcaster in respect of programmes;

(b) they must be clearly identified as such by the name and/or logo of the sponsor at the beginning and/or the end of the programmes;

(c) they must not encourage the purchase or rental of the products or services of the sponsor or a third party, in particular by making special promotional references to those products or services.

2. Television programmes may not be sponsored by natural or legal persons whose principal activity is the manufacture or sale of products, or the provision of services, the advertising of which is prohibited by Article 13 or 14.

3. News and current affairs programmes may not be sponsored.

Article 18

1. The amount of advertising shall not exceed 15% of the daily transmission time. However, this percentage may be increased to 20% to include forms of advertisement such as direct offers to the

public for the sale, purchase or rental of products or for the provision of services, provided the amount of spot advertising does not exceed 15%.

2. The amount of spot advertising within a given one-hour period shall not exceed 20%.

3. Without prejudice to the provisions of paragraph 1, forms of advertisements such as direct offers to the public for the sale, purchase or rental of products or for the provision of services shall not exceed one hour per day.

Article 19

Member States may lay down stricter rules than those in Article 18 for programming time and the procedures for television broadcasting for television broadcasters under their jurisdiction, so as to reconcile demand for televised advertising with the public interest, taking account in particular of:

(a) the role of television in providing information, education, culture and entertainment;

(b) the protection of pluralism of information and of the media.

Article 20

Without prejudice to Article 3, Member States may, with due regard for Community law, lay down conditions other than those laid down in Article 11 (2) to (5) and in Article 18 in respect of broadcasts intended solely for the national territory which may not be received, directly or indirectly, in one or more other Member States.

Article 21

Member States shall, within the framework of their laws, ensure that in the case of television broadcasts that do not comply with the provisions of this chapter, appropriate measures are applied to secure compliance with these provisions.

CHAPTER V

Protection of minors

Article 22

Member States shall take appropriate measures to ensure that television broadcasts by broadcasters under their jurisdiction do not include programmes which might seriously impair the physical, mental or moral development of minors, in particular those that involve pornography or gratuitous violence. This provision shall extend to other programmes which are likely to impair the physical, mental or moral development of minors, except where it is ensured, by selecting the time of the broadcast or by any technical measure, that minors in the area of transmission will not normally hear or see such broadcasts.

Member States shall also ensure that broadcasts do not contain any incitement to hatred on grounds of race, sex, religion or nationality.

CHAPTER VI

Right of reply

Article 23

1. Without prejudice to other provisions adopted by the Member States under civil, administrative or criminal law, any natural or legal person, regardless of nationality, whose legitimate interests, in

particular reputation and good name, have been damaged by an assertion of incorrect facts in a television programme must have a right of reply or equivalent remedies.

2. A right of reply or equivalent remedies shall exist in relation to all broadcasters under the jurisdiction of a Member State.

3. Member States shall adopt the measures needed to establish the right of reply or the equivalent remedies and shall determine the procedure to be followed for the exercise thereof. In particular, they shall ensure that a sufficient time span is allowed and that the procedures are such that the right or equivalent remedies can be exercised appropriately by natural or legal persons resident or established in other Member States.

4. An application for exercise of the right of reply or the equivalent remedies may be rejected if such a reply is not justified according to the conditions laid down in paragraph 1, would involve a punishable act, would render the broadcaster liable to civil law proceedings or would transgress standards of public decency.

5. Provision shall be made for procedures whereby disputes as to the exercise of the right of reply or the equivalent remedies can be subject to judicial review.

CHAPTER VII

Final provisions

Article 24

In fields which this Directive does not coordinate, it shall not affect the rights and obligations of Member States resulting from existing conventions dealing with telecommunications or broadcasting.

Article 25

1. Member States shall bring into force the laws, regulations and administrative provisions necessary to comply with this directive not later than 3 October 1991. They shall forthwith inform the Commission thereof.

2. Member States shall communicate to the Commission the text of the main provisions of national law which they adopt in the fields governed by this Directive.

Article 26

Not later than the end of the fifth year after the date of adoption of this Directive and every two years thereafter, the Commission shall submit to the European Parliament, the Council, and the Economic and Social Committee a report on the application of this Directive and, if necessary, make further proposals to adapt it to developments in the field of television broadcasting.

Article 27

This Directive is addressed to the Member States.

Done at Luxembourg, 3 October 1989.

For the Council
The President
R. DUMAS

Appendix III

Council of Europe draft Convention on transborder broadcasting

This document contains the text of the European Convention on Transfrontier Television adopted by the Committee of Ministers of the Council of Europe on 15 March 1989.

The Secretariat of the Council of Europe draws attention to the fact that the formal decision to open this Convention for signature — which can only be taken if none of the representatives in the Committee of Ministers objects — will be on the agenda of the extraordinary meeting of the Committee of Ministers on 22 March 1989.

European Convention on Transfrontier Television

Preamble

The member States of the Council of Europe and the other States party to the European Cultural Convention, signatory hereto,

Considering that the aim of the Council of Europe is to achieve greater unity between its members, for the purpose of safeguarding and realizing the ideals and principles which are their common heritage;

Considering that the dignity and equal worth of every human being constitute a fundamental element of those principles;

Considering that the freedom of expression and information, as embodied in Article 10 of the European Convention on Human Rights, constitutes one of the essential conditions of a democratic society and one of the basic conditions for its progress and for the development of every human being;

Reaffirming their commitment to the principles of the free flow of information and ideas and the independence of broadcasters, which constitute an indispensable basis for their broadcasting policy;

Affirming the importance of broadcasting for the development of culture and the free formation of opinions in conditions safeguarding pluralism and equality of opportunity among all democratic groups and political parties;

Convinced that the continued development of information and communication technology should serve to further the right, regardless of frontiers, to express, to seek, to receive and to impart information and ideas whatever their source;

Being desirous to present an increasing range of choice of programme services for the public, thereby enhancing Europe's heritage and developing its audiovisual creation, and being determined to achieve this cultural objective through efforts to increase the production and circulation of high-quality programmes, thereby responding to the public's expectations in the political, educational and cultural field;

Recognizing the need to consolidate the common broad framework of regulation;

Bearing in mind Resolution No 2 and the Declaration of the First European Ministerial Conference on Mass Media Policy;

Being desirous to develop the principles embodied in the existing Council of Europe Recommendations on principles on television advertising, on equality between women and men in the media, on the use of satellite capacity for television and sound radio, and on the promotion of audiovisual production in Europe.

Have agreed as follows:

CHAPTER I

General provisions

Article 1: Object and purpose

This Convention is concerned with programme services embodied in transmissions. The purpose is to facilitate, among the parties, the transfrontier transmission and the retransmission of television programme services.

Article 2: Terms employed

For the purposes of this Convention:

(a) 'Transmission' means the initial emission by terrestrial transmitter, by cable, or by satellite of whatever nature, in encoded or unencoded form, of television programme services for reception by the general public. It does not include communication services operating on individual demand.

(b) 'Retransmission' signifies the fact of receiving and simultaneously transmitting, irrespective of the technical means employed, complete and unchanged television programme services, or important parts of such services, transmitted by broadcasters for reception by the general public.

(c) 'Broadcaster' means the natural or legal person who composes television programme services for reception by the general public and transmits them or has them transmitted, complete and unchanged, by a third party.

(d) 'Programme service' means all the items within a single service provided by a given broadcaster within the meaning of the preceding paragraph.

(e) 'Audiovisual works of European origin' means creative works, the production or co-production of which is controlled by European natural or legal persons.

(f) 'Advertisement' means any public announcement intended to promote the sale, hire or rental of a product or service, to advance a cause or idea or to bring about some other effect desired by the advertiser, for which transmission time has been given to the advertiser for remuneration or similar consideration.

(g) 'Sponsorship' means the participation of a natural or legal person, who is not engaged in broadcasting activities or in the production of audiovisual works, in the direct or indirect financing of a programme with a view to promoting his/her name, trade mark or image.

Article 3: Field of application

This Convention shall apply to any programme service transmitted or retransmitted by entities or by technical means within the jurisdiction of a party, whether by cable, terrestrial transmitter or satellite, and which can be received, directly or indirectly, in one or more other parties.

Article 4: Freedom of reception and retransmission

The parties shall ensure freedom of expression and information in accordance with Article 10 of the European Convention on Human Rights and they shall guarantee freedom of reception and shall not restrict the retransmission on their territories of programme services which comply with the terms of this Convention.

Article 5: Duties of the transmitting parties

1. Each transmitting party shall ensure, by appropriate means and through its competent organs, that all programme services transmitted by entities or by technical means within its jurisdiction, within the meaning of Article 3, comply with the terms of this Convention.

2. For the purposes of this Convention, the transmitting party shall be:

(a) in the case of terrestrial transmissions, the party in which the initial emission is effected;

(b) in the case of satellite transmission:

   (i) the party in which the satellite up-link is situated;

   (ii) the party which grants the use of the frequency or a satellite capacity when the up-link is situated in a State which is not a party to this Convention;

   (iii)the party in which the broadcaster has its seat when responsibility under subparagraphs (i) and (ii) is not established.

3. When programme services transmitted from States which are not parties to this Convention are retransmitted by entities or by technical means within the jurisdiction of a party, within the meaning of Article 3, that party, acting as transmitting party, shall ensure, by appropriate means and through its competent organs, compliance with the terms of this Convention.

Article 6: Provision of information

1. The responsibilities of the broadcaster shall be clearly and adequately specified in the authorization issued by, or contract concluded with, the competent authority of each party, or by any other legal measure.

2. Information about the broadcaster shall be made available, upon request, by the competent authority of each transmitting party. Such information shall include, as a minimum, the name or denomination, seat and status of the broadcaster, the name of the legal representative, the composition of the capital, the nature, purpose and mode of financing of the programme service the broadcaster is providing or intends providing.

CHAPTER II

Programming matters

Article 7: Responsibilities of the broadcaster

1.   All items of programme services, as concerns their presentation and content, shall respect the dignity of the human being and the fundamental rights of others.

In particular, they shall not:

(a) be indecent and in particular contain pornography;

(b) give undue prominence to violence or be likely to incite to racial hatred.

2.   All items of programme services which are likely to impair the physical, mental or moral development of children and adolescents shall not be scheduled when, because of the time of transmission and reception, they are likely to watch them.

3.   The broadcaster shall ensure that news programmes fairly present facts and events and encourage the free formation of opinions.

Article 8: Right of reply

1.   Each transmitting party shall ensure that every natural or legal person, regardless of nationality or place of residence, shall have the opportunity to exercise a right of reply or to seek other comparable legal or administrative remedies relating to programmes transmitted or retransmitted by entities or by technical means within its jurisdiction, within the meaning of Article 3. In particular, it shall ensure that timing and other arrangements for the exercise of the right of reply are such that this right can be effectively exercised. The effective exercise of this right or other comparable legal or administrative remedies shall be ensured both as regards the timing and the modalities.

2.   For this purpose, the name of the broadcaster responsible for the programme service shall be identified therein at regular intervals by appropriate means.

Article 9: Access of the public to major events

Each party shall examine the legal measures to avoid the right of the public to information being undermined due to the exercise by a broadcaster of exclusive rights for the transmission or retransmission, within the meaning of Article 3, of an event of high public interest and which has the effect of depriving a large part of the public in one or more other parties of the opportunity to follow that event on television.

Article 10: Cultural objectives

1.   The parties shall ensure, where practicable and by appropriate means, that broadcasters reserve for European works a majority proportion of their transmission time, excluding the time appointed to news, sports events, games, advertising and teletext services. This proportion, having regard to the broadcaster's informational, educational, cultural and entertainment responsibilities to its viewing public, should be achieved progressively, on the basis of suitable criteria.

2. In case of disagreement between a receiving party and a transmitting party on the application of the preceding paragraph, recourse may be had, at the request of one of the parties, to the Standing Committee with a view to its formulating an advisory opinion on the subject. Such a disagreement shall not be submitted to the arbitration procedure provided for in Article 26.

3. The parties shall undertake to look together for the most appropriate instruments and procedures to support, without discrimination between broadcasters, the activity and development of European production, particularly in countries with a low audiovisual production capacity or restricted language area.

4. The parties, in the spirit of cooperation and mutual assistance which underlies this Convention, shall endeavour to avoid that programme services transmitted or retransmitted by entities or by technical means within their jurisdiction, within the meaning of Article 3, endanger the pluralism of the press and the development of the cinema industries. No cinematographic work shall accordingly be transmitted in such services, unless otherwise agreed between its rights holders and the broadcaster, until two years have elapsed since the work was first shown in cinemas; in the case of cinematographic works co-produced by the broadcaster, this period shall be one year.

CHAPTER III

Advertising

Article 11: General standards

1. All advertisements shall be fair and honest.

2. Advertisements shall not be misleading and shall not prejudice the interests of consumers.

3. Advertisements addressed to, or using children shall avoid anything likely to harm their interests and shall have regard to their special susceptibilities.

4. The advertiser shall not exercise any editorial influence over the content of programmes.

Article 12: Duration

1. The amount of advertising shall not exceed 15% of the daily transmission time. However, this percentage may be increased to 20% to include forms of advertisements such as direct offers to the public for the sale, purchase or rental of products or for the provision of services, provided the amount of spot advertising does not exceed 15%.

2. The amount of spot advertising within a given one-hour period shall not exceed 20%.

3. Forms of advertisements such as direct offers to the public for the sale, purchase or rental of products or for the provision of services shall not exceed one hour per day.

Article 13: Form and presentation

1. Advertisements shall be clearly distinguishable as such and recognizably separate from the other items of the programme service by optical or acoustic means. In principle, they shall be transmitted in blocks.

2. Subliminal advertisements shall not be allowed.

3. Surreptitious advertisements shall not be allowed, in particular the presentation of products or services in programmes when it serves advertising purposes.

4. Advertisements shall not feature, visually or orally, persons regularly presenting news and current affairs programmes.

Article 14: Insertion of advertisements

1. Advertisements shall be inserted between programmes. Provided the conditions contained in paragraphs 2 to 5 of this Article are fulfilled, advertisements may also be inserted during programmes in such a way that the integrity and value of the programme and the rights of the rights holders are not prejudiced.

2. In programmes consisting of autonomous parts, or in sports programmes and similarly structured events and performances comprising intervals, advertisements shall only be inserted between the parts or in the intervals.

3. The transmission of audiovisual works such as feature films and films made for television (excluding series, serials, light entertainment programmes and documentaries), provided their duration is more than 45 minutes, may be interrupted once for each complete period of 45 minutes. A further interruption is allowed if their duration is at least 20 minutes longer than two or more complete periods of 45 minutes.

4. Where programmes, other than those covered by paragraph 2, are interrupted by advertisements, a period of at least 20 minutes should elapse between each successive advertising break within the programme.

5. Advertisements shall not be inserted in any broadcast of a religious service. News and current affairs programmes, documentaries, religious programmes, and children's programmes, when they are less than 30 minutes' duration, shall not be interrupted by advertisements. It they last for 30 minutes or longer, the provisions of the previous paragraphs shall apply.

Article 15: Advertising of particular products

1. Advertisements for tobacco products shall not be allowed.

2. Advertisements for alcoholic beverages of all varieties shall comply with the following rules:

(a) they shall not be addressed particularly to minors and no one associated with the consumption of alcoholic beverages in advertisements should seem to be a minor;

(b) they shall not link the consumption of alcohol to physical performance or driving;

(c) they shall not claim that alcohol has therapeutic qualities or that it is a stimulant, a sedative or a means of resolving personal conflicts;

(d) they shall not encourage immoderate consumption of alcohol or present abstinence or moderation in a negative light;

(e) they shall not place undue emphasis on the alcoholic content of beverages.

3. Advertisements for medicines and medical treatment which are only available on medical prescription in the transmitting party shall not be allowed.

4. Advertisements for all other medicines and medical treatment shall be clearly distinguishable as such, honest, truthful and subject to verification and shall comply with the requirement of protection of the individual from harm.

Article 16: Advertising directed specifically at a single party

1. In order to avoid distortions in competition and endangering the television system of a party, advertisements which are specifically and with some frequency directed to audiences in a single party other than the transmitting party shall not circumvent the television advertising rules in that particular party.

2. The provisions of the preceding paragraph shall not apply where:

(a) the rules concerned establish a discrimination between advertisements transmitted by entities or by technical means within the jurisdiction of that party and advertisements transmitted by entities or by technical means within the jurisdiction of another party; or

(b) the parties concerned have concluded bilateral or multilateral agreements in this area.

CHAPTER IV

Sponsorship

Article 17: General standards

1. When a programme or series of programmes is sponsored in whole or in part, it shall clearly be identified as such by appropriate credits at the beginning and/or end of the programme.

2. The content and scheduling of sponsored programmes may not, under any circumstances, be influenced by the sponsor in such a way as to affect the responsibility and editorial independence of the broadcaster in respect of programmes.

3. Sponsored programmes shall not encourage the purchase or rental of the products or services of the sponsor or a third party, in particular by making special promotional references to those products or services in such programmes.

Article 18: Prohibited sponsorship

1. Programmes may not be sponsored by natural or legal persons whose principal activity is the manufacture or sale of products, or the provision of services, the advertising of which is prohibited by virtue of Article 15.

2. Sponsorship of news and current affairs programmes shall not be allowed.

CHAPTER V

Mutual assistance

Article 19: Cooperation between the parties

1. The parties agree to render each other mutual assistance in order to implement this Convention.

2. For that purpose:

(a) each Contracting State shall designate one or more authorities, the name and address of each of which it shall communicate to the Secretary-General of the Council of Europe at the time of deposit of its instrument of ratification, acceptance, approval or accession;

(b) each party which has designated more than one authority shall specify in its communication under subparagraph (a) the competence of each authority.

3. An authority designated by a party shall:

(a) furnish the information foreseen under Article 6, paragraph 2 of this Convention;

(b) furnish information at the request of an authority designated by another party on the domestic law and practices in the fields covered by this Convention;

(c) cooperate with the authorities designated by the other parties where this would enhance the effectiveness of measures taken in implementation of this Convention;

(d) consider any difficulty arising from the application of this Convention which is brought to its attention by an authority designated by another party.

CHAPTER VI

Standing Committee

Article 20: Standing Committee

1. For the purposes of this Convention, a Standing Committee shall be set up.

2. Each party may be represented on the Standing Committee by one or more delegates. Each delegation shall have one vote. Within the areas of its competence, the European Community shall exercise its right to vote with a number of votes equal to the number of its Member States which are parties to this Convention; the European Community shall not exercise its right to vote in cases where the member States concerned exercise theirs, and conversely.

3. Any State referred to in Article 29, paragraph 1, which is not a party to this Convention may be represented on the Committee as an observer.

4. The Standing Committee may seek the advice of experts in order to discharge its functions. It may, on its own initiative or at the request of the body concerned, invite any international or national governmental or non-governmental body technically qualified in the fields covered by this Convention to be represented by an observer at one or part of one of its meetings. The decision to invite such experts or body shall be taken by a majority of three-quarters of the members.

5. The Standing Committee shall be convened by the Secretary-General of the Council of Europe. Its first meeting shall be held within six months of the date of entry into force of the Convention. It shall subsequently meet whenever one third of the parties or the Committee of Ministers of the Council of Europe so requests, or on the initiative of the Secretary-General of the Council of Europe in accordance with the provisions of Article 23, paragraph 2, or at the request of one or more parties in accordance with the provisions of Articles 21, subparagraph (c), and 25, paragraph 2.

6. A majority of the parties shall constitute a quorum for holding a meeting of the Standing Committee.

7. Subject to the provisions of paragraph 4 and Article 23, paragraph 3, the decisions of the Standing Committee shall be taken by a majority of three-quarters of the members present.

8. Subject to the provisions of this Convention, the Standing Committee shall draw up its own Rules of Procedure.

Article 21: Functions of the Standing Committee

The Standing Committee shall be responsible for following the application of the Convention. It may:

(a) make recommendations to the parties concerning the application of the Convention;

(b) suggest any necessary modifications of the Convention and examine those proposed in accordance with the provisions of Article 23;

(c) examine, at the request of one or more parties, questions concerning the interpretation of the Convention;

(d) use its best endeavours to secure a friendly settlement of any difficulty referred to it in accordance with the provisions of Article 25;

(e) make recommendations to the Committee of Ministers concerning States other than those referred to in Article 29, paragraph 1, to be invited to accede to this Convention.

Article 22: Reports of the Standing Committee

After each meeting, the Standing Committee shall forward to the parties and the Committee of Ministers of the Council of Europe a report on its discussions and any decisions taken.

CHAPTER VII

Amendments

Article 23: Amendments

1. Any party may propose amendments to this Convention.

2. Any proposal for amendment shall be notified to the Secretary-General of the Council of Europe who shall communicate it to the member States of the Council of Europe, to the other States party to the European Cultural Convention, to the European Community and to any non-member State which has acceded to, or has been invited to accede to this Convention in accordance with the provisions of Article 30. The Secretary-General of the Council of Europe shall convene a meeting of the Standing Committee at the earliest two months following the communication of the proposal.

3. The Standing Committee shall examine any amendment proposed and shall submit the text adopted by a majority of three-quarters of the members to the Committee of Ministers for approval. After its approval, the text shall be forwarded to the parties for acceptance.

4. Any amendment shall enter into force on the 30th day after all the parties have informed the Secretary-General of their acceptance thereof.

CHAPTER VIII

Alleged violations of this Convention

Article 24: Alleged violations of this Convention

1. When a party finds a violation of this Convention, it shall communicate to the transmitting party the alleged violation and the two parties shall endeavour to overcome the difficulty on the basis of the provisions of Articles 19, 25 and 26.

2. If the alleged violation is of a manifest, serious and grave nature which raises important public issues and concerns Articles 7, paragraphs 1 or 2, 12, 13, paragraph 1, first sentence, 14 or 15, paragraphs 1 or 3, and if it persists within two weeks following the communication, the receiving party may suspend provisionally the retransmission of the incriminated programme service.

3. In all other cases of alleged violation, with the exception of those provided for in paragraph 4, the receiving party may suspend provisionally the retransmission of the incriminated programme service eight months following the communication, if the alleged violation persists.

4. The provisional suspension of retransmission shall not be allowed in the case of alleged violations of Articles 7, paragraph 3, 8, 9 or 10.

CHAPTER IX

Settlement of disputes

Article 25 : Conciliation

1. In case of difficulty arising from the application of this Convention, the parties concerned shall endeavour to achieve a friendly settlement.

2. Unless one of the parties concerned objects, the Standing Committee may examine the question, by placing itself at the disposal of the parties concerned in order to reach a satisfactory solution as rapidly as possible and, where appropriate, to formulate an advisory opinion on the subject.

3. Each party concerned undertakes to accord the Standing Committee without delay all information and facilities necessary for the discharge of its functions under the preceding paragraph.

Article 26 : Arbitration

1. If the parties concerned cannot settle the dispute in accordance with the provisions of Article 25, they may, by common agreement, submit it to arbitration, the procedure of which is provided for in the Appendix to this Convention. In the absence of such an agreement within six months following the first request to open the procedure of conciliation, the dispute may be submitted to arbitration at the request of one of the parties.

2. Any party may, at any time, declare that it recognizes as compulsory *ipso facto* and without special agreement in respect of any other party accepting the same obligation, the application of the arbitration procedure provided for in the Appendix to this Convention.

CHAPTER X

Other international agreements and the internal law of the parties

Article 27 : Other international agreements or arrangements

1. In their mutual relations, parties which are members of the European Economic Community shall apply Community rules and shall not therefore apply the rules arising from this Convention except in so far as there is no Community rule governing the particular subject concerned.

2. Nothing in this Convention shall prevent the parties from concluding international agreements completing or developing its provisions or extending their field of application.

3. In the case of bilateral agreements, this Convention shall not alter the rights and obligations of parties which arise from such agreements and which do not affect the enjoyment of other parties of their rights or the performance of their obligations under this Convention.

Article 28: Relations between the Convention and the internal law of the parties

Nothing in this Convention shall prevent the parties from applying stricter or more detailed rules than those provided for in this Convention to programme services transmitted by entities or by technical means within their jurisdiction, within the meaning of Article 3.

CHAPTER XI

Final provisions

Article 29: Signature and entry into force

1.   This Convention shall be open for signature by the member States of the Council of Europe and the other States party to the European Cultural Convention, and by the European Community. It is subject to ratification, acceptance or approval. Instruments of ratification, acceptance or approval shall be deposited with the Secretary-General of the Council of Europe.

2.   This Convention shall enter into force on the first day of the month following the expiration of a period of three months after the date on which seven States, of which at least five member States of the Council of Europe, have expressed their consent to be bound by the Convention in accordance with the provisions of the preceding paragraph.

3.   A State may, at the time of signature or at any later date prior to the entry into force of this Convention in respect of that State, declare that it shall apply the Convention provisionally.

4.   In respect of any State referred to in paragraph 1, or the European Community, which subsequently express their consent to be bound by it, this Convention shall enter into force on the first day of the month following the expiration of a period of three months after the date of deposit of the instrument of ratification, acceptance or approval.

Article 30: Accession by non-member States

1.   After the entry into force of this Convention, the Committee of Ministers of the Council of Europe, after consulting the Contracting States may invite any other State to accede to this Convention by a decision taken by the majority provided for in Article 20 (d) of the Statute of the Council of Europe and by the unanimous vote of the representatives of the Contracting States entitled to sit on the Committee.

2.   In respect of any acceding State, this Convention shall enter into force on the first day of the month following the expiration of a period of three months after the date of deposit of the instrument of accession with the Secretary-General of the Council of Europe.

Article 31: Territorial clause

1.   Any State may, at the time of signature or when depositing its instrument of ratification, acceptance, approval or accession, specify the territory or territories to which this Convention shall apply.

2.   Any State may, at any later date, by a declaration addressed to the Secretary-General of the Council of Europe, extend the application of this Convention to any other territory specified in the declaration. In respect of such territory, the Convention shall enter into force on the first day of the month following the expiration of a period of three months after the date of receipt of such declaration by the Secretary-General.

3. Any declaration made under the two preceding paragraphs may, in respect of any territory specified in such declaration, be withdrawn by a notification addressed to the Secretary-General. The withdrawal shall become effective on the first day of the month following the expiration of a period of six months after the date of receipt of such notification by the Secretary-General.

Article 32: Reservations

1. At the time of signature or when depositing its instrument of ratification, acceptance, approval or accession,

(a) any State may declare that it reserves the right to restrict the retransmission on its territory, solely to the extent that it does not comply with its domestic legislation, of programme services containing advertisements for alcoholic beverages according to the rules provided for in Article 15, paragraph 2, of this Convention;

(b) the United Kingdom may declare that it reserves the right not to fulfil the obligation, set out in Article 15, paragraph 1, to prohibit advertisements for tobacco products, in respect of advertisements for cigars and pipe tobacco broadcast by the Independent Broadcasting Authority by terrestrial means on its territory.

No other reservation may be made.

2. A reservation made in accordance with the preceding paragraph may not be the subject of an objection.

3. Any Contracting State which has made a reservation under paragraph 1 may wholly or partly withdraw it by means of a notification addressed to the Secretary-General of the Council of Europe. The withdrawal shall take effect on the date of receipt of such notification by the Secretary-General.

4. A party which has made a reservation in respect of a provision of this Convention may not claim the application of that provision by any other party; it may, however, if its reservation is partial or conditional, claim the application of that provision in so far as it has itself accepted it.

Article 33: Denunciation

1. Any party may, at any time, denounce this Convention by means of a notification addressed to the Secretary-General of the Council of Europe.

2. Such denunciation shall become effective on the first day of the month following the expiration of a period of six months after the date of receipt of the notification by the Secretary-General.

Article 34: Notifications

The Secretary-General of the Council of Europe shall notify the member States of the Council, the other States party to the European Cultural Convention, the European Community and any State which has acceded to, or has been invited to accede to this Convention of:

(a) any signature;

(b) the deposit of any instrument of ratification, acceptance, approval or accession;

(c) any date of entry into force of this Convention in accordance with the provisions of Articles 29, 30 and 31;

(d) any report established in accordance with the provisions of Article 22;

(e) any other act, declaration, notification or communication relating to this Convention.

In witness whereof the undersigned, being duly authorized thereto, have signed this Convention.

Done at ..., the ..., in English and French, both texts being equally authentic, in a single copy which shall be deposited in the archives of the Council of Europe. The Secretary-General of the Council of Europe shall transmit certified copies to each member State of the Council of Europe, to the other States party to the European Cultural Convention, to the European Community and to any State invited to accede to this Convention.

APPENDIX

Arbitration

1. A request for arbitration shall be notified to the Secretary-General of the Council of Europe. It shall include the name of the other party to the dispute and the subject matter of the dispute. The Secretary-General shall communicate the information so received to all the parties to this Convention.

2. In the event of a dispute between two parties one of which is a Member State of the European Community, the latter itself being a party, the request for arbitration shall be addressed both to the Member State and to the Community, which jointly, shall notify the Secretary-General, within one month of receipt of the request, whether the Member State or the Community, or the Member State and the Community jointly, shall be party to the dispute. In the absence of such notification within the said time-limit, the Member State and the Community shall be considered as being one and the same party to the dispute for the purposes of the application of the provisions governing the constitution and procedure of the arbitration tribunal. The same shall apply when the Member State and the Community jointly present themselves as party to the dispute. In cases envisaged by this paragraph, the time-limit of one month foreseen in the first sentence of paragraph 4 hereafter shall be extended to two months.

3. The arbitration tribunal shall consist of three members: each of the parties to the dispute shall appoint one arbitrator; the two arbitrators so appointed shall designate by common agreement the third arbitrator who shall be the chairman of the tribunal. The latter shall not be a national of either of the parties to the dispute, nor have his usual place of residence in the territory of either of those parties, nor be employed by either of them, nor have dealt with the case in another capacity.

4. If one of the parties has not appointed an arbitrator within one month following the communication of the request by the Secretary-General of the Council of Europe, he shall be appointed at the request of the other party by the President of the European Court of Human Rights within a further one-month period. If the President of the Court is unable to act or is a national of one of the parties to the dispute, the appointment shall be made by the Vice-President of the Court or by the most senior judge to the Court who is available and is not a national of one of the parties to the dispute. The same procedure shall be observed if, within a period of one month following the appointment of the second arbitrator, the Chairman of the arbitration tribunal is not designated.

5. The provisions of paragraphs 3 and 4 shall apply, as the case may be, in order to fill any vacancy.

6. Two or more parties which determine by agreement that they are in the same interest shall appoint an arbitrator jointly.

7. The parties to the dispute and the Standing Committee shall provide the arbitration tribunal with all facilities necessary for the effective conduct of the proceedings.

8. The arbitration tribunal shall draw up its own Rules of Procedure. Its decisions shall be taken by majority vote of its members. Its award shall be final and binding.

9. The award of the arbitration tribunal shall be notified to the Secretary-General of the Council of Europe who shall communicate it to all the parties to this Convention.

10. Each party to the dispute shall bear the expenses of the arbitrator appointed by it; these parties shall share equally the expenses of the other arbitrator, as well as other costs entailed by the arbitration.

Appendix IV

List of EBU members and approved observers
at 1 January 1989

Active members:	38 in 32 countries
Associate members:	60 in 37 countries
Total	98 in 69 countries
Approved observers:	1

Active members

1. Radiodiffusion-Télévision Algérienne (Algeria)
   grouping: Entreprise Nationale de Télévision (ENTV)
   Entreprise Nationale de Radiodiffusion Sonore
   Entreprise Nationale de Télédiffusion
   Entreprise Nationale de Production Audiovisuelle
2. Arbeitsgemeinschaft der Öffentlichrechtlichen
   Rundfunkanstalten der Bundesrepublik Deutschland — ARD (Germany)
   grouping: Bayerischer Rundfunk
   Hessischer Rundfunk
   Norddeutscher Rundfunk
   Radio Bremen
   Saarländischer Rundfunk
   Sender Freies Berlin
   Süddeutscher Rundfunk
   Südwestfunk
   Westdeutscher Rundfunk
   Deutsche Welle
   Deutschlandfunk
   Deutsches Fernsehen
   RIAS Berlin
3. Zweites Deutsches Fernsehen — ZDF (Germany)
4. Österreichischer Rundfunk — ORF (Austria)
5. Belgische Radio en Televisie — BRT (Belgium)
6. Radio-Télévision Belge de la Communauté Française — RTBF (Belgium)
7. Cyprus Broadcasting Corporation (Cyprus)
8. Danmarks Radio (Denmark)
9. Egyptian Radio and Television (Egypt)
10. Antena 3 de Radio SA (Spain)
11. Radiotelevisión Española — RTVE (Spain)
    grouping: Radio Nacional de España
    Televisión Española

12. Sociedad Española de Radiodifusión — SER (Spain)
13. Oy Yleisradio AB — YLE (Finland)
14. Organismes français de Radiodiffusion et de Télévision - OFRT (France)
    grouping: Télévision Française 1
             Antenne 2: France
             France-Regions 3
             Canal Plus
             Radio France
             Télédiffusion de France
15. Europe 1 (France)
16. Elliniki Radiophonia Tileorassi — ERT (Greece)
17. Radio Telefís Éireann — RTE (Ireland)
18. Rikisutvarpid — RUV (Iceland)
19. Israel Broadcasting Authority (Israel)
20. Radiotelevisione Italiana — RAI (Italy)
21. Jordan Radio and Television — JRTV (Jordan)
22. Radiodiffusion Libanaise/Télé-Liban — RL/TL (Lebanon)
23. Libyan Jamahiriya Broadcasting — LJB (Libya)
24. Radio-Tele Luxembourg — RTL (Luxembourg)
25. Broadcasting Authority — Malta/Xandir Radio (Malta)
26. Radiodiffusion Télévision Marocaine (Morocco)
27. Radio Monte Carlo (Monaco)
28. Norsk Rikskringkasting — NRK (Norway)
29. Nederlandse Omroepprogramma Stichting — NOS (Netherlands)
    grouping: Algemene Omroepvereniging
             Stichting De Evangelische Omroep
             Katholieke Radio Omroep
             Nederlandse Christelijke Radio Vereniging
             Vereniging Arbeiders Radio Amateurs
             Vrijzinnig Protestantse Radio Omroep
             Televisie Radio Omroep Stichting
             Veronica Omroep Organisatie
30. Radiodifusão Portuguesa — RDP (Portugal)
31. Radiotelevisão Portuguesa — RTP (Portugal)
32. British Broadcasting Corporation — BBC (United Kingdom)
33. United Kingdom Independent Broadcasting — UKIB (UK)
    grouping: Independent Broadcasting Authority
             Channel 4 Television
             Association of Independent Radio Contractors
             Independent Television Association — ITV
             grouping: Anglia Television
                      Border Television
                      Central Independent Television
                      Channel Television
                      Grampian Television
                      Granada Television
                      HTV
                      London Weekend Television
                      Scottish Television

            Television South
            Television South West
            Thames Television
            Tyne Tees Television
            Ulster Television
            Yorkshire Television
            Independent Television News
            TV-AM

34. Sveriges Radio (Sweden)
    grouping: Sveriges Television
               Sveriges Riksradio
               Sveriges Lokalradio
               Sveriges Utbildningsradio

35. Société Suisse de Radiodiffusion et Télévision — SSR (Switzerland)

36. Radiodiffusion-Télévision Tunisienne — RTT (Tunisia)

37. Turkiye Radyo Televizyon Kurumu — TRT (Turkey)

38. Radio Vaticana (Vatican)

39. Jugoslovenska Radiotelevizija — JRT (Yugoslavia)
    grouping: Radiotelevizija Beograd
               Radiotelevizija Ljubljana
               Radiotelevizija Novi Sad
               Radiotelevizija Pristina
               Radiotelevizija Sarajevo
               Radiotelevizija Titograd
               RAdiotelevizija Zagreb
               Radio Jugoslavija

Associate members

1. Saudi Arabian Broadcasting and Television Service (Saudi Arabia)

2. Australian Broadcasting Corporation (Australia)

3. Federation of Australian Commercial Television Stations (Australia)

4. Special Broadcasting Service (Australia)

5. National Broadcasting Authority of Bangladesh

6. Caribbean Broadcasting Corporation (Barbados)

7. TV Globo (Brazil)

8. Canadian Broadcasting Corporation/Société Radio Canada (Canada)

9. CTV Television Network (Canada)

10. Corporación de Televisión de la Universidad Católica de Chile (Chile)

11. Korean Broadcasting System (Korea)

12. Munhwa Broadcasting Corporation (Korea)

13. Radiodiffusion-Télévision Ivoirienne (Ivory Coast)

14. United Arab Emirates Radio and Television (UAE)

15. United Arab Emirates Radio and Television Dubai (UAE)

16. Capital Cities/American Broadcasting Companies — ABC (USA)

17. CBS Inc (USA)

18. Corporation for Public Broadcasting/Public Broadcasting Service/National Public Radio/American Public Radio (USA)

19. National Broadcasting Company — NBC (USA)
20. Turner Broadcasting System/Cable News Network (USA)
21. United States Information Agency (USA)
22. WFMT (USA)
23. Radiodiffusion-Télévision Gabonaise (Gabon)
24. Groenlands Radio (Greenland)
25. Asia Television Ltd (Hong Kong)
26. Radio Television Hong Kong (Hong Kong)
27. Television Broadcasts Ltd (Hong Kong)
28. All India Radio (India)
29. Islamic Republic of Iran Broadcasting (Iran)
30. Iraqi General Establishment for Radio and Television (Iraq)
31. Jamaica Broadcasting Corporation (Jamaica)
32. Asahi National Broadcasting Company (Japan)
33. FM Tokyo Broadcasting Company (Japan)
34. Fuji Television Network (Japan)
35. Mainichi Broadcasting System (Japan)
36. National Association of Broadcasters in Japan (Japan)
37. Nippon Hoso Kyokai — NHK (Japan)
38. Nippon Television Network Corporation (Japan)
39. Tokyo Broadcasting System (Japan)
40. Kuwait Broadcasting and Television Service (Kuwait)
41. Radio Television Malaysia (Malaysia)
42. Malawi Broadcasting Corporation (Malawi)
43. Mauritius Broadcasting Corporation (Mauritius)
44. Instituto Mexicano de Television (Mexico)
45. Televisa (Mexico)
46. Nepal Television Corporation (Nepal)
47. Radio New Zealand (NZ)
48. Television New Zealand (NZ)
49. Oman Directorate-General of Radio and Television (Oman)
50. Pakistan Television Corporation (Pakistan)
51. National Broadcasting Commission of Papua New Guinea (PNG)
52. Compania Peruana de Radiodifusión (Peru)
53. Qatar Television and Broadcasting Service (Qatar)
54. Office de Radiodiffusion Télévision du Sénégal (Senegal)
55. Sri Lanka Broadcasting Corporation (SL)
56. Organisme de la Radio-Télévision Syrienne (Syria)
57. Radio Tanzania-Dar es Salaam (Tanzania)
58. Corporación Venezolana de Televisión (Venezuela)
59. Radio Caracas Television/Radio Caracas Radio (Venezuela)
60. Zimbabwe Broadcasting Corporation (Zimbabwe)

Approved observers
1. Israeli Educational Television (Israel)

Appendix V

Joint declaration on Audiovisual Eureka

The Ministers or representatives of 26 European States as well as the President of the Commission of the European Communities, meeting in Paris on 2 October 1989,

following the initiative of the President of the French Republic and the conclusions reached at the European Council at Rhodes in December 1988 by the Heads of State or Government of the Member States of the European Community,

recalling the work already undertaken in the Council of Europe and its role in the cultural and audiovisual field,

aware of the importance of a coordinated and effective organization of the development of a coherent, dynamic and open audiovisual market taking into account the cultural character and impact of the audiovisual sector,

convinced that the response to the cultural, technological and industrial challenges arising from changes in communications techniques and the growing need for audiovisual programmes lies primarily in the mobilization of professionals and their dynamism,

desiring to bring about the strengthening and greater competitiveness of programme industries in Europe, while respecting the cultural identity and the interests of the creators,

affirming their common will to develop cooperation in the cultural and audiovisual field throughout Europe,

attentive to the views and proposals of the professionals in this sector on the occasion of the European Audiovisual Conference organized jointly by the French government and the Commission of the European Communities,

concerned to give due attention to projects which can encourage the diffusion of the cultures and languages which constitute the richness of Europe,

attached to the principle of the free development and full flowering of creative capacities from all European countries,

wishing to pay particular attention to countries having a limited geographical or linguistic coverage in Europe and to preserve the pluralism of European cultures,

(1) have agreed to take the necessary steps for the establishment of a series of measures entitled 'Audiovisual Eureka' having the objectives of encouraging:

(a) the emergence of a more transparent and dynamic audiovisual market on a European scale;

(b) the launching of actions and concrete cooperation projects of interest for the future of the European audiovisual programme industry, including its technological aspects, with the objective of strengthening the capacity of European enterprises to create and produce and of promoting their competitiveness;

(c) the widest possible distribution of European programmes, the multiplication of exchanges within Europe and the increase of Europe's share of the world market;

(d) the development and the widest possible diffusion of production from countries having a limited geographic or linguistic coverage in Europe;

(e) the promotion of European technologies, particularly in the field of HDTV, for the production and transmission of films and audiovisual programmes;

(2) intend, within the limits of their powers, to take appropriate measures and to implement coherent policies with a view to promoting appropriate general conditions and a legal environment favourable to the creation, production, co-production and exchange of films and audiovisual programmes in Europe, these being the decisive factors for the success of Audiovisual Eureka;

(3) propose to consult each other, and continue, within the competent institutions, the examination of the particular conditions for the development of a coherent and dynamic audiovisual market on a European scale, respecting their international commitments,

(4) intend to examine the possibility of taking additional measures in support of Audiovisual Eureka;

(5) recall that Audiovisual Eureka is aimed at all enterprises and bodies contributing to or participating in the process of conception, finance, production, distribution or transmission of European films and audiovisual programmes;

(6) decide to establish an Audiovisual Eureka Coordinators' Committee, composed of the representatives of the governments of the participating States and the Commission of the European Communities. The Secretary-General of the Council of Europe is invited to designate a representative to participate in its work. The Committee will draw up its Rules of Procedure. It will have the task of giving further examination to the content and the objectives of Audiovisual Eureka, and of regularly evaluating its results. Based on the individual coordinators' consultations with the professional circles, the Committee may develop recommendations designed to improve the market structures and ground rules of the audiovisual industry. To this end, the Committee will examine in particular the various suggestions put forward at the European Audiovisual Conference. It will be responsible for proposing, whenever there is a need, the convening of ministerial meetings with a view to adopting new guidelines or measures designed to promote Audiovisual Eureka;

(7) decide on the creation of a small and flexible Audiovisual Eureka secretariat, which will be able to benefit from the logistic support of the Commission of the European Communities. The Council of Europe is invited to examine what logistic support it could offer to this secretariat. Under the responsibility of the Audiovisual Eureka Coordinators' Committee, the secretariat will have the tasks of:

(a) convening and preparing the meetings of the Audiovisual Eureka Coordinators' Committee;

(b) assisting interested enterprises and other bodies to establish, in liaison with the Coordinators, contacts with partners for Audiovisual Eureka projects of participating States;

(8) agree to entrust the Audiovisual Eureka Coordinators with:

(a) circulating information relating to Audiovisual Eureka projects submitted to them;

(b) facilitating contacts between enterprises and other bodies of the participating countries;

(c) providing the Audiovisual Eureka Coordinators' Committee with all information relating to the description of projects and their conformity with Audiovisual Eureka objectives and criteria;

(d) encouraging the implementation of Audiovisual Eureka projects;

(9) ask the Audiovisual Eureka Coordinators' Committee to examine questions relating to the institution, role and organization of a European Audiovisual Observatory, as well as the modalities of its establishment and functioning, in cooperation with the professionals of this sector. The tasks of this Observatory — which could utilize in the best way the existing resources of participating States and European institutions — could be to collect and process existing information and statistics as well as to define possible further needs. These data should be placed at the disposal of the professionals and of the Audiovisual Eureka Coordinators' Committee so as to promote a better view of the market and greater transparency and to facilitate the implementation of Audiovisual Eureka projects. The Council of Europe is invited to examine what measures could be taken to support the activities of this Observatory.

Paris, 2 October 1989

Annex I

Objectives and criteria
applicable to Audiovisual Eureka projects

The projects presented by enterprises and other interested bodies will have to meet objectives and criteria which will be defined at a later stage by the Audiovisual Eureka Coordinators' Committee.

The definition of these objectives and criteria should draw on the following principles:

(a) encouraging the exchange and the widest possible circulation of European works on cinema or television screens or through videocassettes, particularly by improving distribution mechanisms within Europe and surmounting the linguistic barriers which separate European audiences;

(b) creating a framework favourable to the financing of the production and co-production of original European works responding to the expectations of European audiences and being competitive on the international market;

(c) increasing contacts between professionals and ensuring the clarity and proper distribution of information in the artistic, legal and economic fields;

(d) adapting forms of training for audiovisual occupations to the new needs of the programme industry, while encouraging the development of creativity and cultural and linguistic identities;

(e) strengthening the competitiveness of European enterprises in the sector, including small and medium-sized enterprises, on the European and world markets;

(f) being implemented within the framework of cooperation agreements applying to enterprises of more than one European country and, wherever possible, at least three European countries;

(g) presenting clearly identifiable positive features arising from cooperation on a European scale, in particular by offering new possibilities of expression or new outlets to European creators and professionals;

(h) containing adequate financial commitments on the part of participating enterprises;

(i) contributing to the development and wider audiovisual diffusion of films and audiovisual programmes of countries with a weak production capacity and having limited linguistic coverage in Europe;

(j) promoting new technologies for the production and transmission of films and audiovisual programmes.

Annex II

**Relations between Audiovisual Eureka,
the European Community, the Council of Europe
and other existing cooperation frameworks**

1. Various concrete initiatives have already been undertaken by the European Community (Media pilot programme, Framework programme for research and development), or by the Council of Europe (Eurimages Fund). Audiovisual Eureka projects are not conceived as a substitute for existing cooperation frameworks, their objective being rather to extend or complement these as appropriate.

2. The European Community will be able to participate in Audiovisual Eureka projects, in particular through its programmes.

3. The Council of Europe is invited to cooperate in Audiovisual Eureka.

4. As necessary the Audiovisual Eureka Coordinators' Committee will check with the competent instances of the technological Eureka on the complementary nature and appropriate synergy of their respective projects.

Appendix VI

Speech by Mr Jacques Delors, President of the European Commission, at the European Audiovisual Conference in Paris, 2 October 1989

Minister of State, Ministers, Ladies and Gentlemen,
The Members of the European Commission and the officials accompanying them came here to help with the organization of the Conference, and above all to learn from those who have responsibilities in this area which the rapporteurs claim has such a bright and at the same time hazardous future.

It is not for me to draw the conclusions of the Conference — Mr Roland Dumas will do that shortly — but to assure you that, in the context of Audiovisual Eureka, which I believe has got off to a good start today, the coordinators and organizers will take account of the proposals that have been made and which — since we must distinguish between the 27 countries present and the 12 forming the European Community, which has its own requirements — we will also endeavour to bear in mind.

Needless to say, after having heard the rapporteurs, much remains unanswered; the questions are so difficult. But of two things I am certain.

First, culture is not another piece of merchandise and should not be treated as such. Secondly, culture can be spread today only if we have mastery of the technological tools.

With respect to the first point: culture is not just another type of merchandise — tomorrow the Twelve will have an important discussion — we cannot treat culture as we would treat refrigerators or even motor cars. *Laissez-faire*, market forces alone cannot suffice. We must sincerely say, no protectionism and no *laissez-faire*.

To our American friends, who took the opportunity three or four days before the conference to attack in the GATT — the body responsible for multinational trade — four countries which had signed the Council of Europe Convention, I would like to ask: do we not have the right to exist? Do we not have the right to perpetuate our traditions, our heritage and our languages? How can a country of 10 million inhabitants, faced with the universality offered by satellites, maintain its language which is a vehicle of its culture? Does not the defence of liberty so loudly proclaimed elsewhere include the effort made by each country, or group of countries, to preserve its identity by audiovisual means?

I admit there is not just one European identity, there are many European identities, but we should at least have the possibility to guard and protect them. If we do not have the talent to do so then it is too bad. To begin with, culture should be treated like other fields. This immediately leads to one conclusion: I am not talking about freedom of movement of works, I wish to discuss the organization of the audiovisual area. Although some may jeer and speak of *dirigisme* or State intervention, many major works that are famous today were commissioned by a powerful man of the day.

We cannot be detached from the organization of the audiovisual area and we have much to do. For example, I recognize that the European Commission has failed to resolve the problem of copyright. I might say that it is the fault of the 12 countries which have not reached agreement. But it is our fault, because it is the duty of all of us to find and propose solutions which, wherever possible, will obtain the consensus of the 12 countries.

The second matter of which I am sure is that culture cannot spread unless we have mastery of the technological tools. What was said regarding the technological stakes is very important. I associate myself with the proposal for a White Paper which would help us to become aware of what is at stake in what we can call an industry, but an industry that is closely linked to our cultural future.

It is not possible to stand aside from the joint venture, on the question of technology, and for my part I could not agree if some countries were to cooperate in the other two areas — organization of the audiovisual area or the promotion of works — while refusing to share in the technological risks to be taken by some European countries.

I now come to the contribution by the Conference. This morning, the representative of Sweden said in connection with the Council of Europe Convention that there was the spectator on one side and the producer on the other. Of course it is difficult, he said, but I tend toward the spectator side; this will enable other policymakers to have a clearer idea of the implications, and to bear in mind that behind the producers, in addition to the national industries, there are also the identity and personality of the people. Thus, the question is therefore particularly complex.

With respect to technology, we now have an instrument, the European Economic Interest Group, and it will be interesting to see who wishes to contribute their efforts and bear their share of the risks with the others. It is all very well and very fine to talk about the European Community, the common house of Europe, while standing on the sidelines watching others play. It will be interesting to see who is prepared to share the technological risks and who prefers the shortcuts offered by other technologies. But believe me, in 10 years time the latter will no longer exist and will not be able to claim they have any ambition.

Mr Solana spoke of the new European industries. He was right, when one considers the improvement in annual turnover, all that is at stake, the increase in added value and the workforce employed. He said, and it is quite true, that the three sectors should have a chance. While most of us are still in the realm of radio waves, studies show that most — nearly all — public-television networks produce at least 50 % of European works. This is to show that, regardless of the appetite of the sector, to quote Mr Drucker, European television networks have an interest in producing European works.

Pluralism is absolutely necessary; criteria will be established to determine what is a European product. It has been proposed that a certificate of European origin should be issued. Who will issue it remains to be seen. After all, all ideas are worth considering.

Then there is the question of financial resources. Here in the reports and in the oral statements we find various solutions that can be applied. Aids, tax incentives, the development of venture capital, financial responsibility of the distributor, all that should be gone into thoroughly and put into action.

An additional proposal has been made, and I agree with it, to set up an independent European observation post. But of course, there should be no ambiguity on this question: should the observation post be independent, should it collect data, should it give information, or should it take action. These are different tasks. In my opinion, the observation post should centralize data, inform those concerned, while the policymakers and those engaged in the sector should take action on their own responsibility.

Incidentally, the Community itself should go further, because the 12 Members are under a more extensive contract than the member countries of the Council of Europe. It should be understood that, while remaining true to the spirit of the greater Europe — since we are talking about television without frontiers which is not limited to the 12 Member States, the Community, because it has its own philosophy and its own aims for society, must establish its own criteria in harmony with its other activities.

Mr Drucker spoke at length about programmes. He stressed the educational aspect of television, and for this purpose proposed a European foundation. One might also underline the importance of information given by the media. He made a clear and useful distinction between the cinema, which is a prototype industry, and television, which is a distribution industry. I hope it will be possible to go further and to ask a simple question: what does the future hold for our children who in general watch an average of two and a half to three hours of television every day and only spend half an hour talking to their parents, then do as best they can at school.

What impact does the audiovisual media have on all this? Is it a market problem or a problem of society? I leave it to each of you to find the answer. In any case, to me the answer is clear, it is a problem for society which should be treated as such and should not simply be regarded as a measurement of popularity.

The European Commission will continue its work. In the case of Audiovisual Eureka, as I said this morning, a distinction should be drawn between two types of action: action to improve the environment for creative artists — these actions are mainly carried out through the Media programme, education, training, improvement of techniques, etc. — and the other aspect of Audiovisual Eureka without which of course there would have been no point in establishing it — this consists of producing more works, especially quality works.

The Commission cannot act directly in the second area. You think, and some in this hall have reminded me of it, we have neither the talent nor the intelligence to choose between two or three projects. We leave this to the audiovisual coordinators.

On the other hand, in the context of the Media programme, we will continue to finance and support the effort to set up this forum, which is already very encouraging, composed of all those who are passionately attached to this new industry and who take part in it, including producers, distributors, creative artists, players and directors. At the next European Council, in the name of the Commission, I will propose the means that we should use to promote the creation of audiovisual works over a period of five years, amounting to ECU 250 million. For all those who are not familiar with the foreign exchange market, and I sympathize with them, this makes about FF 1 750 million over five years, in other words Media multiplied by four.

This will demonstrate our continued attachment to establishing a European audiovisual market. I must repeat though, that all these aspects form a whole. I say this for the 27 countries represented (even though I am only acknowledging in passing the political importance of these 27 countries, I am the last to underestimate this factor at a time when we are in particular trying to develop cooperation with Poland and Hungary to help them in their remarkable effort to modernize their economy to reinforce their liberty). I say again, the three aspects are linked: technology, organization of the audiovisual area, and the development of audiovisual production. If, unfortunately for Europe, one of these aspects were to be forgotten, the overall structure would be jeopardized, and with its destruction all the gold and all the diamonds of European creativity would go to waste.

Appendix VII

Charter of the Association of Commercial Television in Europe (ACT)

I – Introduction

The Association of Commercial Television in Europe (ACT) was founded by five large private distributors to serve as a platform for all television distribution companies whose resources are derived solely from commercial revenue, including subscriptions.

It was vital to create such an association in view of the far-reaching changes currently affecting the European audiovisual scene.

The new technological developments, in particular those concerning satellite television, and the political will to set up a large market in the audiovisual sector, have highlighted the need to move away from the national regulatory field and to set up a flexible and liberal regulatory field at European level.

The new guidelines also imply a change in attitude, a task to which the ACT will contribute. Indeed, despite the valuable contribution of some organizations in the audiovisual industry, such as the European Advertising Tripartite and European Group of Television Advertising, the regulations adopted so far have always been in favour of the public sector.

Members of the ACT would like balance to be restored by drawing the attention of the various bodies to the essential contribution made by the private sector, not only as a stimulus for the market but also as a means of developing the European identity and cultural heritage.

This presupposes an understanding of the basic principles that underlie the philosophy and operating mechanism of commercial television.

II – Characteristics of private television

Advertising and sponsorship are vital for distributors, since these sources of financing depend on investment which may be made in the production of quality programmes likely to appeal to the public.

Contrary to the generally accepted notion, advertisers are not only interested in reaching a mass audience. They also invest in a broadcasting time aimed at specific groups.

As the essential intermediary between television viewers and advertisers, the distributor must offer throughout the day a range of programmes that is varied and up to the quality expected by the public.

The acceptance or rejection by television viewers of various opinions and social origins, the talent of creative writers and the economic constraints on distributors create market laws. The latter dictate the main lines of programming adopted by the commercial distributor.

III – Contribution to the European identity

The commercial nature of their activities gives private distributors cultural and economic legitimacy in European society. They make an important contribution to these two sectors.

(1) *Cultural legitimacy*

Private television participates in European social and cultural changes. It not only reflects existing diversity but gives it an impetus by expressing the constantly evolving aspirations and expectations of the people.

Live television, private television is also a free space offering viewers the widest range of programmes.

Being obliged to respond to viewers' wishes, private television is both an expression of popular sovereignty and a guarantee of pluralism.

(2) *Economic legitimacy*

Commercial television is a powerful motor for the development of the market economy:

(i)   it contributes to the qualitative and quantitative growth of the production of European programmes;

(ii) it provides better information for consumers through advertising;

(iii) it plays an increasing role in job creation in all the sectors directly or indirectly linked to its activities.

IV – Problems

The members of the ACT believe that, if market conditions in the programme production section and in the advertising sector are favourable, they are bound to improve substantially their contributions to the development of the audiovisual industries.

The conditions are as follows:

(1) *Creation of an environment favourable to the production of programmes*

Apart from specific national markets like the United Kingdom, the programme market in Europe is extremely small and demand considerably outstrips supply.

130 000 hours of programmes are broadcast in Europe each year whereas only 25 000 to 30 000 hours are produced there. The difference is made up by imports, mainly from the United States, Australia and Japan.

This gap is certainly increasing on account of the rapid multiplication of operators and programme time, although the latter factors do not generate an increase in audience numbers.

The ACT considers that two main factors are at the basis of the general *malaise* in the European audiovisual industry: the first concerns regulations, the second structures.

Regulations

To promote investment in the production of quality programmes likely to appeal to viewers in preference to imported programmes, European governments should adopt regulatory frameworks that will regulate the market without suffocating it under the weight of too many constraints.

The ACT is nevertheless concerned about current contradictions between the wish to create a European audiovisual market by governments and supranational bodies on the one hand, and the rigidity of the regulatory means mobilized for the purpose.

The quota policy illustrates this restrictive approach.

The ACT considers that quotas for programmes will only result in artificially swelling the volume of programmes produced to the detriment of quality.

Preference should be given to the development of contractual policies and self-regulating rules already applied in the sector.

Structures

In addition, the ACT considers that the weakness of the European audiovisual market is linked to the structural problems. At the root of the problem of the audiovisual industry in Europe is the inability of market structures to encourage production at European level and the export of programmes to the world market.

Investing in the production of programmes is a high-risk activity calling for substantial capital. Programmes continue to be produced at national level for a national market.

Apart from the United Kingdom, on account of language factors, the European industry does not have the necessary economic capacity to finance a massive production of expensive high-quality programmes for placement on foreign markets.

This tendency towards the subdivision of the market is aggravated by the contradictions between the various fiscal laws and the existence of a series of subsidies and aids granted by the various countries to support their own national market.

(2) *Creation of an environment favourable to advertising*

Television advertising and sponsorship play a fundamental role in the development of a strong European audiovisual sector. Nevertheless, television advertising is regarded with mistrust by many European governments, and is subject to detailed and pointless restrictions.

The ACT is convinced that, to benefit from the economic and financial advantages of advertising, a minimum of regulatory action — that takes account of national rules issued by the industry itself — is essential at European level.

The Community proposal for a Directive and the Council of Europe Convention on cross-frontier television (which has already been endorsed) confirm the need to facilitate access by all European viewers to programmes broadcast on the European continent. The ACT is therefore in principle in agreement with the declared aims of both these instruments.

However, aware that the Convention and the Directive are the result of compromise, we reaffirm our preference for more liberal European regulations based on the following principles:

1. *Country of origin:* television advertising should be able to circulate freely throughout Europe, the sole responsibility resting with the country of origin of the broadcast.

203

2. *Uniform regulations:* television advertising should be subject to the same restrictions as those imposed on advertising in the other media.

3. *Minimum standards:* a minimum regulation should be adopted at European level to ensure that television advertising remains distinct and clearly recognizable compared with programmes, and that certain standards of taste and decency are maintained.

V – Conclusions

Private television companies have a specific role to play in the construction of a strong European audiovisual industry and, through the ACT, they express their belief in this ideal.

Nevertheless, to carry out this role, private distributors need to evolve in a stable market capable of stimulating competition in the context of controlled development.

In most European countries, creation of a private television sector is the result of awareness by governments of public demand. Commercial television is none the less a media like the others with its own growth problems. It is up to the governments to assist in its development and not to crush it under restrictive measures likely to limit its competitiveness and consequently limit its capacity to participate in the effort to promote the production of programmes.

Essential bibliography

Documents, and particularly books, on audiovisual issues become obsolete in the time it takes to write them. The following is a far from exhaustive list of recent reference works.

1. Bate, S.B. *Television by satellite: Legal aspects*, Oxford 1987.

2. De Bens, E. and Knoche, M. (eds.). *Electronic mass media in Europe: Prospects and developments*, Reidel, Dordrecht, 1987.

3. *Distribution and export of low-budget films in the European Community*, EFDO, Hamburg, 1988.

4. Europe 2000: quelle télévision?, Rapport du Groupe de prospective sur la télévision européenne, European Institute for the Media, Manchester, 1988.

5. The European advertising and media forecasts, *International advertising expenditure: Trends and forecasts to 1992*, December 1988.

6. *EAMF, European agencies, television and advertising expenditure update,* June 1989.

7. *The impact of new communication technologies on the media industry in the EC countries,* (FAST Research programme) Vrije Universiteit Brussel, Brussels, 1986.

8. Kuhn, R. *The politics of broadcasting*, Croom Helm, Kent, 1985.

9. Lange, A. and Renaud, J.L. *L'avenir de l'industrie audiovisuelle européenne*, The European Institute for the Media, Manchester, 1988.

10 Lhoest, H. *Les multinationales de l'audiovisuel en Europe*, IRM/PUF, 1986.

11. Locksley, G. *TV broadcasting in Europe and the new technologies*, Commission of the European Communities, 1988.

12. Logica Consultancy. *Satellite television receivers: The European market*, London, 1988.

13. Logica Consultancy. *Television broadcasting in Europe towards the 1990s*, London, 1987.

14. McQuail, D. and Siune, K. *New media politics*, Sage, London, 1986.

15. *Nouveaux programmes et communication audiovisuelle,* CNCA/Mission Cable, Paris, 1986.

16. Pelton, J.N. and Howkins, J. (eds.). *Satellites International*, Stockton Press, New York, 1988.

17. Rogers, E.M. and Balle, F. (eds.). *The media revolution in America and in Western Europe*, Ablex, New Jersey, 1985.

18. Silj, A. with M. Alvarado, J. Bianchi, R. Chaniac, T. Fahy, M. Hofmann, G. Mencucci, B. O'Connor, M. Souchon, A. Torchi. *A Est di Dallas. Telefilm USA ed Europei a confronto.* ERI, Rome, 1988.

19. *Stories come first,* International Institute of Communications (Report for the Media programme of the European Commission, London, 1988.

The most valuable source for study in the sector remains specialized magazines:

Cable & Satellite Europe (UK); Channels (USA); Bulletin de l'IDATE (F); Les dossiers de l'audiovisuel (F); Mediaperspektiven (D); Revue de l'UER; Immagine e Pubblico (I); Problemi dell' informazione (I); Screen Digest, Screen International (UK); Variety (USA); Videodoc (B).

Works published in the

Document

series

Common standards for enterprises

Florence NICOLAS
with the cooperation of Jacques REPUSSARD

79 pp. – ECU 9
ISBN 92-825-8554-9 CB-PP-88-A01-EN-C

The single financial market

Dominique SERVAIS

53 pp. – ECU 6
ISBN 92-825-8572-7 CB-PP-88-C03-EN-C

A guide to working in a Europe without frontiers

Jean-Claude SÉCHÉ

253 pp. – ECU 18.50
ISBN 92-825-8067-9 CB-PP-88-004-EN-C

Freedom of movement in the Community
Entry and residence

Jean-Claude SÉCHÉ

69 pp. – ECU 7.50
ISBN 92-825-8660-X CB-PP-88-B04-EN-C

Individual choice and higher growth
The aim of consumer policy in the single market
Eamonn LAWLOR

Second edition

72 pp. – ECU 8
ISBN 92-826-0087-4 CB-56-89-869-EN-C

1992: The European social dimension
Patrick VENTURINI

119 pp. – ECU 9.75
ISBN 92-825-8703-7 CB-PP-88-B05-EN-C

Guide to the Reform of the Community's structural funds

104 pp. – ECU 11.25
ISBN 92-826-0029-7 CB-56-89-223-EN-C

1992 and beyond
John Palmer

95 pp. – ECU 8
ISBN 92-826-0088-2 CB-56-89-861-EN-C

Works published in the

european perspectives

series

Telecommunications in Europe

Herbert UNGERER
with the collaboration of Nicholas P. COSTELLO

259 pp. – ECU 10.50
ISBN 92-825-8209-4   CB-PP-88-009-EN-C

The European Monetary System
Origins, operation and outlook

Jacques van YPERSELE
with the cooperation of Jean-Claude KOEUNE

New edition (in preparation)

The European Communities in the international order

Jean GROUX and Philippe MANIN

163 pp. – ECU 5.25
ISBN 92-825-5137-7   CB-40-84-206-EN-C

Money, economic policy and Europe

Tommaso PADOA-SCHIOPPA

215 pp. – ECU 8.95
ISBN 92-825-4410-9   CB-40-84-286-EN-C

The rights of working women in the European Community

Eve C. LANDAU

244 pp. – ECU 5.25
ISBN 92-825-5341-8   CB-43-85-741-EN-C

Lawyers in the European Community

293 pp. – ECU 15.48
ISBN 92-825-6978-0   CB-48-87-290-EN-C

Transport and European integration

Carlo degli ABBATI

229 pp. – ECU 15.48
ISBN 92-825-6199-2   CB-45-86-806-EN-C

Thirty years of Community law

Various authors

498 pp. – ECU 15
ISBN 92-825-2652-6   CB-32-81-681-EN-C

The Community legal order

Jean-Victor LOUIS

New edition (in preparation)

Also available:

European Economy – No 35

The economics of 1992

22 pp. – ECU 16
SSN 0379-0991   CB-AR-88-035-EN-C

European Economy – No 36

Creation of a European financial area

Liberalization of capital movements and financial integration in the Community

12 pp. – ECU 16
SSN 0379-0991   CB-AR-88-036-EN-C

Social Europe – Special edition

The social dimension of the internal market

15 pp. – ECU 4.20
SBN 92-825-8256-6   CB-PP-88-005-EN-C

Energy in Europe – Special issue

The internal energy market

59 pp. – ECU 12.70
ISBN 92-825-8507-7   CB-PP-88-010-EN-C

Energy in Europe – Special issue
Major themes in energy

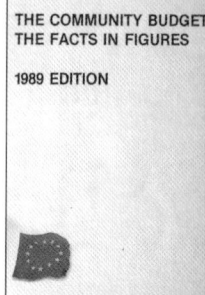

62 pp. – ECU 12.70
ISBN 92-826-0724-0

CB-BI-89-004-EN-C

The Community budget: The facts in figures

1989 Edition

103 pp. – ECU 10
ISBN 92-825-9716-4

CB-55-89-576-EN-C

Panorama of EC industry 1989
Over 125 sectors of manufacturing and service industries in focus

710 pp. – ECU 21
ISBN 92-825-8435-6

CO-52-88-784-EN-C

Europe in figures

1989/90 Edition

64 pp. – ECU 6
ISBN 92-825-9457-2

CA-54-88-158-EN-C

Community public finance
The European budget after the 1988 reform

116 pp. – ECU 10.50
ISBN 92-825-9830-6

CB-55-89-625-EN-C

Employment in Europe

1989

76 pp. – ECU 11.25
ISBN 92-825-9769-5

CE-55-89-366-EN-C

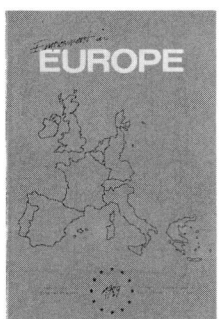

INFO 92

The Commission of the European Communities database focusing on the objectives of the Single Market

Help Desk $\begin{cases} \text{fax} & + 32\ (2)\ 236\ 06\ 24 \\ \text{phone} & + 32\ (2)\ 235\ 00\ 03 \end{cases}$

Research on the

"Cost of non-Europe"

Basic findings

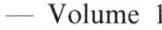

— Volume 1

Basic studies: Executive summaries

578 pp. – ECU 53.25
ISBN 92-825-8605-7

CB-PP-88-B14-EN-C

— Volume 2

Studies on the economics of integration

652 pp. – ECU 57
ISBN 92-825-8616-2

CB-PP-88-C14-EN-C

— Volume 3

The completion of the internal market:
A survey of European industry's perception
of the likely effects

309 pp. – ECU 25.50
ISBN 92-825-8610-3

CB-PP-88-D14-EN-C

— Volume 4

The "Cost of non-Europe"
Border-related controls and administrative formalities
An illustration in the road haulage sector

280 pp. – ECU 22.50
ISBN 92-825-8618-9

CB-PP-88-E14-EN-C

- Volume 5 (Part A-B)
The "Cost of non-Europe" in public sector procurement

Part A: 552 pp.
ISBN 92-825-8646-4; CB-P1-88-F14-EN-C
Part B: 278 pp.
ISBN 92-825-8647-2; CB-P2-88-F14-EN-C

Part A + B: **ECU 120**
ISBN 92-825-8648-0

- Volume 6
Technical barriers in the EC: An illustration by six industries
The "Cost of non-Europe": Some case studies on technical barriers

242 pp. – ECU 21
ISBN 92-825-8649-9   CB-PP-88-G14-EN-C

- Volume 7
The "Cost of non-Europe": Obstacles to transborder business activity

154 pp. – ECU 12.75
ISBN 92-825-8638-3   CB-PP-88-H14-EN-C

- Volume 8
The "Cost of non-Europe" for business services

140 pp. – ECU 13.50
ISBN 92-825-8637-5   CB-PP-88-I14-EN-C

- Volume 9
The "Cost of non-Europe" in financial services

494 pp. – ECU 120
ISBN 92-825-8636-7   CB-PP-88-J14-EN-C

- Volume 10
The benefits of completing the internal market for telecommunication □ services □ equipment in the Community

197 pp. – ECU 17.25
ISBN 92-825-8650-2   CB-PP-88-K14-EN-C

— Volume 11

The EC 92 automobile sector

350 pp. – ECU 27.75
ISBN 92-825-8619-7

CB-PP-88-L14-EN-(

— Volume 12 (Part A-B)

The "Cost of non-Europe" in the foodstuffs industry

Part A: 424 pp.
ISBN 92-825-8642-1; CB-P1-88-M14-EN-C

Part B: 328 pp.
ISBN 92-825-8643-X; CB-P2-88-M14-EN-C

Part A + B: **ECU 120**
ISBN 92-825-8644-8

— Volume 13

Le « Coût de la non-Europe » des produits de construction

168 pp. – ECU 14,25
ISBN 92-825-8631-6

CB-PP-88-N14-FR-(

— Volume 14

The "Cost of non-Europe" in the textile-clothing industry

256 pp. – ECU 21.75
ISBN 92-825-8641-3

CB-PP-88-O14-EN-(

— Volume 15

The "Cost of non-Europe" in the pharmaceutical industry

182 pp. – ECU 13.50
ISBN 92-825-8632-4

CB-PP-88-P14-EN-(

— Volume 16

The Internal Markets of North America – Fragmentation and integration in the US and Canada

176 pp. – ECU 13.50
ISBN 92-825-8630-8

CB-PP-88-Q14-EN-(

Special price for the complete series: **ECU 360**

European Communities — Commission

Audiovisual production in the single market

by Matteo Maggiore

Document

Luxembourg: Office for Official Publications of the European Communities

1990 — 206 pp. — 17.6 × 25.0 cm

ES, DA, DE, GR, EN, FR, IT, NL, PT

ISBN 92-826-0268-0

Catalogue number: CB-58-90-481-EN-C

Price (excluding VAT) in Luxembourg: ECU 10.50